RONNIE HAWKINS
Last of the Good ol' Boys

HAWKINS & GODDARD

Stoddart

First published in 1989 by
Stoddart Publishing Co. Limited
34 Lesmill Road
Toronto, Canada
M3B 2T6

CANADIAN CATALOGUING IN PUBLICATION DATA

Hawkins, Ronnie
    Last of the good ol' boys

ISBN 0-7737-2296-3

1. Hawkins, Ronnie. 2. Rock musicians – Canada –
Biography.   I. Goddard, Peter.   II. Title.

ML420.H38A3 1989   784.5'4'00924   C89-094428-8

Typesetting: Tony Gordon Ltd.

Printed and bound in the United States of America

This is dedicated to the one I love

Thanks to Wanda, Don Tyson, Melanie Noviss, the folks at Vernon Computer Rent-All, Kym Adams, Kathleen Sloan, Dave Booth, Mitch Potter, Linda Larsen, Kare Grant, all the Hawks, Levon Helm, Backstage Productions International, Sandra Tooze, Jack Stoddart, all the rockers, Walt Grealis and Stan Klees — two men who have spent their lives building a music industry in Canada — all the other people who have gone out of their way to help Canadian artists, and Lisa Morgan and the rest of the folks down there in Fayetteville.

CONTENTS

When we were kids, we used to slip around here and there and get into those watermelon patches to get one to eat. Well, Mr. Winters — he's the farmer who owned those watermelon patches and had a '37 Ford pickup that I wanted — one day that old farmer caught us and said, "Now look, boys, I know you been taking those melons, so I'm going to give you a warning now. I poisoned one of those watermelons out there in that field and I'm the only one who knows where it is. If you want to take a chance and eat the fucker, and kill yourself, well you just go on ahead."

Damn. And he knew where it was, too! Well, I had to do something. Just had to. The next morning I came to that old farmer. "Let me tell you something, Mr. Winters," I said. "Now there are two poisoned watermelons out there in that patch and I'm the only one who knows where the other one is. So do you want to negotiate?"

Damn, but we were young and wild and rockin' in those days.

— Ronnie Hawkins

I

ONLY AN HOUR TO ORGY TIME, GIRLS

*Wherein We Meet Our Hero in His Proper Domain,
and We Have a Night Club Boogie with the Good Old Boys
and Hear "Forty Days" One More Time*

THERE IS NO OTHER PLACE TO START our story but here, where so many of us started in so many back seats, and where so many songs started — and the *reasons* for songs started — which is to say, here in a blasted cold parking lot somewhere between rows and rows of parked Ford Escorts and mid-sized Chevies where, as I try to clear the smoke and booze out of my head, I hear someone asking:

"Are you gonna get laid?"

A reasonable question at the best of times, it takes on extra urgency tonight what with the chap asking the question, a tall, six-foot-two galoot of a guy, standing awkwardly while simultaneously taking one epic piss, gulping down a micky of rye, and all the while — as if it were a breath-taking circus act — holding a knife, a long, eight-inch-plus knife which looks like it was intended to skin nuclear submarines. Finishing, he flicks the empty bottle underneath a nearby Cavalier and attends to his business still wielding the knife perilously close to his tender parts.

"With luck," I reply.

"Me, too," he says, straightening up. He's staggering, so drunk he couldn't grab his ass with two hands. "I'm at Stelco," he continues, in reference to the local steel mill. He totters, suddenly off balance, and I grab his arm. "Jesus goddamn," he grumbles. "But isn't this the night for it? Isn't this a beautiful, goddamn night for it?"

Yes indeedy. It sure is. We both lean back on a Mustang Cobra, 5 litres under the hood, light-ended in bad weather but hard-muscle quick with good summer traction. In Burlington, Ontario, now that it's closer to winter than fall, a cold, wet, silvery sheen glazes everything from the parking lot south to Lake Ontario. In this weird white plastic light, the world looks Saran-wrapped. Ronnie's worked worse nights than this. He's worked better. In either case, once you're inside the club, he makes you forget what's outside.

"So what are you doin' here?" he asks. "You with the band or sumthin'?" I'm surprised. He makes me think back.

"You know," I say, "I almost was. I almost was."

But not with *this* band exactly. Back inside Clancy's Live, a vast, squat concrete-block bunker "featuring a 600 sq. ft. sunken dance floor," I find the band in question trying to figure out how four grown men can fit into a dressing room about the size of an interstate toll booth. Not this exact band. Hell, the kid on lead guitar, Robin Hawkins, wasn't even born when I thought I had my chance some quarter century earlier. Robin looks at the dark strawberry-color walls as he opens up the guitar case, and shrugs. "There's another room," he says, "back there with Dad." His smile grows sly. "And all the groupies."

It's 9:15 P.M. and Clancy's Live is getting so crowded you'd have to go outside to change your mind. Burlington, a dormitory suburb for commuters to Hamilton and Toronto, is one long seventies-modern mall alongside the highway. And through that particular miracle of shopping-mall taste, Clancy's Live gives you a sense of what an officers' club near the Arctic circle would be like: cold, clean and Formica hard. The guys are lined up two deep at the long bar just inside the entrance; a pair of local cops are talking to a bouncer. Everyone looks anxious. The Persian Room at the posh Plaza Hotel it is not. If you were to come back in the next few days you could catch the Grass Roots for three nights or Peter Noone of Herman's Hermits, or a production of *Beatlemania* boasting Broadway origins. But the people all around are not a sixties crowd: newly affluent, always cautious and thirty-something. Not these. They drink too hard and too well for that. They take to all their pleasures too easily: heads back laughing, flirting, patting backs and bums. You are sure lookin' gooooood tonight. Son of a bitch!

"I tell you hon," says one woman to another, their dates gone outside for the moment. "I know he wants it. He wants it real bad."

Whatever exactly it is he wants, *he* must be prepared to cope with a woman who's spread out like cold supper (as they say), weighing in at about 190 pounds, with quivery forearms the size of cured hams.

"He's tried some stuff, too," she says. "He'd be real sweet but I was a good girl. I wouldn't let him get past third base."

It's Saturday night. Let's get drunk and be somebody. Some folks here are not out of their twenties, some are nearer their sixties, yet what everyone has in common is this deep-rooted need to bust loose. And the time's coming closer.

But not before everyone in the band has finally struggled into tuxedos, had a beer or two and begun the nightly ritual of waiting. Because they know that somewhere out back, inevitably surrounded by the girls who are curious about him and those who know better than to be curious; circled in by the men who love him, or just have to be near him for the action; by the aging party animals and con artists, the car salesmen, ex-pickers, the wackos, and still more of the girls, his girls, is Ronnie Hawkins, Robin's dad and the star attraction. And until he gets his sweet old ass out on stage, there ain't no show.

If you have never met or heard of Ronnie Hawkins — and living in Canada where this good old Arkansas boy has put down roots for some thirty years, this has become a near-impossibility — you might have trouble getting a fix on exactly who he is: Elvis, Santa Claus and Robert E. Lee all rolled into one; rock 'n' roll godfather for two generations of misfit musicians. Mr. Dynamo! The one Yank Canadians happily claim as their own.

This is not entirely accidental. For someone who's been in the business of selling himself — "the legend in his spare time," as

3

his T-shirt says — he's managed to never allow himself to be pinned down. He likes it like that. He can be as independent as a hog on ice when he wants to be. It gives him room to maneuver. I mean, damn it all, *he* knows he's a legend. All that's really left for everyone else to sort out is, What kind?

"I'm not as good as I once was. But I'm as good once as I ever was."

He's the tough guy with the softest hands you've ever seen. He's lived high on the hog, had three Rolls Royces, money to burn and John Lennon as a house guest, yet he's never entirely left Hawkins Holler and the family dirt farm far behind. He's made and lost millions, but if the truth were told, all he really wants when it's all over is a little log cabin up around Beaver Lake north of Fayetteville, Arkansas, not too far from Neal's Cafe and all that to-die-for sweet chicken. He's a Canadian institution who's still part of the Confederacy.

Rompin' Ronnie has a handsome face, framed by a salt and pepper beard that hides the clean, handsome angle of his fine jaw. He was dazzling good-looking as a kid. "But that wasn't it," says an old girlfriend from back in his university days. "There's handsome and there's dangerous handsome, and he sure was the latter." Now his shoulders are rounder, so's his belly, but still there's nothing soft about him. It's his eyes. He has a boxer's eyes. They don't blink. Like many a great fighter he refuses to not see what he's doing, to go blank even for a second. If he's pissed off at you, he glares; when he's happy, those eyes shine. But they're always on.

By 9:45, Clancy's Live is full of balloons and Rompin' Ronnie's on stage.

"Heeyyyyyyy!"

He's probably the only man on earth who can make a simple black-on-black tuxedo look . . . well, down home. Like dress overalls, or something. Maybe it's the big old loopy country hat he's wearing. Maybe it's the sly, cockeyed smile, and all the false courage from those doubles of dark rum and Diet Coke. Maybe baby.

"The more you drink, the better we sound," he laughs, and for the zillionth time in his life he swings into his very first hit, the very same tune that "took us from the hills and the stills and put

4

us on the pills": "Forty Days."

And damn if it isn't half-again as fast as he's ever done it before. I've heard bands sweat over this song. A Who's Who of rock stars have sweated over this song. Like Roy Buchanan, King Biscuit Boy and Robbie Robertson. David Foster has sweated buckets trying to pluck the wrist-crippling sixteenth-notes out of the piano. Anyone who ever played in a real rock 'n' roll band from the late fifties until the Beatles arrived sweated over this song. But the latest edition of the Hawks tosses it off without even crinkling their shirts. Damn. So this is progress.

"Heeyyyyyy!" shouts Ronnie to this pretty little woman dancing right in front of him. "You keep on like that and you'll be pregnant before morning!" The balloons, selling for $1.50 each (maybe it's for all that high-priced helium), stick up over tables like some alien form of stalagmites. They have different colors signifying a full range of sexual preparedness — surely superfluous at a Ronnie Hawkins show.

Watching all this is a sad-sack-looking boy named J.K. Gulley and his very pregnant wife. J.K. Gulley, formerly of Elmvale, Ontario, is signed to the same company, Backstage Productions, that manages Hawkins. And tonight he's being given a "showcase" with the Hawks, which means he can sing a couple of songs from his new album and in doing so acquaint everyone with his enormous sad eyes and sad-sack hat.

But before J.K. Gulley has his chance Robin Hawkins, the youngest son and heir apparent, has just jumped on a solo that has the dancers stumbling over their feet as they listen. This is truly tasty. Heaven knows how often the kid has been helped, scolded, prodded, whatever, by the old man, but Jesus, is he on his own tonight. Playing lead guitar with the Hawks, whose history embraces the likes of Roy Buchanan and Robbie Robertson, is layered with tradition the equivalent of being concert master with the Berlin Philharmonic. It may not be the only gig in the business. But you've got to follow a lot of class acts.

The Hawk looks back at his son and listens, a kind of patented, show-bizzy grin on his lips, before he jolts the mike back to his face, finishes his signature song, and snaps the band into the next one, written with himself in mind, "I'm Living a Life I Can't Afford."

5

"Oh, I'm working all the time . . . "

And he still is. And he still grumbles about having to get his "tired old ass out on the road" again. But he's at peace with it now, the same way long-distance runners finally get past the pain of the running and set their eyes on the rest of the course.

"Burlington hasn't changed one little bit," Ronnie cracks. "It still has the most beautiful women — and the ugliest men — I've ever seen."

Four women push their way to the front of the stage. From a couple of tables back and from the way they dress, they look like teenagers, as if their clothes were wearing them, not the other way around: perky clothes, with lots of up-lift here and tight curves there. Clothes which suggest, "Go ahead you poor fool, go ahead, try and touch — if you dare." A closer look, however, suggests they're nearer forty than twenty and they're absolutely in control.

The Hawk has a sixth sense about such things. He always has. No wonder women like him: he likes what they like in themselves. From where I'm watching him, there's no way he can easily see the four of them. But he does. Indeed. It's taken him a fraction of a second to notice this mini-entourage and it perks him up right away. Girls! Lawd almighty!

"You want it fast?" he yells.

Yeahhhh!

"Or slow," he growls.

This is a cue for his Chuck Berry medley ("one of my heroes in the fifties") as the band shifts into another gear and finds another level of overdrive for "Roll Over Beethoven," "School Days" and "Maybelline." Showtime. Time for the Hawk to take care of business, which he does with perhaps the most backhanded compliment in show business history, bringing on J.K. Gulley, sad eyes, sad hat, old before his time, with, "He's a lazy old booger." J.K. Gulley smiles sadly, and without mentioning his terrible cold, sings his two hits. Or at least, the sweet pop ballads he hopes will *become* hits.

All the time, at the back of the stage stands the Hawk — watching, listening, still part of the show. By now he's brought on stage too many kids he barely knew who've gone on to "the big time" — and these were kids whose talents he could never understand, singers, guitarists, sex symbols on the rise he figured had

6

about as much chance to make it as "an amoeba's fart in a typhoon." Then, too, he's also introduced too many bums with talent who crashed and burned somewhere along the way and ended up phoning him some desperate Sunday morning begging a couple of hundred bucks so they could score some dope.

It's not as if he's given up trying to sort out what sells or what doesn't sell these days. He still has ears, right? It ain't nuclear physics we're talking about, it's rock 'n' roll. Still, you can predict. He just knows how wacko things can get out there, when some skinny jazz-loving piano player who would rather hear Miles Davis and Spencer Davis can go on, exactly as David Foster did, to be your big time star record producer. Gulley's songs prove to be as mildly soulful as he is, which is to say they'll sound much better on radio. Polite applause attends his departure and there's a buzz through the crowd waiting for the Hawk to get back to the mike.

"This is for all the boys down at Larry's truck stop," he shouts. "They're all alcoholics." There are few towns he's played in or near where he doesn't know at least one good old boy who views the Hawk's yearly gig as a prime chance for a king-sized blow-out. Here, it's a handsome, middle-aged fan, all smiles and silvery hair, who looks like he's got his fashion tips mainly from Johnny Carson. "Hey-O!" the boys from good old Larry's place howl. "Hey-O!" Another round for the boys at Larry's truck stop.

Maybe the best time of night is halfway through it, when the band takes a break, no one in the crowd is too drunk, too tired or too riled up yet, and the Hawk can, in the manner befitting legends in their spare time, receive visitors and in his own dressing room have another double dark rum with Diet Coke. Or two.

The smoke in the office of Clancy's Live is thick enough to chew on. Some of it's even legal. On Hawk's left is a woman he introduces only as "one of Bob Dylan's old ladies." On his right is a slim, attractive woman with a bright face, in a jump suit. She looks like she could be selling something, or maybe just keeping up appearances. She's the wife of the late musician Ray Smith surrounded by her three boys and their womenfolk. A tray of drinks appears as Ray Smith's old lady starts to thank Hawk for letting them come backstage. For years her husband, who died in 1979 at only forty-five, was on the same circuit as Ronnie, as they crossed paths time after time. Smith, smart enough not to cut across the Hawk's turf, gave his act a lot more uptown polish. Ray wore a tuxedo while the Hawk was still into buckskins. Ray, however, was still only a local celebrity while the Hawk ... why, he saw himself in much grander terms, as did his fans. Now, sitting back at his leisure, his crowd all around him, he defers to Ray's wife. He's all very old fashioned and southern about it, saying, "Uh-huh," and, "Yes, well, old Ray ... " By now the smoke has reached health-hazard density. Occasionally someone official with the club, or close to the band, pokes his head through the door, and each time the smile on his face freezes the minute he smells the air. No one inside notices. The Hawk is beaming.

"Hawk," says a boy in a sweater, "you're sounding really good tonight. I'm amazed you're sounding so good."

The Hawk doesn't hear him — or at least pretends not to hear him. It's no time for intimations of mortality.

Making my way back to the table, I find a striking woman with blond hair and vivid blue eyes in a tailored denim skirt outfit, light blue and tight around her hips. She's in her late forties, early fifties maybe, and tells me she's here with her daughter because she used to babysit Harold Jenkins's kids when he lived not far from here, "up Hamilton Mountain — that's before he became Conway Twitty."

Jenkins — that is, Twitty — can claim the distinction of luring the Hawk to Canada in the first place, telling him how much money could be made in the clubs around Hamilton and Toronto. But Conway Twitty, all the gold records and all, is still not in the Hawk's class for this woman. She talks about Twitty as if he were working at Larry's truck stop. But the Hawk — oh, her eyes light up.

I want to ask her her name, to know more about her. But some good old boy in his mid-thirties shyly asks her to dance and finding a spot he begins to twirl her around and around in a very old-fashioned, fifties way with her skirt flaring out from her legs as she turns. It's as light and pretty as ballet with her. And right then and there it's clear as day that he's crazy about her, although she never looks at him.

"Here's a song your granddaddy danced to," announces the Hawk, introducing "Bony Moronie," the 1957 hit for Larry

Williams on Specialty Records. His voice keens over the notes. Conway Twitty's babysitter is out there twirling in blue, the young man watching her as if his heart would break.

Between songs Robin has to tune his guitar and his dad, maybe sensing that the end of the night's not that far off, snaps impatiently at him: "Goddamn it, son." He wants him to get a move on. Next comes "Days Gone By," the first slow one of the night, then "Down in the Alley" a mid-tempo draggy blues kind of thing which yields to "Odessa," vintage Hawkins, with the band echoing back his words, "Odessa baby."

Odessa was a black hooker Hawkins, Levon Helm and the boys in the band knew back in Helena, Arkansas. The song was written not only out of respect for her sexual prowess, but for her fine cooking. In fact, these days, what with everyone growing older, her pork chops would bring a tear to the eye faster than anything else she had to offer.

Finally, the woman in blue, with the slightest shake of her head, turns down the last dance of the night and the guy slinks away as if he's been kicked in the behind as Hawkins, after introducing the musicians in the band, launches into "Who Do You Love."

Hawk snarls out the words over the familiar Bo Diddley riff. Hey-O the truck stop boys. Everybody's up on the 600 square feet of sunken dance floor, and I tell you, if you didn't know better you'd swear you could go outside that door right now and you'd be just down the road from Toad Suck, Arkansas.

Finally, it's over. Nothing is emptier than a rock 'n' roll club after closing, and it's beginning to get to me, the stale smell of beer and all those square feet empty dance floor, so I figure it's time to find my way home. Hawkins will know how to get back to the hotel. So I find my way through the kitchens and into the bar at the back where — but of course! — there he is, holding court, coming down from the night's high.

As much as he's part of the action, as much as he's the grand instigator of it all, just as often as not he's off in the wings, watching it all happen. He'll say anything about anyone, including himself, if he feels it's the truth and has to be said. It's only a few nights since Roy Orbison died at the relatively young age of fifty-two. Radio, TV and the press have all outdone themselves to eulogize this sad, pasty-faced Texan with the tube full of black

hair and his signature dark glasses. But not Hawkins. He knew
Roy well and liked him, too, but wasn't about to be swept along
with the wave of instant, ready-mix sorrow, even when I suggested
that Orbison had died unexpectedly early.

"I mean, he didn't drink or anything like that," I offered.

"Hmph," replied the Hawk. "Roy drank real heavily. Terrible at
times. Sure he drank. Probably it was because of the women."

"The women?"

"Claudette, mostly. The one he wrote the song about," he said.
"The one who died in the motorcycle accident — his wife. You
see," explained the Hawk leaning closer, "that Claudette was a
real wild one. A real wild one. Roy didn't know that."

But then there are the stories he'll tell on himself just as quickly.
"I remember one time I went to this old gal's farm," he says. "She
was into breeding all kinds of animals. There was every kind you
can imagine. Now let me explain that I never did get much from
marijuana. It didn't affect me much. Some people would take one
little puff and they'd be gone. High. But me — I just get a little
sleepy, that's all. Well, at this farm, I was sitting there having a
smoke when this dog came up to me so I started patting this dog's
back. And damn, but don't you know I started dozing off because
of this special cigarette.

"One of my friends came up and replaced the dog with a tiny
little horse. It looked exactly like a horse except its legs weren't
even two feet tall. So when I woke up I'm staring at this li'l horse
when it should've been a dog. And I turned to one of the guys who
was there with me. 'Goddamn, tell me that this horse is standing
in a two-foot hole.' And I'm thinking to myself that maybe there
is something to this marijuana after all!"

He's in the farthest corner, nearest the door, the band to his right,
three new women near him to his left. They're young, up for
anything, giggly and testing. What's going to happen next? Years
ago film director Martin Kahan started following him around for
a documentary he was shooting. They went to gigs. They went to
parties. They went on the road together and . . . nothing! Not one
decent orgy to talk of.

"And I've been with you for five months," Kahan complained. "But son," said the Hawk, "you ain't been around for *six* months, now, have you?"

So as the women chatter, the Hawk suddenly leans over to the one farthest away from him — the better to try out his stage whisper — and asks, "You into whips and chains and things?" He sits back, looks down the table with that mile-wide country grin of his.

"Depends," ventures one girl.

He glances at her. Damn. She could be serious.

Minutes later the signal's given and we all get up to move on, the Hawk having invited everyone back to his room in the motel nearby. The women are invited, too.

"These days," he says, leaning heavily across the table, "the difficulty is not talking them into it. It's talking them out of it."

We're further from Toad Suck than any of us know, I guess — from the good old days and the good old ways. The hotel's dead quiet during the night — but I sure listen for the telltale sound of groupies swooping down the hall. The next day everyone heads east, the Hawk to do another radio show on the never-ending business of being larger than life.

There are two histories of rock 'n' roll: two approaches, two attitudes. The one we've come to know best — the one the majority of rock histories, reviews and interviews have as their basis — is the one which views the process from the outside in; where the "key" figures, the songwriters, the singers, the trend-setters and the producers, the bosses and the hustlers, who stretched the ever-elastic boundaries of the permissible, are judged by their impact on others, and hence by the scope of their success: the records sold, money made, the power, fame and media currency.

This is the history of results. But there's more to this music we're talking about than that. Rock 'n' roll is a process. It's not just what's done, but the *way* it was done, and why. It's a music where what happens live in a club counts for as much as what happens in a recording studio; where the understanding of the music as it's *lived*, night after night in joint after joint, is what matters. And it's here, with this understanding of rock 'n' roll history, that Ronnie

Hawkins need not long for the big time — because he's already there. Just trace back the piano players alone who've pumped out those knuckle-fracturing high notes for him in "Forty Days" and you'll have a cross-section of the history of rock 'n' roll piano: from Larry Gowan back to Richard Manuel and Garth Hudson in The Band; from David Foster back to Scott Cushnie, who has worked with Aerosmith and other bands; from Dwayne Ford to Gene Taylor who ended up with the Blasters and Doug Sahm; and back to Bill King and before him one of the greatest rock 'n' roll piano players of them all, Stan Szelest; and finally to Will "Pop" Jones. They've been hired and fired by the Hawk. God knows how he's yelled at them and loved them and gotten drunk with them. Some have never come back. Some can't stay away. But they all carried along the idea he has about what rock 'n' roll is.

André Hodier, the French jazz critic, noted years ago that with a few exceptions, the creative aspects of most jazz musicians' careers begin to erode after they pass forty. With rock, it's long been believed to happen much sooner — don't trust anyone over thirty — which certainly caused Peter Townshend, Bruce Springsteen, Mick Jagger and others no end of second thoughts. Of course, in neither case it's true. Only recently are we coming to understand what longevity means in rock 'n' roll — that, while you can't do all those tight-hipped backflips you once did, it doesn't mean you've forgotten what that bitty old rock 'n' roll tune you're singing is all about.

One thing's sure, Ronnie Hawkins hasn't forgotten.

Ronnie didn't come to rock 'n' roll as I did — by listening to an original, like him — but as one of those who was there at the beginning, who wired it together out of high hopes, static and passion. To understand this, as I aimed to do during the year we spent on and off together following this night, you have to reconstruct where rock 'n' roll came from in his imagination.

You have to trace his instincts back to the first blues he heard riding in on the radio waves at night; to the jazzed-up hillbilly country music — soon to be called rockabilly — he found at concerts and shows; to Uncle Delmar fiddling, and back to all those wicked Saturday night square-dance tunes the good old pickers around Huntsville, St. Paul and Hawkins Holler would

12

reel off: pieces like the "Arkansas Traveler," "Ole Dan Tucker" and "The Devil's Dream."

And this too you have to understand: music is only a part of it. He grew up as the last medicine shows and minstrel shows still criss-crossed backwoods America; when some sharp-talking potion-pusher or silvery-tongued hayseed vaudevillian would come and stand high and mighty on top of a wagon, with his "poet's voice and rascal's grin," as the Arkansas poet Diane Taylor evokes him. "Taste the dust and feel the magic," she urges. Understand what it was like. Believe! Because back then you'd want to believe. Believe! Because that rascal poet would hold you spellbound as he slicked you silly into sampling the tangy therapeutic values of some privately blended elixir. Ronnie didn't need a sip of any nostrum to tell him that the potion's magic was curiously similar to that found in a bottle of Jack Daniels. He didn't want to. Sheeeit, he understood right off what those dimes and quarters were really paying for.

The show.

You'd better believe it! It was the hustle, the yarn-spinning and leg-pulling that got him. And the minstrel shows were very little different. Sentimental songs, saucy sayings and sassy patter. "Folks," called out the 'interlocutor,' "Step right up. We got you a dancer here to dance your blues away. Leaps, legsplits, backflips, good God almighty. We've got it all, right here!"

So this is who he is, Rompin' Ronnie. Singer, showman, songwriter and party animal without peer; organizer of bands, teacher of traditions, dad and Big Daddy all at once. The list goes on and on: agitator, provoker and charmer. Yet more than any of these, to me he's Mister Interlocutor in that wandering vaudeville he's made of his life; standing up there on stage, the host, the mover, making the introductions — the streamlined, throughly modern, rockin' version of all those good old backroads charmers with their promise of a better life. You see, Ronnie doesn't forget their promises. And he has one of his own. The big time — that's Ronnie's version of the promise and like heaven itself it's always been *just* out there beyond reach even if he can almost touch it, there in pink and powder blue, just waiting for him.

Robbie Robertson, remembering how the Hawk was always pushing, pushing, pushing, thinks of him as a cheerleader. John

Lennon, while sitting in the Hawk's living room, described him to me as "a force." Get close to him and you're drawn into the party, where he's always playing the host.

And that's what he does in this book.

At times you find him up front alone in the spotlight, sweet-talking you dizzy with all his stories, tales and yarns — talking alone because there's no one else who could possibly do it better. At times he steps aside to call on those he knows, the carnival of folks he keeps around him, the men, women, buddies, pickers, producers, fans, all his very own Mr. Tambos and Mr. Bones, to step into the spotlight for their versions of what happened. Why, sometimes theirs is the same as Ronnie's own version. Amazing!

Then again, he's one of those people with whom the razzle dazzle of his imagined life is exceeded only by the real thing. With him, you sometimes *have* to start with the unbelievable — because it's true.

II

DADDY WAS A ROCKER

In Which We Discover the Joys of Fayetteville, Arkansas, Visit Hawkins Holler and Run Some Corn Liquor in a Model A Ford

TO GET TO HAWKINS HOLLER you go about a half century back in Arkansas history, from Tyson Farms' modern aluminum sheds near Beaver Lake north of Fayetteville down the interstate and along the mile-and-a-half of hard dirt road off Highway 23. Here in the foothills of Whittemore Mountain young Ronnie used to help out in the family's home-grown lumber operation. The two-lane blacktops which got you this far follow the curve of the low hills that rise higher the nearer you get to the Ozark National Forest and bitty places like Combs, Brashers Switch and St. Paul where you find Ahart's Grocery-Cafe-Cabins. You pass by as you go: trailer homes and the Full Gospel Church; single-lane bridges and low, squat barns; Tiny Town Gospel Lighthouse and signs for Charolais cattle and the University of Arkansas football team, the Razorbacks: "Go Hogs Go." Victory Free Will Baptist Church.

The land, nearer to the middle of America than most, was settled late. According to most local histories, Frank Pierce in 1819 had the honor to become the first white man to look at the low rolling hills which were to surround the new county seat. Named Washington Courthouse at first, the burgeoning little town was renamed Fayetteville after the town in Tennessee from which

15

James Buchanan and John Woody, two of the earliest townsfolk, had come. (The Tennessee town itself like others throughout the United States had been named after the pro-American French general, Lafayette.) Ironically, the Hawkins clan came from yet another Fayetteville — Fayetteville County, Georgia. And they came to be rooted in Arkansas only after a tragedy.

Edward Hawkins, leaving his parents Nathaniel and Charlotte back in Georgia, was looking for a place to get a fresh start with his young wife, the former Missouri Bice, and their two babies, William Edward Augustus — Ronnie's grandfather "Billy" — and little Louisa. But Missouri died as their wagon train pushed north and west from Alabama, and they carried her remains part way in a coffin made of wagon timbers. They settled in St. Paul — the old St. Paul, that is, the town that's long gone about two miles from the current St. Paul and just down the road a bit from Fayetteville. There, generations later, Ronnie would sit in the barbershop belonging to to his dad, Jasper, and listen to the shoeshine man, Buddy Hayes, "pop the rag" as he shined the shoes, singing the blues. For Ronnie, musical memories are as strong today as those barbershop afternoons and the popping of that rag.

The uneven land, modest valleys alternating with modest stretches of prairie, was rich in forest: oak, walnut, spicewood and ash; mulberry, paw-paw, black locust and cherry. St. Paul was soon to become the site of an important logging industry. Edward, a big, powerful man who had hauled his own wagon part of the way through the Ozarks after his mules dropped dead, carved out a living for the family doing some mill work whenever he had to. Being a single father only made life more difficult, and in 1877 he married again. He and Emmy Bowle produced five more children. Theirs wasn't the only Hawkins clan, though. Other unrelated Hawkins families were eventually to settle in or near the Ozarks, most prominent among them the Hawkins sawmilling family in southwest Missouri. But Ronnie's ancestors, locals agree, weren't like the others bearing the same name.

"What I can say about *this* Hawkins family," a woman minding a store just west of St. Paul tells me, after I've stopped to ask directions, "is that they worked real hard, *real* hard, and at work that'd break the backs of other men. They've done their share of drinking in their time and some even did more than their share;

and they loved music. Wasn't a Hawkins I knew couldn't play something: a fiddle, a guitar, what have you." Sure enough, not a hundred years after he'd settled in St. Paul, Edward's family was to have its impact on music when his two great-grandsons, Ronald and Dale, helped create the wildest music man had ever heard — rock 'n' roll.

Others arriving in the Fayetteville area by trail from Cane Hill or by the Huntsville road were like Edward and his family: men and women wanting to make a go of it on their own. From the earliest days, strangers arriving in this brave new land soon began to remark in letters back home about something common to all those who'd settled there — their stubborn, unflinching, independent streak. Not a few arguments were settled by violence. "Shooting, stabbing, knocking down and dragging out appear to be the order of the day at present in this place," Steward Case, a young clerk at James Sutton's store just in from Indiana, noted in a letter he sent back home in 1840. "Almost everyone you see is armed to his teeth at all times."

Murder and other time-honored forms of mayhem eventually became a thing of the past as the good citizens of Fayetteville determined that they could be just as respectable as any of those fine folks back east. By the 1860s, the town could brag about its many fine general stores and the new Arkansas College. It had become a banking center as well. Van Horne's Fayetteville Female Institute was a bustling concern in its new residences on the northwest corner of Dickson Street and College Avenue.

Unlike many other small towns, anxious to embrace the coming era of business and commerce, Fayetteville was never willing to forget the "finer things." Its uninterrupted support of its many and varied colleges foretold the local prominence of the University of Arkansas, today very much the center of the town's activities. By the 1850s, Fayetteville finally had the "pretensions" of society, as one diarist noted. The Butterfield Coach line connected the area with the world beyond, the line's stage meeting the train in southern Missouri and joining up with the river barges at Van Buren to the south. Fancy foods came north from New Orleans. Machinery came from Cincinnati. Merchants went as far as Philadelphia and New York to place their orders. Why, there wasn't much you couldn't get in Fayetteville, and what you couldn't get you probably didn't need.

So the loyalties in as worldly a town as Fayetteville were profoundly divided when on May 6, 1861, Arkansas became the eighth state to leave the Union. Some families had sons in the armies of both North and South, and the hostilities which raged on battlefields well away from Fayetteville came home after the war and often lived on for a generation or two. Arkansas's country folk came to distrust both sides about equally. To maintain their beloved independence, the men and boys from the hills at first refused to leave the Union. They owned few slaves, after all — although slavery was carried on in the area — and felt little kinship with the richer landowners who did. The firing on Fort Sumter led them to support Secession but again only out of an ingrown defiance, this time against the invading forces from the North. Although the town retained no particular military importance, it proved to be in the way of both armies and was occupied, pillaged, destroyed, then abandoned by both sides throughout the conflict. Eventually a rebuilt Fayetteville rose from the ashes of the old. But some things never changed. Rejoining the Union after the war only made them even more certain they'd been right in wanting their independence: the carpetbaggers from the North were as bad as the looting Confederate forces during the war.

In the Reconstruction years it was easier to be a dyed-in-the-wool outlaw than to be a northern entrepreneur or southern gentleman. Quantrill's Raiders hid out in the Ozarks, as did the Dalton Gang. Jesse James and his henchman Cole Younger had no difficulty whatsoever finding friends, a place to hide out or a jug of corn mash deep in the Ozarks near Fayetteville, St. Paul or Huntsville. His hosts knew Jesse was an outlaw, but he helped out poor folks with a bit of money now and then and he was a good church-going boy for all that; indeed, brother Frank eventually became a Baptist elder. The truth was, many of Jesse's "hosts" felt a bit like outlaws, too. At least they followed no particular law but their own. They were cut from the mould of Edward Hawkins, who on December 12, 1863, signed the "Presidential Amnesty Oath" to, in effect, become a loyal supporter of the Union side. They may have gone through the motions of fitting in. But they never did, not really.

Yet this cussed independence gives the "Creation State" a

larger-than-life quality. Arkansas folks like to "spin the windy" or "stretch the blanket" on occasion, especially at the expense of all those who only think of them as poor, dumb hillbillies. Take the Fillyloo bird, or the Gillyloo as it's sometimes called. Some folks may not believe that such a wondrous creature exists deep in the Ozark Mountains. These same folks may not want to believe this bird can fly backward and sometimes upside down, or that on occasion it has carried off local girls who otherwise would have no other way of explaining why they didn't come back the other night. Then again these folks don't understand the Arkansas hills. Another Ozark flying critter, the Giasticutus, is said to be powerful enough to haul cattle up into the sky. Around Boone County, and Searcy County, too, sightings of the Gowrow have been reported, all twenty-foot long with its big tusks. And just let these eastern skeptics doubt for a moment that the local "white mule," also known as "white lightning," is consumed for recreation and not for its well-known therapeutic effects.

The bustling little city Ronnie Hawkins grew up in was left relatively unscathed by the Great Depression. No bank was forced to close and if money was scarce, people took to trading with their neighbors for what they wanted. The hundreds of miles of good road which eventually helped local industry and tourism — and helped run local moonshine north into Missouri or west to Oklahoma — were built by Franklin D. Roosevelt's Civilian Conservation Corps. The Palace Theater was packing them in for double bills. The town had its own baseball team, the Educators (later renamed the Bears), playing in the now-defunct Arkansas-Missouri league. Folks got by.

Ronnie Hawkins's earliest memories are full of play, kin folks all around, parents he knew loved him — and moving. Always moving. He was born in Huntsville, Arkansas, January 10, 1935. He grew up between there and St. Paul, until the third grade. "My folks never had much," says Ronnie, "but we got by. We sure did."

"I remember it was late at night and my father woke me up," says Winnifred Laws — "Bobbie" — Ronnie's sister. "I was about five-and-a-half years old and my father said I had a new baby brother. Dr. Carl Beebe was the doctor who delivered him. It was a very cold night. We were living in Huntsville. I even have a

19

picture of the house he was born in. It's still there. We moved to St. Paul when Ronald was about nine months old and we lived there until he was about four years old, when we moved back to Huntsville where he went to first grade. My father was a barber in Huntsville and my mother was a schoolteacher. This was in very hard times. My father left the barbershop when Ronald was nine months old and went to St. Paul and did itinerant work. He picked apples and went through the hayfields in Kansas and did whatever jobs he could do.

"When Ron was little, just two or three years old, my father was working for a man named Dean Myers. Father worked all day for fifty cents. One day I took Ronald up to where he was working, hauling rock. That's what he did all day long. Ronald and I noticed some honey — they had honey bees at that farm. A little bucket of honey was thirty-five cents. So our father gave almost his whole day's work for a bucket of honey for Ronald and me. And he carried Ronald home — it was about three miles — on his shoulders.

"Economics was the reason we eventually moved to St. Paul. My father was unemployed. He had lost his barbershop somehow. So we moved to St. Paul so that my mother could teach in that part of the country. From the time Ron was two to when he was four she taught at a place called Boston, and also a place called Dripping Springs. Ronald and I were with her. We boarded out with the people — Cindy and Jim Bennett, wonderful old country people. They took care of Ronald and when he was three we lived with my grandmother Hawkins's brother and his wife, Aunt Martha and Uncle Jim Witt."

The Hawkins family was always on the move, Winnifred remembers. "Then we moved back over to Huntsville, Arkansas, and my mother taught around there. This time we were moving because mother had new jobs. Those three years, dad was just working anyplace he could. But when we came back over to Huntsville, he got another barbershop."

Now living in San Diego, Winnifred is a noted art expert and was for years the dean of Queens College, New York. Like Ronnie, she keeps promising herself she's going to move back to Fayetteville. "Our parents were really the most wonderful people," she says. "In their own different ways. My father was one of the kindest people I've ever known — he was a great influence on me. Neither he nor my mother ever spoke a harsh word to either Ronald or me. We never ever had a fight in our lives.

"My father was totally uneducated. He never went to school. He was restricted in his way of earning a livelihood. He had to do barbering, which he learned as a young apprentice, or he had to do manual labor. My mother was sort of the Rock of Gibraltar. She kept it together with those teaching jobs. She always wanted both Ronald and me to have an education. And we did. Ronald went to university for five years and I went for a long time.

"It was our mother who kept us going as far as education is concerned. Our father gave us a lot of practical sense. He was a very ingenious person, making do with whatever there was, and he was a wonderful provider for the family in his own way. He would go hunting and fishing and take us with him. Always thinking about our welfare, always."

Ronnie takes up the story: "Finally we moved into Fayetteville, not far away, where the University of Arkansas is located. Now, I'm not much for history. I've lived all the history I'll ever need. But the short and simple version of my early days is this. I went to high school in Fayetteville, then to the University of Arkansas when I was seventeen for arts and sciences, but I switched after my first year to physical education. Before I was through, though, I dropped out to go with my bands.

"The name Hawkins goes back to England and the kings who had trainers for their hawks. They used falcons to hunt with. The name started out as 'Hawkin' but it changed over the years. My mother's maiden name was Cornet, but I didn't hang around them. I hung around the Hawkinses because of the music. Grandfather Cornet was one of those real stern men. He worked his ass off: made sure everything was right, and made sure all his kids were educated even though education didn't mean too much to a lot of people in those days. Even when I was growing up there were six-year-old kids plowing and hoeing."

"They was hardy hillbillies," remembers Eugene Schieffler, a lawyer who married Ronnie's great aunt before moving to Helena. "Ronnie was a natural musician and he had some uncles who were natural musicians too. They got by when they had to. When Jasper, his daddy, was young he and his brothers would go to Kansas to

21

work in the wheat when they needed hard cash. Ronnie had hard times but he got by."

"My Aunt Annabelle's husband had his own sawmills," says Ronnie, remembering all the work he put in. "My other uncle, Uncle Eddie, went further. He'd buy a big farm with no house on it, put up a sawmill there and set up an old V-8 engine that ran the sawmill. He'd go in, cut the trees, build big chicken houses, raise chickens, build a big house, build a big farm on 100 acres or whatever and then sell it. And that's how he made his living. A good living. He was a hard worker, putting in fourteen-hour days. And he was half-blind — a skunk had hit him in the eyes with its spray. The doctors couldn't help, and for years he couldn't read anything. Years and years later he got glasses that he could see with. But for thirty years he didn't have glasses.

"My great-granddad founded Hawkins Holler, although it wasn't called that then. He got the land free to work it and then he had kids and they could take a piece and run it. It ended up being all Hawkinses. They all worked together when I was a little kid. Each farm had a hundred or two hundred acres. For a while everyone made railway ties. There ended up being some twenty-five or thirty Hawkins families around that area until the war came along and everybody went into the army; everyone went this way and that. The one who has been through it all and remembers everything is my aunt, Annabelle."

"My husband and I moved here, to Hawkins Holler, in '39," says Annabelle Hawkins, sitting proudly upright in the old family chair, in the same low-ceilinged house she helped build. "We had three kids when we moved here and my youngest daughter was born here. I taught school here for forty years and I also taught near here at St. Paul. Then I went to New Mexico and I taught junior-high English there for twelve more years in Almagordo, New Mexico."

Reluctantly, she turns off her favorite soap opera. The very real heat from the artificial fire in the hearth cuts through the damp. "Ronnie's mother, Flora, had bought the house in New Mexico," Annabelle continues, "and Jasper, Ronnie's father, joined us and barbered there for a year or two before he came back to Arkansas, to Springdale. They weren't legally separated — they just didn't live together too much of the time. Maybe I shouldn't mention this, but Ronnie's father had a problem with alcohol, you know. Jasper would drink a whole lot and things might have been a lot worse if it hadn't been for Ronnie's mother, who just took over and saw that the family was taken care of. She was a good business woman. She worked all the time.

"All the Hawkinses had a great sense of wit and humor. Ronnie's mother was more serious so he got his wit from his father. Flora never made Ronnie go to church, but she always went. His father, though, took care of him a lot when he was little."

"My mom and dad were total opposites in so many ways," remembers Ronnie. "Mom was almost a fanatic about religion, while dad was a total redneck, total, and he didn't care for church much. Mom went to church all her life. She even got some sort of commemoration from one church for never having missed a service."

There's more to his memories of his parents than fondness. Indeed, there's a kind of wide-eyed admiration. For him, his mother may have been the most independent woman he's known. As for his daddy — he was more of a hell raiser than Ronnie will ever be:

Did mom ever have to watch dad! One time, when we were living in Huntsville, dad was running around with one of the local red hot mamas. He'd gone out in the car and slipped over to St. Paul with this mama and there they were, together in a big parking area.

Well, there was this guy named Carl Presley. He was a mover and a rocker also. He was married to a beautiful woman but he was out slipping around with high school girls, too. He had a car, a Chevy convertible that had a rumble seat, so mom got him and they drove to St. Paul and caught dad up there with this old gal. Mom got out of the car and walked up to the door and said, "Don't you come home."

Of course dad tried to explain that he was just giving this gal a ride. But they were *parked.*

I remember a time much later — this would be in the late sixties — when I came back home and I caught him in bed with two women. He was sixty-five at the time, and they were both under forty. They were naked as jaybirds. He stood there with his Jockey shorts on with his crotch hanging down to his knees. And he was wearing his old false teeth and he was chewing gum, with that plate just a-flapping.

"Son, don't get the wrong idea," he said. "These are your relatives and it's cold."

This was the time I had Jay Smith and John Till in my band. They couldn't believe it. Dad was a rocker. He was a ladies' man. Those old blue-hairs went for him like they do me. I don't really know why he and momma never divorced. Momma was religious so I guess she stayed, as the Bible says, for better or for worse. She was old school. She believed that once you get together with someone, even someone like dad, you stay together. Today they'd be divorced and not think anything of it, but nobody got divorced in those days.

I'll tell you something: mom and dad died five months apart in 1978. Dad died first in March. I was done there in Fayetteville when he died and at the time mom was fine. Only months later they gave me a call and said, "Momma's in bad shape in the hospital — you'd better come." But by the time I got there, she had passed away.

I don't know if I'm religious, but I can see how religion held a lot of people together. Old dad never trusted any preacher, I'll tell you that. And he was right about most of them most of the time, too. He thought people used you, and he'd been through a lot. He'd caught too many preachers doing naughty things. One day Oral Roberts, the preacher from Oklahoma, came through the area. We all had to go over where he'd set up his tabernacle. Oral was healing everybody; dad was there drunk. We were all watching. "Heal *me*, goddamn you!" dad yelled, getting out of his chair.

And that was that. After a while, poor mom would never ask him to go to church because he'd go drunk and get to acting up. And that was something you did not do in the South, act up in church.

But something would bug dad and he'd say, "Oh shit," and walk out in the middle of the service.

I didn't drink much until I was past forty and to this day I don't like the taste of whiskey. I drink it to numb my head, that's all I ever did it for. Why drink? I mean, in the bands I had, we had dreams of conquering the world. I had these dreams until I was well into my thirties. We worked day and night trying to get better. Goddamn, we practiced more than any band in the world. Drinking just got in the way.

I guess the Hawkinses are very impulsive. If they drink they'll drink to the extreme. If they smoke they'll smoke to the extreme. Whatever they do they do to the extreme. All the men on the Hawkins side were drinkers, smokers, fighters, boozers, and all the women they married were religious fanatics, just about. These women didn't drink, didn't smoke; they worked day and night. But all the Hawkinses were musical. They played all the time. I can't remember ever not being able to pick up the guitar. The rest of the family, they'd have guitars and fiddles and banjos.

At first Winnifred and Ron didn't know what to make of their dad's drinking, but were determined early on not to do it themselves. "I knew from the time I was a little girl that alcoholism is an illness and that my dad really wanted to quit drinking," says Winnifred. "Drinking is one of those things that runs through the Hawkins family, all the way back to my great-great-grandfather.

"As a girl, my mother was very outgoing but she became a little more quiet and solemn and introverted as she got older, I think because of the burdens and the hardships she had raising us. She had a hard time. Everybody did back then, though. You worked for something like thirty dollars a month. But she was a wonderful woman. I think of her spirit now, when I get to feeling sorry for myself once in a while. I think of what my mother and father endured.

"Mother moved us to Fayetteville — our first address was 615 Ida Avenue — in 1944, simply so that I could go to university. But then I got married in December 1944, shortly after we moved to Fayetteville, when I was fifteen years old. That shattered the family.

"As things turned out," Winnifred goes on, "my mother and I both went to university. She went to college in the summertime when she wasn't working. When she first started teaching, nobody ever heard of a teacher going to college. She went on and finished university and her master's degree in education before she went to New Mexico. Meanwhile my dad worked and earned what he could in the barbershop. They just sort of lived together but separately, if that makes any sense. He lived his life and she lived her life but they both lived together. Back then, it was not like it is now when if you don't get along you just split. Back then they made the best of things.

"The thing that really kept her going was school. She enjoyed learning. Dad gave us a lot of practical sense. Mother gave us the ability to keep on striving and forging ahead. Daddy taught us to do the best we could with what we had. In their own ways they both gave us a lot."

"Now when it came to music," says Ronnie's Aunt Annabelle, "Ronnie's grandmother was musical. Very musical. Evidently the music was her side of the family because some of the other Witts are musicians as well. But we had to work a lot in the Depression and we didn't have much time to expose our kids to things like music. The family didn't think Ronnie would ever amount to anything, even to play music. I never had an idea what he wanted to be, either. The family didn't know he'd be musical although I do remember he was always just singing and carrying on. When he was a kid he used to lie in bed every morning and sing."

"I can't remember when I first wanted to start playing music," Ronnie comments. "It was there forever. On Sunday afternoons in particular the Hawkins family would take turns being at different cousins' houses. And everyone would bring food and we'd sit around and tell stories and make music. The stories and the music always seemed to go together. And maybe there was a little drinking, too, as my dad and a few of the older guys would slip out back for some moonshine."

But it's not the boozing he remembers best, it's the music making:

Delmar Hawkins, my uncle, was a good one. He actually played with me for three or four weeks, later on, when I had the Shamrock Club. He played fiddle but he borrowed Claude Chambers's bass to play with us. We weren't even using bass much at that time because Claude, who was our bassist, couldn't always play with us. But Delmar was such a great musician he just got on stage at

26

rehearsal and never missed two notes during the whole set, just slapping that goddamn bass. That's Delmar. That's how good a musician he was. He never even really knew the material we were doing because he was more of a country player. But he had no problem with it.

I was only five or six at the time that Delmar became really big as a musician. His nickname was Skipper — Skipper Hawkins. He'd gone to California and he really had it made. He was drinking a lot then but he was still playing and making $300 a week when my dad was hauling rock on a government work project for seventy-five cents a day. He burned himself out in California and Las Vegas and started showing up for the dates drunk. But for a while there he'd come home for a week or two driving a brand new Cadillac and wearing brand new clothes and I knew that's what I wanted to be.

He's the reason I started a career in music, I guess. The other Hawkinses, well they only played weekends and made a couple of bucks. But Uncle Delmar actually made a living on music. We all could hear him on network radio out of Tulsa.

Eventually he spent every penny he made on whiskey and was divorced because he was running around with all sorts of women. So his wife left Arkansas and went to Louisiana and that's how come my cousin Dale Hawkins and his brother Jerry ended up in Louisiana. Dale came back for a few summers to visit grandma with me in Hawkins Holler.

Now, when it came to music, I'd been playing since I was a kid. Playing, singing — doing something. I was in high-school operettas and did little fairs and stuff like that since I was ten, eleven years old. I had no serious plans at that time but people knew I sang.

One of the first shows I did something on featured Hank Williams. It was in Fort Smith, not far from Fayetteville, in the forties. I was young, still in grade school. Old Hank, he was so drunk he couldn't do anything on stage. At that time they'd let kids get up and perform with his band. Free, of course. So I got up and did the Burl Ives songs I knew and some Stephen Foster: "Beautiful Dreamer," and "Camptown Races." At this time I'd learned everything dad could teach me. I could play three or four chords in three or four keys on the guitar. I faked it a little bit, too.

You see, I was too busy trying to do backflips and do the show and learn the songs to concentrate on the music part of it. "Do da, do da." Even back then I knew that every important white cat — Al Jolson, Stephen Foster — they all did it by copying blacks. Even Hank Williams learned all the stuff he had from those black cats in Alabama. Elvis Presley copied black music. That's all Elvis did. That's all I did. That's all those cats in Memphis were trying to do: take those blues songs and copy them and make them commercial. Shit, Pat Boone sold more records than Fats Domino doing Fats Domino songs.

But music wasn't the only thing I was interested in. Damn, no! There were cars and girls. Girls like my babysitter. I was about eleven and she was eighteen years old. That's an old woman for an eleven-year-old. And she was beautiful. She was my first love and she was married. She'd married into one of those rich southern families. Her husband was a little weird. He'd already gone through college but she was so beautiful that he married her although he was getting the kind of master's degree where you had to go out on field trips to study. He was studying geology, I think, and he'd go on these field trips for a month or two at a time to Peru or someplace else in South America. So there she was in her little apartment, just married, eighteen: the babysitter.

Mom had to work all the time. Dad worked all the time, too. We lived in the basement of the same apartment building on Ida Street that this girl lived in. This was during the war, before Mom and Dad bought their place on West Maple. So when I came in from school one time they asked her, "Can you keep an eye on him?"

"Oh, I'd love to have company," she said. "I'll fix him a little sandwich or something to eat."

Well, it didn't take long till she started to teach me *everything* that there was to know about making sandwiches. You understand. And boy, after a while everyone was sure I had the strictest parents in school. When school let out the first thing everybody else did was play a little softball or something before they went home to eat, right. But not me, man; I *ran* home. Every one was really impressed. They said, "Your folks are so strict they don't ever let you out."

I like to think that's the reason I didn't become a professional ball player or some sort of athlete. I had pretty good ability but I didn't practice much because I always went home to get babysat. I don't think I was ever found out, although mom was suspicious 'cause I was being babysat so much.

True to the spirit of his times, Ronnie's fascination with nubile babysitters and hot pop music was matched — at times surpassed — by his passion for cars. No one can remember the Hawk not having a car, neither his relatives nor the buddies who knew him as a kid. But for him the passion was more than the usual need for instant exhilaration and escape the car offers. No. Ronnie loved cars not for what they offered but for what they were — mobile bits of Americana, or something. Damn, he didn't know. He just felt it.

And it wasn't just any car. Hell no. An old car. He just knew he loved the *feel* of the old cars, the way he could feel the engine work. Vintage sedans, trucks — he found it nearly impossible to pass an old shed and spot the up-curve of an old fender without wanting to go in and take a look and, just as likely, try to buy whatever was there.

To this day, when Ronnie goes back to visit Claude Chambers, the first bass player in his first real band, the two of them will go out to the shed behind the tiny bungalow Claude shares with his mom and spend a few minutes just gazing at the old car radios or clocks Claude has been fixing. For Ronnie was hooked on cars early. Real early.

"My first car was a 1929 Model A," he recalls. "I delivered telegrams for Western Union with it. I had the car and my driver's license when I was twelve. Back in Arkansas in the 1940s, twelve-year-olds could drive with special permission, because if they weren't allowed to drive a lot of kids couldn't get to school. When all the schools consolidated into a system, buses were used to take all the kids who'd gone to little schools to the bigger schools. That's when the driving age went up. But before that, you saw all sorts of young kids out driving cars."

Certainly, as soon as he was allowed to young Ronald got himself a set of wheels. He remembers with a slow, sly smile:

Because I had a car, I found myself a really good way to make money: I ran liquor. It wasn't moonshine exactly, just bottles of booze. I started when I was only fourteen and I kept at it until I was nineteen or twenty. That's how I made my money for the clubs I bought into.

I knew all the bootleggers around, so the run from Missouri to Oklahoma was easy. The others running whiskey were driving big Cadillacs. Not me. I made most of my whiskey money driving my Model A. It was a coupe so you could put six cases of whiskey in it. The state police were looking for the big Cadillacs, doing spot checks. They'd catch those big cars coming through with trailers filled with whiskey and the police would kick the shit out of the guys they caught. I never got stopped, not once. They didn't stop a Model A with a kid in it.

I went to Missouri to get the whiskey. The Missouri state line is only about sixteen miles from Fayetteville, and just across the Missouri line gas was half price, cigarettes were half price and whiskey was half price. Things are still like that; it all has to do with the taxes. I was running the whiskey into Oklahoma. Arkansas had liquor but Oklahoma was dry — though it had booze cans, bootleggers and private clubs where liquor was sold.

The club owners were giving me like fifty to a hundred dollars a run. I was making more money than anybody my age in the world at the time. If I made three runs that would be $300 a day. For my daddy, making seventy-five dollars a week as a barber was a big week. Everybody — the gangsters and everyone else running whiskey — warned me, don't buy a Cadillac and don't start spending money. People will ask where you got it. So what I did was become a silent partner with Dayton Stratton in some bars and clubs. He was old enough to own a bar, while I was just a kid and I couldn't. But he didn't have the cash and I did.

People didn't know why I suddenly had enough money to buy a couple of bars. I was clever. I said that I'd sold a car or swapped a hotrod.

Ronnie's cousins Landon and Don Hawkins, who lived for a while out in Hawkins Holler where there was no electricity or indoor plumbing, were dazzled by their cousin back in town. Landon particularly. Ronnie, he thought, "had the world by the tail. He was good looking, athletic, funny: a real kidder. Ronnie had a Model A Roadster which was as finely tuned as a fiddle and he'd do just about anything as an excuse to drive it around town. He took over a paper route just so he could drive that car. He delivered telegraphs. He drove moonshine, although there was the added incentive of making some fast money."

"We all went to Fayetteville High," Ronnie remembers. "I was in the last graduating class at the old high school. They had no integration then. There weren't blacks in high school when I was there and not many blacks in university. I don't know where the blacks went to school. You never much thought about them back then.

"But I sure was listening to lots of music: the blues. There weren't any record stores around that would dare sell it, so we'd have to listen to it on the radio. It was like a signal from someplace else. And I listened *hard* to that music. Real hard. After a while, I knew I had to find out more about it. Hell, I had a car. Memphis was just down the road. Memphis had Beale Street, the home of the blues for me. Beale Street was beautiful back then. Everybody was dressed up. Everybody had style. Everybody was staying alive making the music I loved. Man, I *knew* I had to go."

III

ESTHER WILLIAMS AND ME

Higher Education, or How to Live Like a Football Hero and Not Have to Play Rough

"IT WAS DURING HIGH SCHOOL that I really started listening to music," says Ronnie. "Black music. I didn't like white country much, though that's pretty much all you could listen to around Fayetteville. Mom and dad listened to Grand Ole Opry but I never did like that stuff as much as the blues. Mel Tillis — who I met back in the fifties, when he was wearing those real funny suits with rhinestones all over them — still gets hot at me whenever he hears me say it."

Ronnie was definitely out of the mainstream back then when it came to his taste in music. He reminisces about his high school days and the influences that shaped his musical career:

The only white country music I liked then was by Hank Williams, Lefty Frizzell and some of the old Jimmie Rodgers stuff. To me they were singers of the soul. The kid that's hot today — Randy Travis — he's a copy of Lefty Frizzell. I listened to some other kinds of music but I liked Muddy Waters and the blues more. I liked Josh White, too. He played blues, the folk blues really. And he wrote most of his own stuff.

My dad worked at a barbershop where they had a little shoe-shine boy named Buddy Hayes. Buddy had a blues band and they used to practice in the back of that barbershop — they were into a sort of Louis Armstrong-New Orleans kind of blues jazz. His piano player played a Fats Waller type of piano. That kind of piano playing has been the basis for the style I've always wanted the piano player in my band to have. Buddy and the rest were the ones who told me that I should buy those old 78s so I could hear some of that old country blues, as they called it: John Lee Hooker, Howlin' Wolf, B.B. King — who was a Memphis deejay at the time — and Muddy Waters.

But I was also learning a lot hanging out down in the black part of town. There was a guy there called Half Pint who had a brother called Little Joe. Half Pint was incredibly talented. I mean, Sammy Davis hasn't got one-tenth of the talent this kid had. He could dance better, sing better, rock better than anybody I'd ever seen and on top of that he was probably the greatest drummer that'll ever come out of the state of Arkansas. He could do anything, this kid. At twelve years old he would dance on street corners for nickles and dimes. I learned a lot of steps off of him. He was doing the duck walk way back then, before Chuck Berry did it. Vaudeville people called it the "camel walk." It's like you're standing still and you're moving.

I was just a kid when I started singing. At first it was with whatever bands came through town. I sang with Roy Orbison's band, and with Harold Jenkins's — that's what he was called before he called himself Conway Twitty. I'd play with pick-up bands, too. I did hundreds of those kinds of shows. They'd get me up there and I'd do some songs, sort of like an opening act might, although they didn't call it that.

It was just after high school when I put my first band together. It started when Harold Pinkerton, who played rhythm guitar, and Bobby Keene — who was the best guitar player in the area at that time — started playing with me. "Pink" and I were in school together. The next two who joined a little later had their own band: Claude Chambers, who played bass, and Herman Tuck, a really good drummer. Jerry Lee Lewis was trying to get Tuck to go with him all the time. Well, they were known musicians, those two, so the rest of us had to hustle around and get all sorts of work lined up before they'd join us for a permanent situation. They were big time compared to us. They were making *ten dollars* a night, sometimes. Hell, the rest of us played for two dollars a night.

But they decided to come with me because I was getting the action. I was getting the little jobs and the girls and damn if I didn't discover right off, that combination gets the musicians. I was playing the better parties. And right from the start we were the Hawks. *All* my bands have been the Hawks.

We played everywhere. We played garage parties and the Huntsville Festival . . . hell, we'd play anywhere they'd let us. Our first job — at least one very near the first — was at the Rockwood Club in Fayetteville. I liked the place so much that a few years later I bought it. We were as good a band as anything else around at that time. That band wouldn't hold up to the bands that came later. These were guys who had other jobs and who played on the side. You can't get real great doing that. You have to play all the time and practice all the time. Everybody in that early band had the potential to do it but nobody did enough with it. We'd just play weekends and the odd Wednesday. That was date night for kids at the university.

We had some really wild times. Damn, Herman Tuck tried to set local records for excessive behavior. But the band broke up when I went into the army in 1957. Herman played with Jerry Lee a bit. He also played with some big bands — you know, dance bands. He was that good, Herman was. But he gave it up after a while. The others did, too.

Even when I was still in high school I was making my trips to Memphis — mainly to buy records and to see what Beale Street was like. I also went down there to check out the music scene, of course. I'd heard of a couple of bands coming through town playing. I'd heard of some of the traveling guitar players. But I had to hear more and that meant getting records. Fayetteville record stores wouldn't even order the kind of records I liked. They said they didn't stock "nigger" music. As for the radio, the regular stations didn't play anything but that who-shit-in-my-saddle-bag country music. That's all you heard from radio around Fayetteville.

For potential tourists back east searching for rural America,

Arkansas was the mythical "Land of a Million Smiles" the state's peppy brochures said it was. Then, too, there was the Arkansas Industrial Development Commission which beckoned new industry with promises of cheap, non-union labor. But for Fayetteville, it was the university itself which proved to be the biggest center of growth. By 1951, the Fine Arts Center, the new addition to campus by Fayetteville-born architect Edward Durrell Stone (best-known for the Museum of Modern Art and Rockefeller Center, both in New York) confirmed the progressiveness of the university and in turn, its importance to the town which was growing up around it.

"The reason I went to university was mainly because of mom," Ronnie explains. "Dad didn't give a hoot about school. He'd say, 'You don't learn it in the goddamn school. You gotta learn it by doin' it.' That was his motto. But momma of course wanted to better her kids."

He was anything but the reluctant student. There was too much action around the university, what with the fraternities and sororities, and all those opportunities to play dances — and meet girls. "I started out in arts and sciences in 1952, but was in that for only a year," says Ronnie. "I wanted to study a little painting, I wanted to study a little acting. Hell, I wanted to be Clark Gable. When I realized I wasn't going to be another Clark Gable, I got into phys ed where I met Rodney Ryan, the head cat. I was his favorite. He might not tell you that, but I was. I just knew it. I caused him a lot of problems, but we had fun. They didn't even have anything when I was there. Now they have facilities second to none. Back then they didn't even have an indoor swimming pool."

Ryan, a smiling, contented man who back then had arms as thick as a woman's waist from hauling ice in the summers, was instantly taken by this budding rock 'n' roller who showed real promise on the track, in the pool, and even some prowess on the rings in gym. Ryan knew that Ronnie's wildness just needed some taming. He liked his spirit — even when it led Ronnie to mimic Ryan in class. What he didn't like was the idea of his potential star pupil flunking out. The day a crucial test was about to start and Ronnie had yet to show up, Ryan hurried across campus and literally hauled Ronnie out of bed.

"He had a Model T," Ryan still recalls. "And he had rigged it so that it could bypass the muffler. We didn't have an anti-noise ordinance then; nevertheless, you just didn't drive cars around without a muffler. Ronnie had this thing rigged that you could just pull a knob if there were cops around and the car would be quiet. When the cops weren't around, what a racket he could make. He could put on a show! If you wanted a diver to put on a clown exhibition on a diving board, you got Ron. He could do some of the best clown acts off the diving board I have ever seen."

"I made a hundred dollars a week one summer as a clown diver," remembers Ronnie. "Esther Williams was MGM's swimming movie star then and she was involved with a swimming-pool company. The company hired her and was using her name so they hired me at a hundred a week to do clown diving for three or four weeks while they were promoting the swimming pool. I wanted to see Esther Williams. I liked her back then; she *could* swim! I never did meet her, but I'll tell you what is really strange. All these years go by and in 1988 I did a movie, *Snake Eater*, with her son Lorenzo Lamas which, so far, has been seen mostly in Europe."

Ronnie's eyes twinkle as he describes how he went to college on an athletic scholarship — without ever turning out for practice:

I lived on a full athletic scholarship when I was at the university — they just didn't know it. I didn't want to pay the tuition, but I went anyhow and I never paid a cent for five years of college. You see, I had a method. Back then they'd give the boys an athletic card with their number on it and their picture. With that card you'd get all your books, all your papers, food, everything. They had the dorm, Gregson Hall, where the athletes stayed and ate. So I made my own athletic card and used Gregson Hall. The result was, I had food, I had books, I had everything. After about two or three years that ol' gal who ran Gregson Hall said, "Son, what do you play?" She'd seen me in there eating every day but she'd never seen me do anything — football, basketball, track or anything. I can't remember what I told her, but I guess by then it didn't matter much. It was my last year before anybody knew anything and by the time they found out it was too late.

The majority of people I grew up with were interested in white country music. But there were some rebels — the ones I was running with who were like me. So I played the music I liked through high school and all through college. I made some money at it but I still needed to make a few runs for whiskey to buy the car I wanted.

Eventually I was making more and more of these whiskey runs and I started saving a little bit of money. I was only seventeen or eighteen by this time, but I was making a couple of hundred dollars a day at least. I wasn't supposed to have any money, at least not that kind of money. In a little town you can't start driving a goddamn Cadillac and start living like a pharaoh if you haven't got a job. You can get away with it in a big city because nobody knows you. But everybody knows everybody's business in a little town. And here I was, just a kid, without a job. So I kept the cash and didn't spend any of it. I had my own little bank. Because everyone was always coming through the house, I built a little hiding place for the money in my '39 Ford Coupe.

There's a space near the fender which in the old days was covered up. So I opened up this space, put a fishing-tackle box in there and then carpeted it over so it looked just like a hump. You'd just have to lift up the rug and there was my money box! And it was fireproof.

A car cost four or five hundred dollars back in the early fifties and the minimum wage around Arkansas was about fifty cents an hour. I would work for fifty cents an hour when I had to, when I wasn't playing or running whiskey. But eventually I was saving enough money to do something with it. And seeing what club owners made off bands, I decided that I should get involved in that end of the business, too. So I started owning clubs — before I was old enough to legally go into them. It was always a question of having the right front man. The first one I owned a piece of was the Tea Table, a little bitty place outside of Fayetteville. It was small but it was the only thing cheap enough for Dayton Stratton and me to get into in the early fifties. Dayton was a friend of mine who was older: my front man. Everything else was too expensive for us. We didn't have it long, just a season or two.

Dayton had a little money himself but mostly he had the know-how and the hustle. I had the money and he had the experience. He'd worked in bars before, as a bouncer and as bartender in Phoenix where his dad was a gangster. He was a beautiful cat. I dug him. I'd like to have him running a bar right now. So he fronted all our operations until I hit twenty-one and could own a liquor licence myself.

We brought Carl Perkins to the Tea Table even before "Blue Suede Shoes" had been released. We got him through this agent who was bugging us all the time: Bob Neal, the one who managed Presley first. Then we had Carl back again after the song came out in '56. After we'd made a little money there, we bought the Shamrock which was the old Bubble Club across from the drive-in theater. I bought it for about $10,000. Bubba Birks led the house band and they played Dixieland every Saturday afternoon. Bubba played piano and harmonica, but he played clarinet for the Dixieland. We had acts come in as well. Bob Neal also managed Roy Orbison, who was at the Shamrock a lot. Roy would come over and jam at the house, too. He even stayed with me a few times.

I ended up owning my first big club, the Rockwood, by myself, however, because Dayton couldn't come up with his part of the money. So he worked for me, getting a salary for looking after everything. Dayton was young, really nice and really tough. He had the hardest left I knew. He never lost a fight.

Someone else who worked at the Rockwood was Ken Brooks. He was six-foot-one and he was tough, too. He fought and won the golden gloves at 126 pounds. That's tough and *skinny*. He was also the funniest human being I knew — I mean, Jonathan Winters and Robin Williams aren't in his league.

There was the night when Kenny was working with the band and we wanted to stay in the Sands Hotel in Fayetteville. But they wouldn't let us stay at that hotel because we were rock 'n' rollers; they wouldn't let us stay even if they knew we didn't tear up anything, didn't break anything and we didn't make noise. I always had my band trying to take care of everything. We were careful of our reputation because we had already lost a lot of gigs in high school just because we played rock 'n' roll music. Well, Kenny knew exactly what to do. He got a friend of his who had this snake farm and he got a couple of dozen black moccasins in some sacks, and slipped them into the pool about five or six in the morning just before it got light. It's only the cottonmouth moccasins which are poisonous, but the black moccasins look just as bad. And of course these people came out in the morning to get into the pool and there's a couple of dozen snakes just going crazy, because they're sick — they're screwed up from the chlorine in the pool. This big old fat woman comes out and she gets on the diving board and she looks down there and screams and falls in. Damn! I mean Johnny Weissmuller couldn't have been any quicker getting out of the pool. Then of course here come the police, the fire department — all because of those snakes. Boy, it stirred up some shit. They couldn't prove anything. They couldn't prove it was us. But I thought it was time we'd better ease on out of there.

After I'd settled in Canada and was married, running the Rockwood became something of a problem. It's hard to look after anything if you're living somewhere else. My wife Wanda looked after the club for a while. I had to stay in Canada because of everything I had going on, and that's when things went haywire in the club. I had to stay away more than I should have. But we had found out that there were things going on at the club that were, well, not exactly like they should have been. So I sent Wanda down to check it out. Well, this time somebody called up immigration to get Wanda out of town, so she wouldn't do any checking up.

But because she was just down there checking the club out — she wasn't on the payroll — legally she could stay. But they were making it rough enough. At that time, whatever money I was making in Canada I was sending every penny down to Fayetteville to keep the Rockwood going. We couldn't figure it out. Things weren't adding up. Friday and Saturday nights were packed; people were lined up. We should have been making a fortune. But the money was going to other people, not us. They were just bleeding us blind.

All the better bands played the Rockwood. Jerry Lee Lewis played there a thousand times, Carl Perkins, Sonny Burgess. The club would hold 800 people. You could walk upstairs where we had dancing and hustling. It had a balcony — a huge place.

Back then Wednesday night was date night. You couldn't date on Monday, Tuesday or Thursday. But the girls could stay out a little later on Wednesday. Now, I had this little girl I went out with. She had to be fifteen years old and was Rex Perkins's youngest daughter. Rex was a big lawyer then. Anyway, at that time not too many parents would let their daughters go out with me at all. I'd have to send somebody else to get the girl and we'd meet somewhere.

Well, that particular night I borrowed a '55 Buick Century from Mr. Blackman. And I picked her up and went out driving near the school when the cops spotted us. But as the cops started to back up, boy we headed out of there, spinning gravel and all that. We ended down at Lover's Lane — that's what they actually called it — and the cops found us. Cars would slip up there onto the dirt roads of the university and have a little privacy. Nobody could afford motels; there weren't that many around, anyway. And not many folks had apartments. What the cops didn't know was that she was the one who'd been doing the driving. So we changed places and I got behind the wheel.

I tried to cross it up — I learned that in racing. You're cutting to the left but your wheels are to the right and you've got to have enough power to scoot it around. That way you can go around faster. Those big cars, you know how hard they are to steer. Next thing, I spun out and hit that ditch . . . and I hit Elmo Ritchie, too. He was one of the sheriffs around there. They chased me and I nearly hit four or five other lovers' cars. I'm going through with my lights off, you see.

"You're gonna kill somebody, hotroddin' around here," the cops told me, when they caught up to us. And later I got the usual lecture about hotrodding from the judge.

At the university, they tried to keep all the kids out of trouble and in their books so they could learn something. Well, there I was trying to do two things and finding I couldn't do both. I'm trying to play music, staying out late, then I'd have to come back to those morning classes. So, after five years at college, just before graduation, in 1957 I finally decided it was better to leave school and get this music thing over with. I could go back to university later and really hustle.

IV

ELVIS? WHAT KINDA NAME IS ELVIS?

ROCK 'N' ROLL CAME OF AGE IN THE CITY — but it was country born and bred. Rock needed the baby-booming Beatles in the sixties to boost it to its mega-billion-dollar status. But its soul was shaped by the Great Depression in the thirties. The hard times from the late twenties through the later thirties helped define what would be heard, how, and who would make it possible. When Ronnie's Uncle Delmar went west to find work as a fiddler, he was following the pattern of migration established in the hungry thirties as millions of men and women left home to better themselves. And the music Ronnie was listening to on KHOG in Fayetteville — Bob Wills and the Texas Playboys' western swing or Hank Snow, or singing cowboys like Gene Autrey — was shaped by two enormous upheavals in America: the mass-marketing of cheap entertainment brought about to dull the pain of the Depression, and the spread of new technology. In 1927, the first great country recordings were made by Jimmie Rodgers, "the singing brakeman," and the Carter Family in Bristol, deep in the heart of the Appalachian mountains on the border of Tennessee and Virginia. The arrival of new recording technology was met with new musical technology: guitarists, replacing the traditional banjo-pickers, were using amplifying hookups not only to boost the sound but to create a different kind of sound, something more electric.

Yet even though regional musicians by the dozens found their way onto record, the major recording companies were slow to pick up on this brand-new interest in old-time country music. Radio sure wasn't, though. Man, oh man, you could hear Cowboy Slim Rinehart sing and Dr. J.R. Brinkley's goat-gland rejuvenation elixirs pitched from as far away as Villa Acuna, Mexico, on station XERF. And folks living in the Midwest swore by the curative powers of Crazy Waters Crystals (a laxative), mostly because of all the great music it sponsored on the "Crazy Barn Dance" broadcast Saturday nights from Charlotte, North Carolina. Of course, there was the "Grand Ole Opry," first on WSM in Nashville and later on NBC.

Not all radio was happy with its country stars. In fact, many stations held off playing this music to the bitter end, says Bill Bolick, who along with his brother Earl made up the Blue Sky Boys. "I suppose it was what they considered a necessary evil; they knew it was popular with most of their listeners and yet they frowned on it very much and, I think, really tried to hold the country musician down."

Yet the popularity of radio's country stars, and the economics of the Depression, forced the recording industry to make drastic changes: it began to sell cheaper records and reach a new audience. RCA came up with a budget line, Bluebird, which specialized in country and "race" recordings. In 1934, Decca came out with a thirty-five cent record format which was so successful that virtually every other company had to cut their costs to stay competitive. These cheaper records in turn appealed to a new kind of audience, a younger audience with current tastes. At first, the Depression restricted movement, as young men and women stayed home as long as they could, where at least they could get free meals and a place to stay. But there soon arose a massive new migration of young people looking for work. Eventually the down-home records mirroring traditional values like home, family and local loyalties — like J.E Mainer's Mountaineers' "Maple on the Hill" or the Monroe Brothers' duet, "What Would You Give in Exchange for Your Soul" — were replaced by ones that reflected this migration.

Country music and its soon-to-be partner, the blues, expressed what it meant to be young, alive and struggling in America. The fifties generation of rock 'n' rollers was weaned on this music — these musics, actually. As much as this new generation stretched it to the limits, it never forgot what either was about, blues or country.

This generation would never be as isolated as its folks. Radio made all kinds of music increasingly available. Even the dumbest shit-kicker in the Ozarks heard the urbane Cole Porter, as well as Woody Guthrie and the other winds of change blowing in from the great and bloody strikes of the Depression like those in the Kentucky coal mines. So while the music business was figuring out what to do with this flood of new sounds — this country-bluegrass-hillbilly-gospel-downhomey-blues thing — all the good ol' country boys were coming back with their own taste of the new South. It might have been a hybrid like Bob Wills's jazzy western swing or the sound of Milton Brown's Musical Brownies. It might have been the kind of hot country fiddle Delmar Hawkins played. Whatever it was, it was hot. Damn!

Long before the executives at RCA Records swallowed hard on their martinis and bet a fortune on some dumb rube from Memphis called Elvis, long, *long* before this sassy young stud in from Fayetteville named Hawkins started recording hits in a New York studio for Roulette Records, backwater America had established the game plan. Have you heard the news? The America no one had ever heard about had just arrived.

What gives the early Sun records or Hawkins's own "Forty Days" their power-punch was not just their energy but the way it was harnessed. Even the disc itself seemed too frail a thing to contain the music. The slam-bang drive of the rhythm and the choppy, high-riding melody line were forced into a tight, classic shape by the inevitable blues-based chord structure. Rockabilly's roots in conservative country music brought to it a rock-ribbed solidity. Its hankering for the blues showed it the way to its freedom. Rock 'n' roll, in becoming simply "rock," would eventually find other musical shapes to explore. But they were all based on what was coming out of the American South and Midwest, mostly, from the late 1940s through the mid-1950s.

Popular music had rarely been so expressive, so unambiguously, sexually, funnily, directly — personal. The musicians' pleasures and passions were not yet fine-tuned or restructured by commercial second thoughts. Back then rockabilly was a dazzling balance of rebellion and acceptance, as a generation of dutiful sons and daughters with "thank you ma'am" on their lips scared the bejesus out of the world as they wiggled their hips.

By the mid-fifties most everyone in rockabilly had come to Memphis, but not everyone recorded there. Little recording studios and local radio stations were cropping up throughout North America. There were King Records in Cincinnati, Jules and Saul Bihari's Modern Records in Los Angeles's Watts area, and brother Lester Bihari's operation in Memphis. Lew Chudd's Imperial label and David and Julian Braund's Deluxe label were both in New Orleans and Norman Petty's Je-Wel label in Clovis, New Mexico, saw early efforts by Roy Orbison and Buddy Holly.

Rockabilly — or "rock-billies" music, a fusion of pure country hillbilly with the new, blues-tinged rock 'n' roll — was a purely mid-fifties confection, a term not often used kindly. Country musicians like Bill Monroe, the father of bluegrass, or western swing's Bob Wills, hated being called "hillbillies" by the uppity easterners or anyone else. And they weren't much more fond of the term "rockabilly" with its double-barreled load of bad connotations. But in truth, the emerging rockabilly style was many styles all at once and there were about as many ways to describe it as there were variations in the music itself. Chess Records continued to call it country and western for their new specialty label but some northern deejays called it country boogie. The Delmore Brothers named their song "Hillbilly Boogie," while the 1947 Jack Guthrie single was called "Oakie Boogie." To Carl Perkins it was "bopping the blues." Ronnie Hawkins only thought of it as his attempt at black music. In some instances it had hints of jazz: "Red Headed Woman" by Sonny Burgess boasted jazz trumpeter Ray Nance. Hank Penny's instrumental, "Hillbilly Be Bop," featured bebop jazz chops from country steel guitarist Speedy West. And Bill Haley's Comets were fronted after 1952 by the hard-driving rhythm 'n' blues saxophonist Rudi Pompeii.

Rockabilly was part of rock 'n' roll's classic period just as surely as Haydn and Mozart crystalized the classical period of that other kind of music. Sun Records' studio in a renovated radiator repair shop at 706 Union Avenue, Memphis, Tennessee, may not have been as swank architecturally as the Esterhazy palace where Franz Joseph Haydn plied his trade, but it nevertheless provided a focus for a music that allowed the expression of pure freedom and yet represented an exercise in decisive form.

Well before rock 'n' roll had in any way become standardized, its rough edges smoothed out into a universally accepted shape, these studios and stations were able to foster myriad rock 'n' rolls: harder and more country in Texas, bluesier in the north and east; Cajun and barrel-house piano rocking out of New Orleans. Often an individual could be the catalyst for a new sound, or a unique recording technique. A hot young engineer like Cosimo Matassa at Deluxe could effect a "sound" as much as hot young session player like bassist Bill Black or guitarist Scotty Moore at Memphis's Sun Records, or bandleader Dave Bartholomew in New Orleans. What fueled everyone's imagination was the feeling that there was a new music in the making, that it had a huge new audience, and that it was exciting in a way no music before it had been exciting. Well before 1951, when Cleveland record-store owner Leo Mintz convinced a deejay on the skids named Alan Freed that there was money to be made through a white jock plugging "race music," dozens upon dozens of producers, songwriters and pickers of all descriptions were frantically trying to harness all the energy they heard around them.

This energy came from everywhere. Post-Second-World-War nostalgia for those "happier" earlier days saw a fascination with old-time Dixieland and hot 1930s boogie-woogie piano which found its way into country music. Arthur Smith ("Guitar Boogie") and Merle Travis ("Sixteen Tons") twined country around the lickety-split boogie beat as country music's emerging generation of Hank Snow, Hank Thompson and Webb Pierce and so many others played it hotter and faster. But no group was affected more than the piano players. The great first generation of rock 'n' roll piano players, Charlie Rich, Merrill Moore, Mickey Gilley and Roy Hall, with Jerry Lee Lewis up front waving the flag, had the fire lit under their careers by boogie woogie.

And this was just one of many musical cross-overs. Bill Haley, a bright young deejay at WPWA up in Chester, Pennsylvania, was taking it the next step: blending hot country (or what he maintained was western swing) with what he knew of rhythm 'n' blues for his single, "Rock the Joint," in 1952. Like Alan Freed in Cleveland, like Atlantic Records' Ahmet Ertegun in New York or Phil and Marshall Chess in Chicago, Haley understood that the migration northward of southern blacks looking for work in industry had brought not only a demand for blues and rhythm 'n' blues but had helped make a generation of white teenagers aware of a music their parents had no idea even existed. He may not have been the idea of the teenage idol that Sam Phillips or Colonel Tom Parker promoted at Sun Records, with his big, round moon face and that weird lick of hair over his forehead. But he was right for the times. When "Rock Around the Clock" came out and was exported around the world via the movie, *Blackboard Jungle*, Haley became rock 'n' roll's first genuine hero. In British singer Ian Drury's wonderful phrase, "Big Bill Haley was the first cuckoo of spring."

But what early rock 'n' roll still needed was a musical focus. Sam Phillips was the man who found it. After all, Phillips had helped make the Chess brothers richer, selling them records by Howlin' Wolf that he himself had cut. He was making the Biharis bigger by sending them B.B. King sides. He survived the best he could by recording Memphis bluesmen like Little Milton Campbell. He knew he could become a lot richer if he could only manage to bridge the gap between black and white music.

He could make "a billion," he kept telling folks, if he could find "a white man with a Negro feel."

If you are of a mind to do so, you can blame what happened next in rock 'n' roll on Dean Martin. That's right. *That* Dean Martin. When Elvis Presley started running over his stuff for Sam Phillips, he offered bits of country and gospel, but there was as much Dean Martin material as anything else. More than music was involved here. We're talking style. Dean Martin had style (and a better voice than most critics have come to recognize). And Dean was so cool he was downright comatose. Elvis wasn't buying all those poolshark's flash duds from Lansky's in Memphis, all pink and black with monster colors and pegged pants, just to find something to do with the dollar-fifty an hour he was making driving a truck for Crown Electric. He was making a fundamental investment that provided the foundation for the emerging "youth culture": ready cash converted to instant style. Elvis was one of pop's first fashion guerrillas, zapping the squares. Looking anti-frantic. Made in the shade. Cool.

This meant diddly-squat to Sam Phillips. All Sam Phillips knew, after this wild young dude had cut a couple of demos for "That's All Right" from Arthur Crudup and put a gloss on Bill Monroe's version of "Blue Moon of Kentucky," was that by 1954 he'd found his man — the singer who was going to make the magic happen. And as for Elvis's hair? That great, structured pile of hair, that *pompadour*? Well, at least the boy was polite, Sam figured.

But Presley brought to Phillips more than just the answer to a musical problem in one neat package. He brought the wrapping. Music and style — only one part was missing.

Presley's rapid ascent up the country charts, then onto package country tours, was quickly noted wherever there was someone waiting for the next musical tremor. But what people really took notice of were the news reports in the music-trade papers or even the smaller dailies which noted that while Hank Snow or the Cowboy Copas had been the stars of the show, it was the lanky young Elvis Presley from Tupelo, Mississippi, who had caused the most commotion, particularly among the young women. Women! Screaming!

Whether RCA's executives knew it at the time they started negotiating for Presley's contract, whether the television produc-ers understood it as they nervously began to lure rock acts onto their shows back east, the essential ingredients for rock 'n' roll were finally in place: music, style — and sex.

Talk to anybody there at the beginning, whether Carl Perkins, Johnny Cash, Sonny Burgess or D.J. Fontana, Elvis's drummer for so many years, they all agree that if Elvis hadn't come along someone would have had to invent him. But he *was* there. And the potent combination of his enormous talent, RCA's enormous promotional budget and its equally enormous gamble on selling him to a non-country audience — the biggest and best gamble in the company's troubled history — made the payoff beyond anyone's wildest imagination. Presley wasn't the first of the modern pop phenoms. Credit there must go to Frank Sinatra. But it was Presley who embodied so many of the factors that went into shaping the new, emerging culture of the latter half of the century: its media-friendliness, its talent for instant synthesis, its penchant for larger-than-life personalities.

Elvis was where the action was, and as quickly as they could, record companies across the continent tried to get their own piece of that action. Sam Phillips, who'd done nicely in his deal with RCA for Presley, started recording a moody farm kid out of Arkansas who played a lot of piano: Charlie Rich. Fred Foster, the bright young producer behind the new Nashville pop label, Monument, finally found the key to recording Roy Orbison, and "Only the Lonely" became their first hit. And in New York, Morris Levy was hearing a lot about another young stud out of Arkansas who, they said, was better looking than Elvis and wilder than stink: Ronnie Hawkins.

"Like a lot of cats," says Ronnie, "I went to Memphis when I was a kid. I went to buy records at first. Then I went to hang out." From the start, Ronnie knew that to be a rocker he had to be where the rockers were:

I discovered Sun when I was buying records because Sun was originally a black label. But when it started to rock, well, I wanted to get a deal with it. Everybody did; everybody wanted to record for Sun and go to Memphis. Maybe if you were really into country music you'd go to Nashville. But if you played what I wanted to play — what the Burnett Brothers played, and Jerry Lee Lewis and all those other cats — then you went to Memphis. Hell, nowadays it would be an easy trip, but back then it was long. And because it was some distance you ended up staying there for a bit, and hanging out, which is how I started meeting all those guys: Elvis, Johnny Cash, Carl Perkins. We were all after the same thing. It wasn't New York or Los Angeles for us. It was Memphis.

But Memphis was a tough town. It was the roughest town to make a living in because there were so many great musicians and so few places to play. There were lots of fights. Johnny and Dorsey Burnett played the most violent, the hottest goddamn music you ever heard. I called it bumble-bee rock 'n' roll because it was so damn fast. They're both dead now but they were the toughest sons of bitches you ever did see. I mean, they wouldn't take any shit from anybody. If someone said something — you know, called them "queers" because they had their hair a half-inch longer than a crew cut — they'd lay their instruments down, come down off the stage and beat the livin' shit out of whoever said it. They were powerful redneck fightin' mothers.

After a while, you got to know where to go. I used to buy my clothes at Lansky Brothers, where Presley used to buy all his stuff until he got so big they started making it for him specially. At Lansky's you could get stuff in pinks and whites and blacks and all the hip colors the guys were wearing back then. The clothes then were sort of a fall-off from the zoot suit days in the forties: peg pants, and the wide knee, long coats with padding to make your shoulders look broader. You could buy pants with pink strips down them. I also bought pointed shoes, in different colors, Italian-style shoes.

Back then my colors were mainly black and red. That was another great thing about Lansky's. Because we were all poor musicians, a lot of their clothes were reversible, for me red on one side, black on the other, so people wouldn't think you just had one suit of clothes. If you'd wear a red shirt, then you'd wear a black reversible vest. We were trying to show we were making it.

But because of all that competition it was tough to really make it. Hell, Buddy Holly came to Memphis and was turned down. Roy Orbison didn't make it there, and he'd already cut "Ooby Dooby" and "Go Go Go."

Then there was Elvis. I met him two or three times down there but nothing ever worked out between us because we were seventeen or eighteen years old and both were trying to do something for ourselves. Later on, just before he died, I heard he used to listen to my old records. But back then he was cocky, real cocky. He was trying to get going like everyone else. And of course I had to be the one to try to get him to change his name. I thought he should change Elvis Presley to a good stage name because, well, "Elvis Presley" didn't sound right. Back then no one had ever heard of a name like Elvis Presley. In fact, I've never heard of it since, except for two or three black dudes named Elvis. So I told him it didn't sound right.

"Elvis, you've got to call yourself 'Rock' or 'Jack' or something,"

I said. "Anything as long as it's not 'Elvis Presley.'"

Well, damn. You know what he told me? Elvis said, "I'm going to make more money than all of you guys put together. And I'm going to make it with *my* name."

And in about three years he did. He was different. It started to happen for him after Sam Phillips put him together with Bill Black who played bass and Scotty Moore on guitar. They were good session guys, fine musicians. Elvis just played a little rhythm guitar. There were just the three of them when they went out on tour because they weren't allowed to have drummers on some of those shows. And then he started playing all the little clubs, the same clubs I've played, in Arkansas, too. And his reputation started growing. In Newport, Arkansas, one day, they canceled Elvis because they were afraid he was too wild for the kids.

He was doing hopped-up country but they didn't have a name for it then. They called it hot country for a little while; later they called it rock 'n' roll. Me, I just called it music. That was it. I had no other name for it. I was trying to copy the blues; it was that basic. But that's what everybody was doing at the time, all the cats — although nobody wanted to admit they were copying the black music.

"Shit," I thought. "What difference does it make if it's black or green or yellow or blue, if it's music everybody likes?"

But the South is so strong with religion, and at that time it was as prejudiced as hell. People in the South did not want white kids dancing to sinful "nigger music," as they called it. Yet there we were, trying to play black music, but it was coming out differently because we couldn't do it right. It was coming out like country rock. We were taking the old rhythm 'n' blues songs and playing them country-style with a black beat. We were doing that with Hank Williams stuff, too. That made it extra tough back then, because there were so many who didn't like what we were doing. I'll tell you something: The most money I ever made for one night in the first three years of my career was the night a cat gave us $300 to *stop* playing. He said we were too wild.

"Son," he told me, "I love Hank Williams, and you're crucifying him and his music."

He gave us $300 to not do anything at a time I was making only seventy-five for playing. We figured we were going to follow him around and set up everywhere he went.

Now Elvis just kept playing and getting bigger and bigger, finally making it to the Louisiana Hayride show. That's when he picked up D.J. Fontana, the drummer. He kept drawing crowds and then, of course, Colonel Tom showed up, and that was that. Elvis was going to become a star.

I met Colonel Tom Parker several times, because at the time he ran some little country carnivals that would come through all the small towns. Colonel Tom had carnival acts and dancing chickens, but one of the biggest things he had going was that medicine of his. Colonel Tom Parker's own special remedy was eighty percent pure alcohol. It was years before the Pure Food and Drug Administration caught up to it. But you could see why he was so successful with his medicine. These were very religious people down there. If you put a gun to their heads telling them they had to drink that whiskey, hell, they'd take the bullet. They didn't drink whiskey, no sir! Meanwhile, their damn iceboxes were stacked to the gills with Colonel Tom's special remedy. Each bottle said right on the label that it was eighty percent alcohol, but that didn't matter. It wasn't whiskey and that was good enough for those religious people.

But it wasn't the good Colonel's remedy that made me feel better — it was those trips to Memphis.

Whenever I was in Memphis in those early days I was tight with guys like Roy Orbison. They used to know a month ahead of time when I was coming through the area, and I'd get ten phone calls inviting me to come on out. But as time went on they didn't call as much and we all just went our separate ways. Roy was different from the others. He was a quiet one. He wasn't a rocker. He was a ballad singer who always wanted to be a rock 'n' roller.

These were the days when I was just starting and was still in university and not sure what was going to happen. But I'd done enough shows back in Fayetteville, and I'd met enough people that they'd heard of me in Memphis. So I got a call from Bill Justis — he's the sax player who had a big hit in 1957 with that instrumental song called "Raunchy" — who was doing artist and repertoire work for Sun Records. He wanted me to do some demos.

People around Memphis were saying nice things about me, I guess. Things like, "This kid's outgrowing everybody." So Sun gave me a shot. Of course, by this time they'd already signed Carl Perkins from Jackson, Tennessee. They'd already signed Johnny Cash who had just come out of the air force and was selling cars. His band, the Tennessee Two, were the mechanics working on those cars.

Then there was Jerry Lee Lewis, who came from Louisiana — he had a real reputation — and Charlie Rich, who was from Arkansas, too. Charlie was good; crazy drunk all the time, but he was good. We never got together to play but I crossed paths with Charlie a lot. He was always one of my favorites but he was always a little weird. All that boozing changed his personality. On some of those early Sun tapes, Jerry Lee's drunk, Sam Phillips is drunk and they get into religion. You never heard such craziness in your life. They'd go into the studio for a week. Carl Perkins would be in there, too and they'd just drink until everybody passed out. Then they'd come back the next day to see if they'd done anything — to see what was on the tapes. And they'd start the whole thing over again. They'd take a couple of pills, drink some Jack Daniels and it would start all over again.

Understand, all through this time Carl Perkins was getting red hot — he and his brothers Jay and Clayton, as well as W.S. Holland, used to perform as The Perkins Brothers Band. They even had their own show on WTJS out of Jackson. Anyway, "Blue Suede Shoes" was the number-one song around. Red Foley had a network of country stations out of Springfield, Missouri, and Carl appeared on Red Foley's show. He was really hot and they had their best break and were going to New York to do the Perry Como show when they had the car wreck. Jay never did recover entirely. Carl had bad injuries to his spine and the crash took off part of his scalp. That's why he had to wear a toupée ever since. He hit the concrete in the crash and it just scalped him. He was two or three years getting over it.

He lost all these great years when he had a number-one record and couldn't do anything about it. That really hurt the most. And it was Elvis who ended up getting a hit with "Blue Suede Shoes," although this was years after Carl had already done it. Elvis ended up over there at Sun, cutting everything, but when Colonel Tom

Parker arrived he saw what Elvis had and he started making sure that what Elvis cut was exclusive, so no one else could record it.

When Bill Justis got me into the studio we cut a lot of demos in about two goddamn weeks. I had his Sun session boys as backup, people who played with Jerry Lee, with Elvis, everybody. We went into the high studio as they called it where they had a one-track board. We all had to gather around one mike but I stood a little closer because I was doing the singing. The first two tunes we cut, if I remember correctly, were "Lawdy Miss Clawdy" and Hank Williams's "Mansion On the Hill." After we'd finished for a while we'd head right down to Beale Street to hear what was going on there. There were a lot of us getting started around Memphis at the same time so we met everyone.

Even though they'd asked me to cut some demos, Sam was so busy with Jerry Lee and Elvis, and they were selling so many records all at one time — it seemed that the yellow Sun label had every pressing plant in the world locked up — they didn't do anything with us. A little later some other record companies were interested. Columbia wanted us to sign with them. And so did Roulette Records, up in New York. So we finally got the deal with Roulette in 1958. But back then I was waiting around for my deal from Sun and when it didn't happen I went back home.

I still had some schooling to do. I had my clubs to think about. And I had a little time to spend with the army.

V

Up and Down Comes Natural . . .

The Legend Teaches the Army a Lesson, Dodges a Shotgun Blast and Confronts a Very Serious Vibrator

WHEN RONNIE AND THE UNITED STATES ARMY enjoyed each other's company, the Hawk was a green kid out of school with rock 'n' roll heroics on his mind. The army merely had Russia, the Korean War and the Cold War on its mind. It was not a match of equals. Ronnie taught the army the kind of moves it never learned in tank training school. The army learned to dance.

Coming in, Ronnie was all prepared to surrender immediately — it didn't matter to whom. Six months later, after Ronnie's stint was barely finished, it was the army's turn to think of surrendering:

In the summer of 1957 I ended up in the army. The American army. Let me tell you, the United States of America had never been safer since Audie Murphy was in it. In those days, America wanted everyone to be ready to fight. You had to do something, somehow, for the military. I wanted to enter it as a prisoner of war, but I don't think they would have gone for that. I spent four years in the National Guard when I was in university, then I volunteered for the regular army. You see, I'd heard that the army was about to change its rules. I'd heard that it wouldn't be much time at all before you'd have to spend a full two years in the regular army. But if I joined before that deadline it would only be six months for someone with all the ROTC training I'd had. I wasn't joining the Green Berets or anything; I got lucky and got in the Special Services, where you go and put on little shows at the officers' clubs, the non-coms clubs and at the PXs. So I went to Fort Smith, Arkansas, for twelve weeks of basic training, then to Laughton, Oklahoma, and Fort Sill, Oklahoma, for the next six months. And it was there I met the Blackhawks and started getting into more trouble then I'd ever been in my entire life — up until then.

Basic training was at Fort Chaffee, Arkansas. The barracks I got assigned to were wretched. Some big dumb old football player had been assigned to it as the sergeant of the barracks and he thought he was R.A. — that's "regular army." These barracks had mostly blacks and Puerto Ricans and this redneck was giving them a real hard time, making them eat cigarettes and all the rest of the shitty things they made recruits do back them. So everyone in the barracks was rebelling.

The Puerto Ricans pretended they couldn't speak English, though as everyone knew, except maybe that dumb old sergeant, you had to speak English to get into the army. The more he tried to make them knuckle under the more they all rebelled. So they put me in charge. I'd also built up quite a lot of P.T. — physical training — points because I was quite athletic in those days. I looked good on paper so I became the sergeant of the barracks. Well, damn, the first thing I did was have a meeting with the two baddest rebels we had. One guy was this huge black dude, about 220 pounds — he looked like Mike Tyson's meaner, bigger brother. The other cat was this skinny Puerto Rican kid, weighing maybe only 120 pounds, but who was a real blade artist. He was a Picasso with a knife. You didn't have to be Einstein to figure out that these were the two guys you had to get on your side, so I appointed them squad leaders.

The army used to harrass you in those days on inspection when they would come around and see how dirty your barracks were. And it was nearly impossible to keep them clean because even if you did have enough time after an inspection was announced, you'd never have enough mops to clean up everything. I mean, there'd only be two or three mops for any one barracks. Next to ours was another barracks full of dumb, football-playing rednecks who kept giving us shit because our barracks were so dirty and we were always getting in trouble. So I decided we'd go out on what you call a midnight requisition – one of those "advance detail parties" the regular army never did find out about – and by the time we got back, we had mops for each and every man in the barracks. We took every mop on the base not nailed down. So everybody in our barracks had a mop under his bed. When they started calling instant inspections we'd have our place shining in minutes. They couldn't believe it. Of course, they never did find those mops.

One night some of those big old football players came across one of our little Puerto Rican cats and beat him up with his own belt. They whipped him so hard across his back and the back of his legs there were huge goddamn blue marks all over him. So I got that big black squad leader of mine and that blade artist and I went over to the sergeant of their barracks.

"Let me tell you something, Hoss," I said to their sergeant, showing him the cats I had with me, "this fucker can bite your leg off, and this little Puerto Rican can throw an apple up in the air and have it peeled before it hits ground. You understand? These two guys will take care of you if you ever mess with any one of us again. Maybe you guys can beat some of us up but a couple of your dumb shitkickers will find themselves dead in the process."

Well, hell, *that* got their respect. So one thing led to another and we went from being the worst barracks to the best in that whole section of the army. We started marching right. We started looking really sharp, especially the Puerto Rican guys. They'd only been rebelling because they'd been treated like dogs. The little old second lieutenant who was in charge didn't notice what was going on — after all, he was from West Point and was as green as a gourd. But the colonel on the base came over and took a look. Well, as it ended up I was named Soldier of the Month and was given a medal by the governor, Orval Faubus.

Next stop after basic training was Fort Sill where I had some real important assignments — like cleaning up after plagues of locusts and swarms — pestilences? — of crickets. And looking for rattlesnakes. This was as close to the regular army as I'd been.

They were selling the rattlesnake venom. They'd also have a great big cook-off — a rattlesnake barbecue. Well, the army sure did that rattlesnake hunt up right. They were *serious*. They'd have you act as if you were bivouacked out in the woods. You'd set up your tents with all your field gear as if you were ready to go to war or something. Then after breakfast each platoon would head to a certain designated area where there were millions of rattlesnakes. Everyone had sacks and sticks, ready to get those damn snakes. You were supposed to take the stick, which had a fork in it, and put it behind the snake's head, then reach down with your hand and pick that snake up and stick it in your sack.

I was the lowest in my class when it came to trapping rattlesnakes. It seems I couldn't find any, not as long as I was in the army. Not one. But there was a perfectly good reason for this. I was asleep in a truck the whole time. I'd lie there in that big old four-by-four, a four-ton four wheel drive truck, that is, until noon when they had a signal to come in; then after lunch I'd go back again for another rest. I had a little mattress up there in the back of the truck. It was nice. I'd just have to make sure there were no rattlesnakes in the truck — and no scorpions in my boots. Scorpions were the worst thing. They love to crawl into your boots. Man, every morning you'd hear some of the cats yelling after they'd stuck their feet down into their boots and got hooked with those scorpion tails. Damn! They made Tarzan sound like a mute.

When I was a kid, folks actually hunted, really hunted. It was almost a necessity to got squirrel hunting, rabbit hunting, and for possum and groundhogs and the like, all to help with the supply of food. Everybody had hound dogs. I can remember way back when I was only four and five years old. I remember how the men used to got out hunting and how they went out fishing. On Sundays they went to church in the mornings and fishing in the afternoon, trying to catch a mess of fish. But I don't remember *anyone* hunting for rattlesnake and I wasn't about to start the trend. No, sir.

I was a sergeant first class, by benefit of the training I had, and I got in with the first sergeant in the regular army. Sergeant Young, he was. We got to be buddies because he liked music — Hank Williams and Lefty Frizzell, some of the same country people I liked. Eventually he got to like some of the rocking stuff I was doing, so I got some soft details. Sergeant Young was different; he knew what it was like to be scared, I guess. He'd been captured by the Japanese and had spent time in a Japanese concentration camp. I remember him telling me that he went into the camp weighing 220 pounds and came out weighing ninety-three. He was tough, he was. And good. He was a master sergeant first class, that's three stripes up and three stripes down with a diamond in the middle. He was the boss in the field artillery. I wasn't counting on learning too much about field artillery, though. I wasn't really counting on a war.

One of my buddies, a guitar player, told me there was a really good black band playing at a club — the Amvets Club — back in Laughton, Oklahoma (Leon Russell's home), where we could go with our weekend passes. Amvets stood for American Veterans of Foreign Wars. It was really a scam but that was the only way it could get to be called a private club. So we went over and watched the band play. After a while I got up on stage and sang two or three songs. The first time I did this it went over pretty good, so after the second and third times the owner of the club approached me. I wasn't in the band or anything but she wanted me to play there every week with them. And Jesus! She was going to pay me and everything. Twenty dollars a night! The big time! After a while she even wanted to be my manager.

Her name was Mary Jo, she was about thirty years old at the time, she was really good looking, and she was making a pot full of money at this club. You see, it was a private club, one of those places that you had to have a membership card just so you could drink. It attracted mostly servicemen, but there were some Indians, too. Because the club was private, you could do anything. Gambling, slot machines, anything. You could get mixed drinks which you couldn't elsewhere because Oklahoma was a dry state. I don't know if politicians in Oklahoma think about it this way, but they can thank the bootleggers for keeping it a dry state. The bootleggers wanted it dry so they could make all that money.

The club wasn't that big, holding maybe 250 people, but it had a nice bar and a good reputation. She kept it that way. If you started a fight you knew two things: not only would you get your head busted but you'd never be allowed back in the club, and it was almost the only action around. Once she told people to quiet

first group he ever played with.
Ronnie is second from the
, first row, in grade one,
tsville, Arkansas.

nie's great-grandfather,
ard, the first Hawkins to settle
kansas.

Music runs in the family: two of Ronnie's uncles, Delmar and Eddie.

Rompin' Ronnie and Carl Perkins in 1957. They drank a bottle a day — the secret to all that en

Uncle Sam needed the Hawk! Sgt. Ronald C. Hawkins, 936th Field Artillery Battalion, Fort Chaffee, Arkansas.

Boys just want to have fun: with Levon Helm at the drums. Oshawa, 1958.

A lean and mean Hawk in 1 with Will Pop Jones at the p

On their first visit to Canada: Hawkins *(left)*, Levon Helm and Jimmy Ray Paulman at the Golden Rail in Hamilton.

Ronnie Hawkins and the Hawks in 1958: the famous camel walk.

"The R R on the front must stand for rock 'n' roll," says Ronnie. (CANADIAN MOTORIST)

Ronnie and John Lennon, with "two of the luckiest girls in the world," Wanda Hawkins and Yoko Ono.

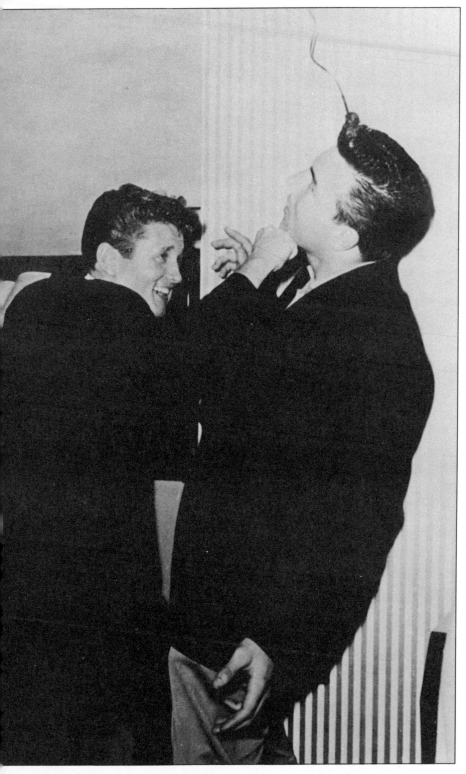

From one champion to another: the Hawk sends George Chuvalo to slumberland.

One of Ronnie's heroes, Walter "Heavy" Andrews, at the Cambridge Hotel in 196[...]

Down deep, a family man: *Clockwise fro[m] left:* Hawkins with Ron Jr., Wanda, Rob[in,] Leah.

down, they did. In case it didn't work, she had a buzzer system which called in the bouncers and they'd go to work on the guy. With army personnel it was different, of course. You'd have to call the MPs. The army was worse than the rest, rowdier and all, what with all those young guys, eighteen, nineteen years old, just out of boot camp, getting drunk and causing trouble because they thought they were the 101st Airborne.

She was doing okay but she felt she still needed bigger crowds and that, I think, that is where I came in. I'd get up on stage with these four black guys and sing things like "Lawdy Miss Clawdy," which Lloyd Price wrote back in the late forties, and "Ooby Dooby" and "Go Go Go" by Roy Orbison. The piano player would do "Kansas City" and I'd do Jerry Lee Lewis's version of "You Win Again," which was originally by Hank Williams. We also did "Let the Good Times Roll" by Shirley and Lee — she was Shirley Goodman and he was Leonard Lee, and they were supposed to be having this big romance in real life, but they weren't. It was only on record. Whatever we did, it sounded like something between the blues and rockabilly. It sort of leaned in both directions at the same time, me being a hayseed and those guys playing a lot funkier. What a band! One hayseed and four blacks.

For a long time we tried to come up with a name for the group. That's back when there were groups called the Cadillacs, the Sevilles and the Penguins. So our guitar player said, "Hey, we might just as well call ourselves 'The Redneck and Four Fuckin' Niggers' because that's what everybody's calling us, anyway." We ended up with the name the Blackhawks, because of that cartoon strip that Marvel Comics had. It was about these flying aces who called themselves the Blackhawks.

The drummer was quite the cat. He was a good drummer; he kept that old fatback-drum back beat rocking. He played a set of drums that must've been fifty years old. He said he'd played with Count Basie, Duke Ellington and for sure he'd been around. He liked a drink now and then, though, and by payday he'd owe his money to the bar; he never had any money. Mary Jo was paying us twenty dollars a night, and we could eat at her club, too. That was real good money for then, but it still didn't go that far. Once we had to get the shocks fixed in the car we were using, and we were told it'd cost a hundred bucks. Well, we didn't have the hundred. "Hell," the drummer said. "A little rockin' never hurt anyone, anyway."

But he had women everywhere! I mean, women *really* liked him. He was one of the ugliest old guys you'd ever seen, but black women dug him, and some white women, too. Now those white women weren't those young Elizabeth Taylors you see around these days, but the type that had the odd tattoo or two. Women didn't show off their tattoos much in the fifties. Nowadays they're as common as a horse turd at a rodeo. But those were tough times. Those were tough women. I still don't know how he did it. It seemed he had a wife or an old lady in every town we played. He never had to rent a motel room. He always had someplace to sleep.

The piano player was trying to imitate Little Richard at that time. Little Richard had a couple of hit records out like "Tutti-Frutti," "Long Tall Sally" and "Slippin' and A-Slidin'" — our piano player used to call it "the Vaseline song." He didn't wear make-up like Little Richard did but he'd stand up like Little Richard and fold his leg up. His name was Rufus, but he didn't like being called that. He wanted something cool, like Pig Meat Markham. Only *he* was called Big Meat Markham. I sang Little Richard's "Lucille" with him. But he played other things as well: "Kansas City" in the real pumping style piano; some Joe Turner things, too. We did all sorts of different music back then, but when we played the rock 'n' roll songs in just the right place, hell, we'd get mobbed. You didn't have to be anybody famous, either. You just had to play it really good, and the kids would mob you.

Our guitar player was a really funny cat. He reminds me now of Richard Pryor. He was a really cool guy, called himself "Pretty Boy" LeRoy Moody. He wore his hair straight, with a mojo rag on to hold his hair back — the style for a lot of black cats back then was to wear their hair straight. He was light skinned, so he told a lot of girls he was Spanish or Indian. He was a real lady killer, and a lot of white girls dug him, although he tried to avoid them to keep out of trouble.

I remember someone back then asked me if I'd ever fucked a black girl. I said, "Well, I thought I had until I saw LeRoy fuck one, then I knew I hadn't."

He was one cat you didn't steal a girl from. Hell, a cocaine dealer couldn't steal a girl from LeRoy Moody and a cocaine dealer can steal anybody's girl. When LeRoy was with 'em, baby, they were branded. When he had to, I mean when were down South, he became really Spanish. He had the accent and everything. He sounded like Fernando Lamas. Man, he had drawing power like Kris Kristofferson when it came to women.

One night I was with his main squeeze at the time, a really beautiful girl, sort of a seventeen-year-old Lena Horne, with a body like Miss America. This night I was just making sure she got to her car safely; the rest of the band were finishing up doing something inside. It had been a wild night. The club had already thrown five or six redneck cowboys out. They were too drunk and they should never have been let in in the first place. They were mouthing off at the band and I'd given the sign so Mary Jo had signaled the doorman and they were thrown out. They'd parked their truck at the Amvets Club, but they went to another club and had gotten even drunker. So there I was, coming out of the Amvets with Pretty Boy's girl, and these five rednecks came up to us, making trouble, saying "nigger" this and "nigger" that. They grabbed us and they were going to kick the shit out of me, and they were going to rape her, for sure. They ripped her dress, grabbed her ass and her tits. Two guys held me. Then a cop car came by. Maybe the club they'd just been at had called the cops on them, maybe it was an accident. That ended it there. I know what would have happened if those rednecks had hurt her. I've seen what guys like LeRoy can do. They'd scrape a dead cat or dog that had been killed on the road and put it in somebody's car as a warning. They'd put a cheap old alarm clock in a little suitcase, and set it on somebody's front porch. I saw it work once. This good old boy came outside, picked up that suitcase and heard that goddamn clock ticking and he practically killed himself getting back in, yelling, "Ohhhh," almost knocking his damn door right off its hinges, running back inside. Five minutes later the sirens were coming from everywhere. Guys like LeRoy could torment a redneck to death.

But by the end of my career with the Blackhawks, before I went back to Fayetteville to start my own band, those dumb old rednecks became friends of the Blackhawks. About six weeks after that incident one of them called me, wanting to apologize. He said they were drunk, all fucked up and all that. He told me they were really sorry, that they really loved our music and he wanted me to talk to Mary Jo to see if they could be reinstated at the club. Maybe that's all they really wanted, but later on whenever we got into trouble with other rednecks those guys were the ones who saved our asses. They were the kind of redneck assholes who had four or five rifles on racks in their trucks and who grew up listening to Bob Wills music. They called what we did "nigger music," but they'd started to like it. It was getting to them. They were our bodyguards for the rest of our careers.

Once a bunch of older redneck farmers — by "older" I mean guys around thirty-five — came into the Amvets Club and got drunk and started booing the music. They started throwing bottles, showing off in front of one another. Well, we had one answer for that shit. We just quit playing and loaded up and started to leave. But as soon as those new redneck friends of ours saw what was happening, they went over to those guys causing trouble and just wiped the place up with them. They broke every stick of furniture in the club to do it, too. Everything. Those clubs were geared to the odd scuffle, you understand. You couldn't hurt the floors at all. And the beer bottles, those big, long-necked old beer bottles, were strong. A bullet couldn't break them. This time, one of those old farmers came at me and I hit him as hard as I could with a beer bottle and he went down. Bleeding bad. The blood spurted to the ceiling every time his heart beat.

To Ronnie, his wild old army days meant more than the brawls, girls and backroad clubs. In his mind, the Blackhawks crystalized the kind of music he wanted to make:

By this time I was developing my act. Before I joined them, the Blackhawks had been playing some really good blues, the older style, the jazz-pop kind of blues like Cab Calloway might've done back in the forties. They'd been together for a long time. I never did know their ages exactly, but they weren't kids anymore. They'd been around. The problem was, they weren't drawing that many people. So after I came along, they had to start playing as close as they could to my material. It came out like the original tunes, but funkier. So instead of doing a kind of rockabilly that was closer to country music, I was doing rockabilly that was closer to soul music, which was exactly what I liked. It was closer to what Chuck Berry was doing, and Little Richard, Fats Domino and Ray Charles. We'd do all the songs which had made it to the hit parade. Sam Cooke had "You Send Me." The Crickets with Buddy Holly had "That'll Be the Day," and we did that, but it always came out funky.

Another thing that helped us get a crowd were all the gymnastics I was doing on stage. I don't know if what I did can compare to what the kids now do on stage — I mean, some of the kids can *fly*. But I could do a double backflip, which was pretty far out. I did other things but the double backflip was the top of my line. I'd do all the front flips, the splits and some tumbling. I'd do a flip right off the stage — what I was doing then was basically the same stuff I ended up doing when I arrived in Canada. When I was at the Concord, on Bloor Street in Toronto, they had the stage right in the middle of the room, because the ceiling was at just the right height for a backflip. They had part of the stage padded, too, in case I missed. I missed about one out of ten times, but all that meant was that I'd fall backwards on my ass. Hell, that became part of the act, too.

Anyway, it was all those backflips I developed with the Blackhawks that later gave me all those names advertisers for clubs like to use, like Jumpin' Ronnie Hawkins and Rompin' Ronnie. I also used to do the camel walk, which goes forward the way Michael Jackson's moon walk goes backward. I used to do it when I sang "Mary Lou." Another thing we used to do was tell all the servicemen back at the base about what was happening at the club, so a lot more people started coming down to yell and clap and eventually it got so crowded that people couldn't get in. You know what that meant: even *more* people started coming because they'd heard you couldn't get in.

That's when Mary Jo offered to manage us and eventually we got to play a few other clubs around the area after my time in the army was over. But things were getting a bit complicated. By now we were even living together as a band — well, most of the time — in the Penthouse. At least, that's what we called it. Actually, it was one big room above an auto-body shop. It was sort of like the army barracks in its way. There were no partitions between the beds, so we hung blankets in between. You could always hear what was going on in the next suite, of course. If you had your special girl with you, you were left alone. But if you picked up someone you wanted to have a little fun with, well, you might want to share the wealth. I'm not saying there were orgies or anything like that. I'd rather call it seven or eight people in love.

There was only one bathroom, and that was down a flight of stairs, where the auto-body cats could use it in the day time. You can imagine what that bathroom was like, covered in grease. There was a shower and a tub, too, but everyone had to line up before we went out to play each night. Because the shop downstairs closed at five each day, the good thing about it was that we could practice and make all the noise we wanted to. You could roar and play, fuck and fart, and it didn't matter. We'd sleep till about noon, because we'd been up real late the night before, and the auto-body guys would get in about seven in the morning. They'd be drilling and pounding and banging, but after a while we became so used to it we'd sleep right through it.

The problem was that some of our guests never got used to it — the girls, I mean. There were lots of girls around our suites in the Penthouse in those days. I had a girl or two of my own there, real pretty girls. You can imagine what it was like for them, and the rest of us, when all the banging started downstairs and everyone would be upstairs, with bodies and bottles and panties strewn everywhere, everyone having fucked their brains out until four in the morning. Agony. It was only okay over the weekends when the body-shop guys didn't show up. Man, then there'd really be a party. Damn! There'd be girls running around naked, and guys running after them trying to get their dicks hard. Those were great nights.

I remember once telling a great guitar player I heard — a black guy, completely unknown but a really great player — that I really felt sorry for him, "Because," I said, "you're black. As good as you are, if you were white you'd be making a billion dollars an hour."

"Aw, shit," he said. "If *you* were black for just one Saturday night, you'd never want to be white again."

Well, living with the Blackhawks and being with all those little girls sure made me think about what the old guitar-playing cat told me. But things were getting complicated. It seems that Mary Jo had an extra job in mind for me: taking care of her. She was an aggressive woman. A business woman. She always dressed well, like she was going to church; she always wore expensive suits. She laughed loud and she was kind of naughty. She had this great, huge mansion of a place and sometimes I'd stay there with her. I got the impression, the *distinct* impression, that if I ever stopped working on her, she would have stopped getting the band jobs. I think she was close to being a nymphomaniac or something, because she was real persistent. Damn. You'd do your best job on her, and you'd get up to go and she'd throw her claws into you and say, "No, you're not through yet." That was downright scary, you know. Scary. And just after you've performed up to your Olympic ability, too. I spent a lot of time in her bathroom hiding and I'd hear through the door, "Yoo-hoo — you're not thro-oo-ough yet."

Jesus, what she didn't teach me! "Ronnie," she told me one night, "Up and down comes natural — it's that other stuff that's got to be learned."

I soon found out what she meant. She had apparatuses in her bedroom. She had one of those *serious* vibrators, the kind you had to kick-start. That bugger was serious. If you plugged it in, there'd be an eight-mile power failure. It had nine speeds forward and thirty-seven in reverse. It'd take Mario Andretti to shift the fucker.

After a while I was driving a Cadillac — her Cadillac — and that pissed off her ex-husband. She'd married this guy twice. But this time around they were really through, although he didn't see it that way, particularly with me driving his ex-wife's Cadillac around. What helped was that her brothers were in the Dixie mafia. They were white guys who ran some illegal booze cans and ran a little whiskey; not big-time Chicago-type gangsters, but small-time crooks. Her ex-husband was a bad guy, too. After she and I had become close we got word that he was going to kill me for fucking his old lady, although this was after their second divorce. He came around a couple of times and told me he was going to send some guys with guns after me. That's when we all started carrying guns, me and all the guys in the band.

Eventually this made us extra leery. We started looking over our shoulders at anything that moved. By this time we thought everybody was out after our asses — hoods, rednecks, old women in wheelchairs, *everybody* looked suspicious. We got to spending so much time looking at the door, checking out who's coming in, it got so we couldn't think. Or play. So Mary Jo called her brothers and they went after her ex-husband. To this day I don't know what happened to him, but all the threatening stopped.

By now, my relationship with her was getting harder and harder to handle. She'd invested a lot of money in our little band. It was about fifteen hundred dollars, but in today's terms that could be easily fifteen thousand — hell, or $150,000. I felt I couldn't leave even though I felt like I had become her goddamn houseboy. She just had to whistle and it seemed I had to come running. The roughest part of all this was here I was, tied down to the boss of the club, while through the door came the best looking young women you ever did see. The only way I could make my intentions known was to whisper in the guitar player's ear and he'd whisper to the girl to meet me somewhere later. Damn, but there got to be a lot of whispering going on. To make it all still worse, Mary Joe wanted me to come home with her every Saturday night. It was part of my unwritten contract. Well, as everyone in the Western world knows, Saturday is the best night for pussy. Always has been. The rest of the week it wasn't too bad dealing with Mary Jo, though. A couple of times she came around to the Penthouse when I had a girl up there, but I'd always say something like, "Don't come up, it's too messy," or "You'll get messed up," and she'd wait until I came downstairs. Eventually, she found out a lot of what I'd been doing, but she forgave me.

The band was starting to go out on the road and play, so I didn't get to see her all that much any longer. Besides, I had enough fights on my hands just playing music. Some of the clubs we played in had chicken wire across the front of the stage to intercept the bottles when someone decided he didn't like something you were doing and threw one in your direction. These were brown-bag clubs. People would bring their booze in those little brown bags and buy their mix at the club. They'd get real drunk and throw the bottles at us.

Those places always had dance floors. They'd squeeze in as many chairs and tables as they could, but they always made sure there was room enough to dance. Why not? Wasn't that the idea, to have a good time, get drunk and raise a little hell? So you can be sure there were a lot of fights, Friday and Saturday nights.

People would expect it. And of course we got involved in quite a few of these fights because people would start smarting off about us being a mixed band. We should've known it was coming. The first night we played outside of Laughton some of the guys got a little drunk and started yelling, "Get those niggers to . . ." — well, I don't recall exactly what it was. We tried to get them to cool down but these rednecks were determined to provoke something. And of course, it was bad for a black cat to try to defend himself. It was bad enough for a black cat to get into a fight but they'd kick the shit out of any black who jumped a white man. It was okay for a white man to jump a black man, but not the other way around.

Not that the guys in the band were going to just stand there. The drummer was an older cat and he'd seen a lot of the bullshit those rednecks were laying on him and he wasn't going to take it, no sir. He was forever saying, "I'll cut the motherfucker." He must've said that a billion times. But he never did it. What he'd do was when everyone would go outside to watch the fights, he'd go over to the tables and drink their drinks. Robbie Robertson was sort of like that, later on. I mean, we'd get into some sort of scrap, the guys in the band and me. All the rest of us would be down there fightin', kickin', clawin' and Robbie would be somewhere else wiping off his guitar strings.

What saved us so many times, in fact what saved us *every* time, was that after playing in the Amvet, we had so many black fans and so many white fans that whenever someone jumped us we had help from both sides. Besides, by then our kind of music was getting hot. Elvis was getting air play, Buddy Holly was hot. Hell, *we* were pretty hot.

The cats in the Blackhawks would con their way out of trouble a lot of times. Around white people, they really played up that whole "yez' m, Missy Smith" black thing, as if they were out of *Gone with the Wind* or something. "Sho' will," they'd say, then they'd turn around and giggle or say, "That motherfucker." They got really good at it, too. They were as good at being Stepin' Fetchit as Stepin' Fetchit. Some old redneck would come up and ask for some dumb old country redneck tune. Here we were playing rhythm 'n' blues, not knowing a thing about it. So the guys in the band would come on real humble, although the rest of us on stage were dying trying not to start laughing. So whoever was doing the talking, maybe Pretty Boy, would say, "I'm very sorry Mistuh John" — that was the trick, always call them by their first names — "I'm very sorry, but we just ain't never played none of that *good* music. We grew up with this other shit and that's all we know. But we'll try the best we can."

Well, hell, that would calm a table of rednecks down. If it didn't we'd have Mary Jo push that button and have them thrown out. As a result of that I learned how to play "Oh, Susannah" on the harmonica. And I can sing all the Stephen Foster songs.

After a while we were working a lot out of Laughton, Oklahoma. But one of the worst scraps we ever got into was in a little town in Texas. It started the night this old boy who owned one of the clubs refused to pay the band. He was the one of those big old hero football players from the southwest conference — Texas, Oklahoma, Arkansas — and in those days it was as popular as the NFL is now. He was paying us ten dollars a man for the night. And he'd let us play all night but after we were through he gave me my ten bucks and said, "Fuck them niggers. I ain't payin' those niggers."

Well, hell, that was back in the days when I'd bust somebody really quick. I just happened to have one of those long-necked beer bottles with me so I busted him in the head with it, grabbed our money and ran. But Jesus, we no sooner got outside when I remembered we'd forgotten our snare drum. Our *three*-dollar snare drum. So we stopped, trying to figure out whether to go back and get that snare or get out of there. Of course, there was the drummer saying over and over how he wanted to "cut" somebody. He was always willing to cut somebody but he wasn't willing to go back in that club and get his own snare drum. And we needed it.

So me and Pretty Boy LeRoy Moody had to go back after that drum. And we got the drum, but what did we see? That old boy I'd just brained was finally getting going. He'd wrapped his head in a bar rag to stop the bleeding — there was blood running all down his face — and he had a goddamn sawed-off shotgun in his hand and was loading it up. You talk about us moving. I always thought I was pretty fast, but that was when I found out that Pretty Boy could outrun me with two watermelons under his arms. Pretty Boy passed me so fast he would have made Ben Johnson look like a standing pigeon. I thought the other guys were going to drive off and leave us because they had the car already going before we got there. It wasn't going anywhere fast, though. It was on gravel and with those tires spinning on the gravel it seemed it wasn't moving at all. We got in just as the shotgun blast hit the back of the car. It didn't break the glass, just peppered the back like BB's. It just goes to prove that a sawed-off shotgun is only good at short range.

Sometimes we had to make some quick getaways when someone came out and found us using our "Arkansas credit card" — that's a siphon hose and a five-gallon can. That's what we needed to get a little gas out of some old boy's car. I mean, money was still tight with us. But we didn't always get gas just from cars. A lot of the farmers then had their own pumps. We'd have a couple of places we'd checked out ahead of time that we'd drop around to at night. You didn't want to hit the same place too often because they'd start to suspect what was going on they'd wait for you. Sometimes they didn't catch you. Sometimes they wouldn't bother measuring their gas until the day it was all gone and they knew it was either leaking or someone was stealing it. I was the only rock 'n' roll singer who belched up gas fumes. I guess that's why I didn't smoke — I was afraid I'd blow my head off. Pretty Boy LeRoy Moody had two five-gallon cans and we'd fill them and hide them in our car. One day we showed up at a place that had dogs. Whoever had checked out this place didn't see the dogs in the daytime. So there was Pretty Boy filling up his tanks when the dogs started coming after him. The lights were going on in the house; the owner was coming out onto the porch with his gun. Anybody else in the world would have left those cans behind, but not Pretty Boy. He ran *over* those dogs carrying those cans. Man, he could've been an Olympic sprinting champion.

LeRoy helped get us out of another jam; or rather, his buddy from Chicago did. This buddy had been born in Mississippi but he'd done well as pimp in Chicago. He'd gone there when he was just young, but he'd fought his way up through a tough section of town. And he'd made it. He drove a huge Cadillac, and at six foot six or seven he was big enough to make Mr. T look like a pygmy. Man, he was classic to look at. He was wearing black shirts and white ties. He had a gold tooth. He had every kind of hat you can imagine. He was tough and, just as good, he *looked* tough.

One night we were playing at a club in Texas and these two or three little sweet things came in. They sat down there right in front of us and well, they started winking at us and pulling their dresses up a bit, and they were sucking the booze off their fingers — stuff like that. Well, sure enough, a bunch of rough-ass rednecks came in and started flirting with these girls. And the girls let these rednecks buy them drinks — they let them buy the whole night long. Well, you know what those old rednecks were planning for those girls. But as soon as we were finished, me and LeRoy and the bass player went over and sat down at a table to have a drink and these girls came over to sit with us, after accepting booze from those other guys all night long. If you don't think that can cause a little tension, try it sometime. So we're sitting there with the girls, and they're smiling and sucking on their fingers and meanwhile, from where those rednecks were sitting, you could hear lots of mumbling and grumbling. We knew something was coming, so we left the table and went through the side door of the club with our equipment. In those days you didn't leave your equipment, even overnight. You took it home with you because there were lots of inside jobs done in those honky tonks. Realize, these clubs were usually run by outlaws. You couldn't exactly count on finding what you'd left behind the night before. By the time we made it outside we found all these pissed-off cats gathered around, saying all sorts of derogatory things. And it was getting worse and worse. I mean, these guys were really pissed off missing out on all that pussy they were expecting — when LeRoy's buddy happens to come by, all six foot six of him.

"Now boys," says the pimp. "Hold it right there. Let's don't have any trouble. If you want to *have* trouble, well trouble's my motherfuckin' name. It's my first name. It's my last name. It's my middle name, too."

You could tell just by looking at this cat that he meant it. So he backed them down, even though there were about four or five of those redneck cats. They could see the scar tissue over this guy's eyes. He was lean and mean.

I only saw him once more. He came back into our area for a couple of months some time later, just checking and looking around. Showing off, you know. He had a big new Cadillac, twenty or thirty new suits. And even more hats. He even had — and this was rare back then — his nails manicured. He'd gone from country boy to a real heavy in Chicago. A month or so later, he'd gone — forever, I guess. At least, I never saw him again.

Generally, we had less trouble when we played black clubs. Fights would break out — maybe somebody would owe somebody else some money and they hadn't paid it back. But that was it. There wasn't anybody calling me "whitey" or anything like that. They were pissed off, all right. They knew they were being mistreated — this was still the fifties, remember. The blacks I knew were getting tired of being kicked around. But when it came to their clubs, they were just out to have a good time. If there was a problem, they'd settle it somewhere else.

The black clubs were usually some barn-like shack, covered in Coca-Cola signs, with chairs inside and a little bar set up, with a dance floor and a jukebox with the best records in the world. Everybody dressed up. We were in those clubs when it was special, a Friday or Saturday night. Our drummer, who was always short of money, would hock his suit for two dollars at the beginning of the week then get it out of hock for three bucks before the weekend. A lot of guys did that.

There was another way black clubs and white clubs were different. You'd walk in a white joint and you'd smell beer and cigarettes; walk in a black place and you'd smell beer, cigarettes — and another kind of smoke. They smoked reefers openly. Even the paper — the brown paper — was made out of marijuana. But if you wanted to smoke it you had to order it directly from the big-time cats who ran the stuff.

Mary Jo was trying to get us better jobs, being our manager. We were branching out, you see. We played at her club, the Amvets, Sunday, Monday, Tuesday, Wednesday and Thursday. But for the important Friday and Saturday nights, we tried to get bookings to different clubs for more exposure. The problem for us, of course, was traveling on the road. These were the days when they had toilets which said "White Only" and "Black Only." *I* could stay anywhere, of course. But we got turned down in a lot of motels because of the rest of the band. We'd arrive, there'd be a vacancy sign, but all of a sudden we'd hear, "It's full, it's booked." And it wasn't any good registering in a motel, then slipping in the rest of the boys to spend the night there, trying to sleep but not being able to because you'd be thinking that at any moment you're going to be caught. These were still violent times. We got kicked out of places a lot of times. There was one place, a motel we were practicing at, where there were all kinds of complaints from the folks all around us. Well, the owner came up to do something all right, but instead of kicking *us* out he kicked out all the people who'd been complaining.

The best time we pulled it off, though, came in one of the fanciest hotels in Houston. This was a place that didn't allow any blacks at all, but Pretty Boy LeRoy Moody came up with an idea. His buddy from Chicago was still with us then. The way it worked was this. I walked in, like some big cattle baron, and LeRoy was my chauffeur. The rest of the band were my servants. I looked really big time, as if I were ready to buy the King Ranch and everything around it. Well, I walked in there and told them I had to have a suite of rooms. I had to have my servants with me — they really dug that in the hotel because they still dug slavery then — and I had to have my own special cook. So they let us up there and we had a party to boggle your mind, and they never found out.

It worked because we paid up front. I told them at the front desk that I was waiting for my plane to get fixed — that if it got fixed we might have to leave in the middle of the night. We got the suite pretty cheap, too. They didn't know what we didn't have. I was carrying a roll of bills with a couple of hundreds wrapped around a lot of one-dollar bills. These were rolls big enough to choke a couple of horses, so they were really impressive. I never did show them what was under those hundreds. When they waited for a tip, I told them, "I'll see you tomorrow."

Another time Mary Jo got us booked on this big package show in Wichita Falls, Texas, headlined by Mickey Baker and Sylvia Robinson, who had "Love Is Strange" out. The show had Paul Anka before he had all the surgery done to his face, Buddy Holly, Ray Charles, Chuck Berry "and many others" — that was us. Just a small-time band, we weren't that impressive going into that first show in Wichita Falls. But we sure were with what we did during the show. In those days, depending on who the promoter was, they'd package a show together with several different acts. The acts didn't get paid much because it was considered good promotion for them. They'd be going into different areas, meeting the disc jockeys, things like that. So they got room and board; basically, that was their pay. And usually they had some orchestra put together that could read the arrangements for whichever acts *had* musical arrangements — as Jackie Wilson did. The rockabillies of course didn't have arrangements. Some, like Buddy Holly, had their own bands. Otherwise, Sam "the Man" Taylor was often the head boss of all the musicians on shows like that. Anyway, on this particular show, we went out and did three songs, but because the crowd wouldn't settle down after we played, they gave us the okay to do five more.

I did "Ooby Dooby," "Go Go Go" and "Lawdy Miss Clawdy." I usually would do one of Chuck Berry's songs but because he was on the show we had to do one he wasn't going to do. We asked him if it was okay. He was kind of a kingpin at the time. Hell, I've always thought he was the William Shakespeare of rock 'n' roll. He got into a lot of trouble later on, with girls and income tax and a lot of other things. They say it's left him a little bitter; that he's pissed off at a lot of things. But he was a kingpin back then, man, for what he was writing. He was nice back then, too, and he played well. Since then I know he's caused trouble with the bands he's played with, ignoring them on stage and all that, but not then. He'd use the orchestra that was there and he sounded even better than he did on record. They'd just play those simple riffs and not try to make it sound like a big orchestra. Because he was a big star, Chuck always had someone looking after him. He usually had a driver and a valet. That was a status thing for a lot of rockers back then — to have your own chauffeur and your own valet who'd look after your wardrobe and do everything for you.

Buddy Holly was different. He was kind of a loner. Back in February of '57 he'd recorded "That'll Be the Day" and "I'm Looking for Someone to Love." But they were just starting to break out as hits, so he was something of a local Texas boy; hell, he'd been recording around Wichita Falls and Lubbock when he was still known as Charles Hardin Holly and was writing and singing with his buddy, Bob Montgomery, as "Buddy and Bob." He stayed by himself. Then there was Paul Anka who sang "Diana." Bill Doggett did "Honky Tonk" — it had been the top rhythm 'n' blues record of 1956.

Ray Charles was also on that show. He was just as starting out. He already had "Hallelujah, I Love Her So" and "I Got a Woman" out. But he hadn't cut "What'd I Say" yet, and that was the one which put him into the white market and made him a big star. But, hell, black music in general hadn't really made it into the white market yet. Our name was two notches higher on the bill than Ray Charles's was. There were a lot of black labels but no black label that sold a lot to whites. Berry Gordy, Jr., who started Motown, was still just working out of his old house in Detroit, with a studio downstairs. He'd had a jazz store which he sold for a little money. He'd made money writing "Lonely Teardrops" with Tyran Carlo for Jackie Wilson, another cat from Detroit who'd gone on his own after leaving Billy Ward's Dominoes. And he borrowed some money from his sister Anna. That's why he called his first record company Anna, the label that cut "Money (That's What I Want)" in 1960. It was sung by Barrett Strong and helped make Berry Gordy, Jr., a really rich guy. It was recorded later on by another little ol' band — the Beatles.

Ray Charles went over okay that night. Everybody went over okay. But *we* were great that night in Wichita Falls. We were the hit of the show and Mary Jo tried to do everything she could to capitalize on it for us. She sent out telegrams to Dick Clark, to Ed Sullivan, to Milton Berle, to everybody, saying we were the hit of the show. She sent out pictures and letters and brochures and the write-ups we were getting in the papers. She even got a letter back from Norman Petty, down in Clovis, New Mexico, who had his own studio and had recorded Buddy Holly. He invited us to do a demo tape but we didn't because we thought we had this other big deal coming up, one that Mary Joe had found which had been arranged with some semi-gangster cats.

But nothing happened with those guys. And so we went back out on the road again and things got tougher and tougher. That's where I got most of my scars — on my legs, my face, everywhere — fighting with the Blackhawks. We were sure we were going to be murdered some night, the prejudice was so strong. They wouldn't even let us rest in the parks, sleeping in our old Buick. As soon as they saw some black dudes in a car, they'd make us leave the park real quickly. Someone would come by and say, "You're only allowed to rest here thirty minutes," or something like that, so we'd have to move on again. Then there was the problem of sleeping five cats in a car. In those days the cars had drive shafts in the back and there was that damn hump in the back in the middle of the floorboard. That hump made it uncomfortable. You padded it with quilts or sleeping bags as much as you could but it was still damn uncomfortable. Except for the drummer. The more I think about him the more I realize what a strange cat he was. I don't think he ever slept. He did other things that were strange, too. He walked without swinging his arms, like he was a zombie, slow, never in a hurry. He had long, long arms for his size — he was about five foot ten. Strange, he hardly ever blinked. He had thick eyelids and always seemed stoned on something, drink or reefer or whatever. But the rest of us didn't worry a hell of a lot about whether he slept or not. We were always so tired always having to be on the move that as soon as we stopped the car we'd be asleep — until they made us move on to the next place.

The Blackhawks were Ronnie's initiation into the real world of rock 'n' roll — and the reactionary, redneck, racist South. You can see by the way his face tenses that sometimes his memories aren't the happiest ones:

One strike we had against us was being in the South, where the prejudice against blacks was the strongest. Even if you had the law on your side, everyone and everything was against you. The law, we found, didn't mean shit. The music was the second strike. Playing rock 'n' roll or rhythm 'n' blues was playing the music of the devil. All the preachers were against it. I remember one preacher who'd heard about what we were doing who came out to try to change my way of thinking.

"Do you believe in God?" he asked me.

"Hell," I replied, "I believe in God as much as the next man but I'm a little leery of his ground crew."

And, of course, being a mixed band, black and white, was a third strike. That was one strike too many. And there was something else — Mary Jo. She was putting even more pressure on me to move in with her permanently. I had the feeling that if I didn't she'd stop backing the band. It was cut and dried with her. I was going to be her houseboy, or no money for the band. And she wanted us to continue, in a way. But the truth was, some of the other guys in the band were tired of the hassles we were having, too. After that big concert we found ourselves back on the same old circuit and we still weren't really making any real money. We were still living below the poverty line, except for what Mary Jo was giving us from the club. The two guitar players had a chance to play with a band in Chicago. Officially, LeRoy played lead in the Blackhawks but the other guy was a lead player, too. They just had different styles. LeRoy played in a B.B. King style. The other guy played slide-guitar stuff and sounded more like Elmore James — he was the one with the electronic feel and could make different sounds on his guitar. He was into sounds as much as notes. So one night we decided that was it. We just walked away from it. We'd played our last dance.

It was really, really sad. Everybody got drunk one final time together and we were crying because we'd come so close. It was such a good band. We knew we were good. We'd played in front of total strangers and all of a sudden those total strangers would come up to the band and start screaming because they *liked* what we were playing. They hadn't heard us on radio. They didn't know who we were. So we knew it was the playing itself that was really getting over to them. It was terribly sad to know that and have to leave that behind. It always is.

We said goodbye and I came back to Fayetteville. The day the Blackhawks split was the day I left Mary Jo. We'd had a gig that night, that last night, and after it she came out with a bottle or two of rare champagne — she liked to drink and smoke a little grass. I spent the night with her. What a night. We went through her entire repertoire of tricks. She was upset, I knew, but not too upset because at the time there was a good chance I was coming back. We talked about my going away to think things over. Maybe some money would come together. Maybe we'd put the band back together again. Maybe, maybe, maybe. So I left. I packed up my old army duffel bag — hell, I didn't have much, just my jeans and my record hop suit — and got a ride back home to Fayetteville in Doug Douglas's noisy old Austin Healey.

I never did see Mary Jo or the Blackhawks again. Of all the bands I've had, the Blackhawks was the only one I never kept up with. I ended up playing with a band who were really good — the one with Levon Helm and Robbie Robertson. They were as good at playing funk as any white band ever was. But the Blackhawks were the easiest to work with, the most fun. Thinking back, when we split, it was the end of an era. Everyone else from that era is either dead, in jail or in a mental institution — and I'm bordering on all three.

VI

WATCH IT BOYS, THERE'LL BE ESKIMOS EVERYWHERE

With Conway Twitty to the Rescue, the Hawk Flies North to Find "Canadia"

RONNIE WASN'T BACK IN FAYETTEVILLE two days when he got a telephone call. "Hey boy," said the voice, "how'd y'all like to be a rock 'n' roll star?" Hell, what the caller down the other end of the line didn't know was that Ronnie was already a rock 'n' roll star. Being with the Blackhawks had convinced him of that. There was only a small matter of getting a new band together, getting some records out and becoming famous to be taken care of. But that was the easy part. The big hurdle had been crossed. He was a star.

And damn, he could already see himself on the prime-time TV when he heard who wanted him: some Memphis boys, session players at Sun Records. The best. Memphis! Goddamn, he told his pals. He was going to Memphis and when he came back, he'd be in the big time; they could just wait and see.

"But by the time I got *down* to Memphis the band had broken up," Ronnie remembers. "Seems they had a sax player, Wee Willie Willis, and he was the one that broke up the band over who was

78

going to be the leader; the leader got ten dollars a session compared to the five dollars everyone else got. They had guaranteed me a hundred a week to front the band, but by the time I got there, there was no more band. But I met their guitar player, Jimmy Ray Paulman, who'd also played with Conway Twitty and the Rockhousers, Billy Lee Riley and the Little Green Men and a lot of other cats. He was the only one in that band who wanted to do something else."

And Ronnie had to come up with something else quick. After all the bragging he'd been doing, he had to end up with a Memphis band somehow. So he and Jimmy Ray starting plotting:

Now I couldn't go right back to Fayetteville after I told everybody that I was going to Memphis to make the big time. If you come back home three days after you left, you've got to hide out for the rest of your life because everybody would ask, "What happened to that big deal?" So I didn't go back. I went with Jimmy Ray to West Helena, Arkansas.

I was with an ol' boy named Donny Stone, a football star from the University of Arkansas. Through him I met Charlie Halbert, a big football fan who owned the Rainbow Inn Motel. So I stayed with, and I worked for, Charlie at his motel. Charlie liked musicians. He'd already helped everybody who was starting out — Elvis Presley, Carl Perkins — everybody. Conway Twitty's dad drove a ferryboat on the Mississippi for Charlie Halbert. That's why he helped Conway. Charlie had letters and pictures of everybody, of him and Elvis, too. And he was good to everybody.

When Charlie had first met him, Elvis didn't make enough money at Charlie's to buy gas to get back to Memphis, so Charlie footed that bill. He had to do the same thing for Carl Perkins. Conway, too. He gave me a job sweeping and cleaning up and helping at the motel to get free room and board. But I had a band to think about and Charlie helped out there, too. It seems that the old harp player, Sonny Boy Williamson, had his equipment in the basement of an old radio station in West Helena, KFFA. Actually, there were two Sonny Boy Williamsons, one who recorded in Chicago and this guy I'm talking about in West Helena whose real name was Rice Miller. He was the one who recorded as the King Biscuit Boy.

79

Anyway, Charlie Halbert knew this cat named Basil, the number-one disc jockey in town. So, to help us out, Charlie called up Basil and said, "Listen, they need to practice somewhere, goddamn it."

You see, they were old drunks together. Besides, Charlie had lots of money — he was one of those money-rollers, a real showoff with it — and Basil owed him practically everything. So we got to use the basement and all of King Biscuit Boy's equipment. That's how, years later, when I heard Richard Newell, the harmonica player from Hamilton, play, I came to give him that name: King Biscuit Boy; he played the blues like Sonny Boy. Richard didn't like the name for years but now I think he understands.

So I started putting my new band together in West Helena. I had Jimmy Ray on guitar. Willard "Pop" Jones was on piano. His eyes were crossed. It was merely a matter of an operation to cut muscles and straighten them out, but his momma told him that if God hadn't meant for him to be crosseyed, he wouldn't be crosseyed. The truth was, if he didn't have that eye fixed he was going to go blind. But he believed what his momma said for four or five years. If he had stayed in Arkansas he'd still believe it and he'd still be crosseyed, or blind. And we were looking for bass and drums. For a while, we used Jimmy Ray's brother on upright bass.

You have to understand the kind of places these boys were coming from. How backwoods they were. They believed things like if you stuck your hand in a sack of rattlesnakes and God was on your side, well, those ol' snakes wouldn't bite you. I'm not sticking my hand in a sack full of rattlesnakes no matter who tells me to or for what reason. But they believed that kind of thing. Real rural.

Will "Pop" Jones was from Maryanna, Arkansas, where he still lives. But he'd heard of this little kid from Marvel, Arkansas. A kid named Levon. Levon Helm. He was only seventeen or eighteen, but already Levon had played with Willard a few times. But he'd never owned a set of drums. He only played snare and a little rhythm guitar. He was still in high school and had a band called the Jungle Bush Beaters. He and his sister had sung a lot as kids. They'd played for Miss Arkansas pageants and things like that. His sister played the washtub bass, he played rhythm guitar and they sang harmony together. He'd started when he was in grade school. By the time he got to high school he could go and get drunk and still keep rhythm just fine, although for years he didn't have a proper set of drums.

Right from the start, Levon played more drums with less licks than any drummer in the world. And he could make it sound right. He liked what I liked in music. He'd grown up with blacks. He had that music. That's his territory. He knew about Sonny Boy Williamson when Sonny Boy lived right there in Walnut Corners. Levon had never met him until he got together with me, but he knew all about him. Hell, he might have been the best guitar player I ever had, too. He was better than Robbie Robertson was early on.

Where Levon came from, in Phillips County, they're ignorant mothers; I mean, they were still in the Civil War there. It was really rural. If it rained back then Levon couldn't get out: his house would be surrounded by water. Even horses couldn't reach him. He'd have to come by boat. So if it looked like it'd be rainy on the weekend, we'd go in early and bring out Levon's clothes and one of his suits. He'd have to stay in town.

That wasn't our only problem. Jimmy Ray's brother was getting ruined all the time. He took snuff and he'd get all hot and drunk and that snuff would be running down his white shirt and his pants while he was slapping that bass. And he and Jimmy Ray were always arguing and fighting. So I said, "We'll make it without a bass for a while until we find the right one," which is how we ended up using Jimmy "Lefty" Evans. Lefty had also worked with Conway and all those same Memphis guys. But he was sort of a flimflam man. He didn't know whether he wanted to be a preacher or not. Preachers made money down there, at least a lot of them did. Even Conway went for preaching for a while to make money. He had his own church, too.

We were playing those little ol' honky tonks in the area, weekends mostly, and like I've been saying all along, they were real brass-knuckle bars where you had to show a razor and puke twice before they'd let you in. The Delta Supper Club, the Silver Moon — places like that around southern Arkansas.

Sometimes we'd work Thursday, Friday and Saturday and all the holidays. The rest of the time we rehearsed, using King Biscuit Boy's equipment until Charlie helped us get some equipment of our own. I knew I wouldn't go back to Fayetteville until the band was ready and we'd be able to outdraw other bands in that area. I didn't go anywhere near Fayetteville for a long time. I had to sell things to get the money to keep going. We worked hard. Levon was the easiest one to get along with. He was always laughing and joking and cutting up. He was the funniest kid you ever saw; he'd laugh about everything. Jimmy Ray Paulman had the most experience. He'd been on tour for a few years with different bands, including Conway Twitty's. He'd even played in Canada. Another reason we rehearsed for a long time was because we had to wait for Levon to graduate from high school. Until then his parents would only let him travel on weekends.

Meanwhile, Dayton was handling the club. I wouldn't go back but I kept in touch. At one point Dayton came down to West Helena to see if I'd come back for a little bit. But I didn't want anybody knowing what I was doing until I returned with a band that could rock. The four of them — Levon, Willard, Jimmy Evans and Jimmy Ray — were that band.

And he owed his career in Canada to Conway Twitty, or Harold Jenkins, as he was still known at the time around the Southern Ontario circuit he helped open up. Conway was a rocker then. He had a fleshy, sensuous face, with full lips and hooded eyes, which to his fans made him one of Elvis's main rivals. The problem was, like the rest of Elvis's rivals, he was waiting for the right break-through record to come along. So in 1958, still waiting, he happened to be on the phone with Ronnie one day. He urged his fellow Arkansas rocker to come north.

"I was playing the Flamingo Lounge in Hamilton, the Brass Rail in London and the Brown Derby and the Le Coq D'Or in Toronto," Twitty remembers. Later, Twitty would tell questioners that he was doing it because he was waiting to have a hit record — the one called "Its Only Make Believe," which he wrote between sets at the Flamingo. Still, he says, "I think everyone was aware that something big was happening and that you were right on the leading edge of it."

"So Conway's agent booked us into the Golden Rail tavern in Hamilton," Ronnie says. "It was in 1958 and for a while it looked like it was going to be a disaster because people were lined up to get *out*. But Dallas Harms, the only Canadian I'd met in Arkansas, saved us when he filled the club with all his friends. Later Dallas went on to write some great hits, including 'Paper Rosie.' The owner brought us back several times.

"But going to Canada, at first we thought we were going to run into igloos, Eskimos and dogsleds. It's the north pole, that's what we thought. Levon's dad even made it worse. He said, 'Those goddamn Canadians up there in Canadia' — that's what he called it, 'Canadia' — 'they're worse than the Mexicans. They'll stick a goddamn knife in ya for a nickel, never mind a dime.' He'd never been out of his own county but that's how he was. He had an answer for everything. Of course, he probably got his ideas in books he'd seen on the Yukon in 1840 and that's what stuck in his mind. But he sure was against us going. He said that in 'Canadia' there's ten months of winter and two months of bad sledding."

Ronnie laughs loudly when he thinks of this, mainly because he's looking out over the unspoiled, tree-lined lake fronting his estate near Peterborough — exactly the kind of "wild" rural retreat Canadians fight to own these days:

But in truth we thought it was going to be wilderness, too. I was college educated but I'd never heard anything about Canada. My only connection was that at one time a bunch of us were going to run off and join the Canadian Air Force because we heard you could join when you were sixteen.

This was the first of my bands that I could call a Memphis band — because we worked there — even though we were from Arkansas. And for rockers like me, when you mentioned Memphis it had a special meaning. Saying you were from Memphis meant you had some connection with W.C. Handy and Beale Street and the blues. White kids were playing the blues, but that was rare anywhere except in Memphis. In those days I never thought of Los Angeles or New York. I only thought of Memphis, for the music. That was the headquarters for what I wanted to do, I thought. I didn't know the business; I just knew that in Memphis they played the kind of music I liked.

I kept hearing stories about what happened to those demos I'd done. I heard that they were going to release this, they were going to release that. All of the sudden though, Colonel Tom showed up,

Elvis went on to RCA and Jerry Lee Lewis became as hot as hell. So Sun only seemed interested in Jerry Lee and everybody else got dropped. Jerry Lee was selling more records than the plants could press. And that became big money for Sun because Sam Phillips owned the publishing rights to most of the songs.

In those days Carl Perkins did a lot of drinking. But no matter how drunk he got he never missed a lick. And Carl was one of the strongest country boys I'd ever seen. He was half drunk one night and bet that he could lift the back of my car off the ground — and he did.

After a while it was obvious the thing with Sun was not happening. We were in Canada by then and an agent had seen us in Toronto. Hell, by that time we'd even done our first record. We'd recorded "Bo Diddley" in a studio in a Hamilton garage as the Ron Hawkins Quartet, in 1958. This agent saw how we were doing in the clubs, what was going on, the excitement. So he called some other agents in Wildwood, New Jersey. So we went over there to play and within a week we were really hot there, out-drawing Sammy Davis, Frankie Laine and Teresa Brewer all put together. Well, when you do that it stirs up agents. It stirs up everybody. So people from record companies started coming down to hear us and we were being asked to audition.

At the same time Morris Levy at Roulette had a few things going. He had his jazz label with Count Basie and all those heavies back then. And he had a little rhythm 'n' blues label where he had Frankie Lymon and the Teenagers, and other black acts. The Roulette label was kept for special acts. Morris sent an agent over to talk to us. He told us how much they were into what we were doing, how much Morris was into rock 'n' roll. He spent a lot of money romancing us. Well, it was new to us because we hadn't had anybody romancing us before. So I decided to go with Roulette because I liked the way Morris cared about us. I'd heard some things about the way Morris operated. I'd heard he practically owned the deejay Alan Freed; that Freed was a gambler, a bad gambler, and that if you wanted him to push a record he liked to be paid in hundred-dollar bills in a brown bag. But I still liked Morris. Still do.

This was in 1958, when we recorded "Forty Days" and "Mary Lou." By then we were so well rehearsed we could just get into the studio and do it. We recorded at the Bell studios in New York, some of the stuff on their early two-track machine, some on the bigger, more sophisticated four-track machine. And we went out promoting ourselves. A lot of rockers had done TV by then, and we did the "Steve Allen Show." Of course they'd never seen anything like us. We had the fiddle pickup we put on that piano which made it ten times louder than an ordinary piano. It didn't sound electric, but that didn't make any difference. It was loud. And of course I was doing the double backflips. The cameras stopped and all of a sudden everybody in the building was watching us play. They'd never seen a monkey act like that. Remember, Steve Allen is a musician. He's a big-time piano player. So there he was watching Willard just banging those keys as hard as he could. It was like a popcorn machine when the hammers started to jump out of that piano. Well, Steve Allen liked it.

I did a lot of different things on stage. It was wild. I added all the stuff from those minstrel shows I'd seen growing up as a kid. I also added stuff I learned from Half Pint. Half Pint's hero was Bill Bojangles Robinson who, I guess, was every black kid's hero. In the movies he was the only black ever to be allowed to do anything more than say "yez' m."

I started meeting a lot of people. Jerry Wexler, who was a journalist working for *Billboard*, got hired by Atlantic Records because he knew all about music industry politics, about buying time and promotion. And there was Dick Clark.

Clark, who'd taken over the "American Bandstand" show on Philadelphia's WFIL from Bob Horn in 1956, was beginning to hit his stride after he'd sold the dance show in 1957 to the fledgling ABC network. He knew the show's potential — and so did the record industry. Every afternoon kids across the continent tuned in to watch the latest dances to the latest records, and the up-and-coming acts. And to this day, Al Bruno remembers how Ronnie Hawkins stunned the "Bandstand" dancers.

"They'd seen a lot of exciting acts on the show," he says. "Jackie Wilson, James Brown, and he was *that* exciting. He had all the moves. And I remember thinking at the time how I'd hate to be the act that ever had to follow him on stage."

Bruno — Albert Victor Joseph Bruneau, from Sudbury — had

already met the Hawk in Toronto. He'd come to meet Clark while working with Conway Twitty and eventually became Clark's musical director. Roulette made sure Ronnie got a chance to do his big hits, "Mary Lou" and "Bo Diddley," on the show, but he was shackled in one way: he couldn't sing live, but had to lip-synch the record. "But even that didn't stop him. He was still wild," says Bruno, now an award-winning country guitar player. "But right from the start I thought there was something else to him, as a singer, I mean. He was a stylist. Everything he did was distinct. Maybe a lot of people didn't see that then, but it was there."

Morris Levy saw it, for sure. Levy, who in 1959 would be grilled for his relationship with Alan Freed as part of the growing anti-payola investigation, groaned at the thought that Ronnie wasn't willing to leave the lucrative club circuit he was developing in Canada. To Levy, Hawkins might've been bigger than Elvis. "Ronnie wouldn't come home. He loved Canada. It broke my heart."

Maybe so, but the way Ronnie saw it, as long as he was on his own turf — Southern Ontario — he controlled his own destiny:

It seems every time someone wanted to sign me they wanted me to move wherever they were. That way they can keep control of you, I guess, keep an eye on you for a while. That's what Albert Grossman wanted when he wanted to sign me — leave Canada and go and live in Woodstock. Fred Foster offered me a million dollars a year if I'd come and live in Nashville. But goddamn, I never liked Nashville. It's a phoney town. Now it's wide open but then they had all those old-school musicians who ran everything. And if you don't go with the clique that was in control, you couldn't do anything. They controlled it all: the Grand Ole Opry — everything. And the guy who was at the head of it all was the Yo-Yo King, Roy Acuff, the one who used to have a Yo-Yo on stage at the Opry.

While we were with Roulette, Morris Levy was grooming Count Basie to be the biggest thing at the time. Morris finally got him booked into the Waldorf Astoria. He was the first black act to perform there and the Count spent about three months getting ready. But when he did appear he changed his whole sound so it would suit the fancy Waldorf Astoria and would be nothing like the kind of rhythm 'n' blues he'd been playing. Well, the people there didn't like it. They wanted to hear Count Basie. He played three days with his new arrangements and it wasn't going over. So he just went right back to the old stuff he'd been doing forever and it drove all the rich people crazy. What he really had was a rhythm 'n' blues band. He had that big ol' singer, Big Joe Williams, who sang the blues. The real thing. Morris was basically a jazz man. If he was given a chance to go see Count Basie or a rock 'n' roll band, he'd go see Count Basie. Because of Morris I spent a lot of time with the Count.

Interesting cat. He wouldn't walk upstairs. If he had to walk upstairs he wouldn't go. If the president had invited him to the White House and he had to walk up a flight of steps, he would not go. But everyone around him always knew that so he had elevators available.

"I did that for the first six years," Basie would say, "and I ain't walkin' upstairs with you no more."

Morris was tied in with Joe Glazier of Associated Booking, one of the biggest booking agents in the world, who started with Louis Armstrong. We got in with him and he helped us, too. He was the one who took me to see that 1959 fight in New York where Floyd Patterson got knocked out by Ingemar Johansson. There I was, sitting in the front row with Joe Glazier. John Wayne was there and so were Johnny Mathis and Johnny Ray who, I found out, were living together at the time. They got drunk and embraced and kissed all through the fight. Johnny Mathis and Johnny Ray. Two of my goddamn heroes — well, I liked Johnny Ray. Johnny Mathis was a little uptown for me.

It was really exciting being down there. But we were so busy by then in Canada, in Toronto, on Yonge Street, that it didn't make much sense to move. We'd come so far.

When Ronnie gets down on himself — which is not too often — he rarely thinks about opportunities he's missed. Other things bug him: friends who don't return his calls, folks who've cheated him — but not missed chances. In fact, nothing burns him faster than hearing that other people believe he deliberately missed chances and shied away from all his big opportunities.

But the one "opportunity" he didn't mind missing was the one which would have taken him back out of Canada and put him into the great all-American let's-find-the-next-Elvis sweepstakes. He knew that's what Morris Levy wanted. He knew that's what everyone wanted. He admits to himself he'd have done it if the money had been right, but it wasn't. At least he didn't have the guarantees that he had working in Canada. And he might have done it if the times had been different. But even as "Mary Lou" spent seven weeks on *Billboard*'s singles charts in 1959, Ronnie could see major changes in rock 'n' roll. With payola scandals and anti-rock 'n' roll crusades heating up, the days of innocence were over. It wasn't a wild adventure any more. It meant big money now. It was increasingly controlled by big business. To survive, musicians had to learn to fend for themselves — to find something that couldn't be easily taken from them. Ronnie found he couldn't control what happened to his records. He could, however, control where he played his music. He knew where he was hot — in the clubs.

In retrospect, we are better able to understand what was going on. We even have a phrase for it. They were days the music "died," or so they say. Not all the music, of course; we still had Tommy Sands and Percy Faith to look forward to. Frank Avalon released "Venus," for anyone who cared. No, they mean *the* music, classic rock 'n' roll, the lean and mean stuff, was gone. It made sense, sort of. Elvis was in the army, and no one was particularly thrilled with the sideburn-less stuff he was releasing like "I Need Your Love Tonight." Buddy Holly, J.P. Richardson — the Big Bopper — and Ritchie Valens were dead after their plane crashed in a cornfield near Clear Lake, Iowa, *en route* to a show. Jerry Lee Lewis had blown his career off the map by guilessly admitting that, sho' nuff, he'd married pretty little Myra Gale Brown, his fourteen-year-old third cousin. ("Of course, we never *could* understand what all the fuss was about," says Ronnie. "We all knew she was twelve.")

Chuck Berry was indicted under the Mann Act for transporting a minor across state lines for immoral reasons. Little Richard, having tossed eight thousand dollars worth of jewelry into Sydney's Hunt River during an Australian tour, renounced the wicked rock 'n' roll life and began studying for the ministry at Oakwood College, a Seventh Day Adventist church in Huntsville, Alabama. No sir, it didn't look good. And it sounded even worse. I mean, there was the *Still More Sing Along With Mitch* album.

Things hadn't exactly come to a standstill, though. Although we didn't know it at the time, George Harrison had just joined the Quarrymen in Liverpool with Paul McCartney and John Lennon. And the appearance of Ray Charles's great hallelujah-shout of a record, "What'd I Say," gave us faith we weren't going to slide back to a radio filled with Florian Zabach playing the "Hot Canary" on his fiddle. But the more you heard of Edd Byrnes and Connie Stevens mewing "Kookie, Kookie, Lend Me Your Comb," the more you came to believe all those who said rock 'n' roll wasn't going to last. It was, all said, a pretty rough time.

Because the end of the fifties saw the emergence of the music and radio industry that is still pretty much in place today. In August 1958, *Billboard*, the influential record-trade magazine, had begun its Top 100 chart, and by the following year radio stations in growing numbers had begun to mirror *Billboard's* rationalization of the irrational by establishing their own Top 40 formats. Rating rock 'n' roll was becoming formalized and, with that, standardized. Soon enough a kid in Port Credit, Ontario, would be hearing the same thing as a kid in Carmel, California. Certainly, pop charts had existed before rock 'n' roll. Certainly, the music and radio industries had exercised considerable control over what was heard. But rock 'n' roll was supposed to be the exception, the rebel music.

It wasn't. The unthinkable was happening. Rock 'n' roll was becoming big business, with even its most vociferous foes, such as Mitch ("Sing Along") Miller, Columbia Records' former director of artists and repertoire, giving in. (Miller, perennial guest on anti-rock panels, signed a deal in 1959 with two of rock 'n' roll's leading songwriters, Jerry Leiber and Mike Stoller.) Parents, professors and psychiatrists alike pummeled rock 'n' roll, as radio stations continued to throw record-busting parties. But these were aftershocks from the main tremor which had come and, apparently, gone.

So, what exactly is Don McLean talking about in "American Pie" when he whimpers that the music died with Buddy Holly? Something was certainly missing. In truth, many things went missing all at once: a sound, a style, an attitude, that delicious chill that comes with potential danger, mixing fast old cars and rock 'n' roll on the radio — all of which can be subsumed under one word: rockabilly. And it wasn't just missing in our imaginations.

Radio stations dropped Jerry Lee like a hot potato, and Carl Perkins and the rest. Only Elvis and the Elvis clones survived, but everyone knew that it wasn't the same. Radio couldn't avoid Elvis and in fact came to welcome the sweeter stuff he was putting out. But deejays and programmers could feel particularly superior when they reckoned they no longer had to play all those weird, snarly-sounding records from all those clodkicking southern boys who probably didn't wear underwear. No sir. Trash Jerry Lee and give me some Peggy Lee.

So at night I'd comb the radio stations out there like some mad scientist looking for a new star to discover, going from one end of the dial to the other, desperate for that one errant little station that hadn't heard the word yet, the station still programming the latest platter from Wayne Cochrane, Fats Domino — *anybody* hot. And for a while there I'd be able to find it, even though I might not be able to hear the call letters and I could never be sure what state it was coming from. But boy, did it sound god. There'd be some madman hootin' and hollerin' out there in the dark, "Cousin" this or "Madman" that, and he'd slap on a tune I hadn't heard before — and and haven't heard since. I'd just catch the singer's name: Malcolm Yelvington . . . or Jimmy Edwards . . . or who? Who was that? But that would be all. Eventually, though, the signal from a bigger station would blot out my sickly connection or bury it in a blizzard of static. Gone. The bigger station was all I could get.

About the same time a similar if less obvious power struggle was going on in the schools, even schools as far away from the action as mine, out there in near-bloody-awful nowhere, west of Toronto. For a while, the rockabilly style had some cachet despite what parents thought and all the nice kids made themselves believe.

Eventually, though, the other side — the nice kids on the decorating committee — started winning. Nothing obvious at first: you might notice that the duck's-ass haircuts were shorter, the girls' dresses not as tight around the hips, even the bulgy pink sweaters a little less . . . bulgy pink. All the Gene Vincents out there started looking a lot like Fabian. Eventually, hanging around the parking lot lost its zing and, well, you started thinking that maybe it wasn't so bad to get out of remedial Latin verbs or whatever to put up streamers for the Sadie Hawkins dance. You started losing your grip and — I don't know how to explain it — after a while, "Tiger" didn't sound like *that* bad a song and Fabian didn't seem that dumb. But then — before we really comprehended what we were doing, before we'd come to realize how we'd lost the faith, before we had entirely forgotten all the dirty parts to "Louie, Louie" — it was over. Rock, classic rock, pompadour piled-on-high piano-pounding rock 'n' roll was through. And those weirdo Beatles from England, who'd learned their guitar stuff from Carl Perkins and harmonies from the Everly Brothers, who needed Roy Orbison to open their shows, came along and almost wiped clean our memories of all that great fifties stuff.

Certainly, classic rock 'n' roll didn't disappear then. It hasn't disappeared now. Any guitarist who's played in a Ronnie Hawkins band owes some debt to the late Roy Buchanan and a lean, classic rockabilly-based style. Hawkins will make sure of it, you can bet. And any band or musician who feels any debt to Creedence Clearwater or the Beatles is touched by rockabilly the way Creedence and the Fab Four were themselves. And George Thorogood, Eddie Van Halen, The Stray Cats, Billy Idol, Shakin' Pyramids and dozens of other musicians and dozens of other bands have kept the tradition alive.

Back then Ronnie was keeping the tradition alive in his own way, in the clubs, throughout Southern Ontario.

"We'd go to Arkansas and play," he tells it, "then we'd come back to Canada. It was back and forth all the time, but we found it was easier in Southern Ontario because of the bars. There were so many bars between Windsor and Montreal, you could practically play a different one every night. And they were better run. A lot of the honky tonks we were playing in the South were run by gangsters. They weren't supposed to have a liquor license so they'd just get the place and put it in someone else's name. It was in these places that we always got into trouble." Ronnie smiles, remembering one incident:

Like the time I burned down that club in Tulsa. We were playing there — it was in 1959 — and after we'd finished for the week, the owner of the club gave us a hot check. We'd heard that he'd flim-flammed a lot of people before us. He'd flim-flammed Ray Charles. The owner figured that he could give you a hot check, you wouldn't have the money to get lawyers and all that and come back and get him. At that time, Leon Russell had the house band in this honky tonk. He was with J.J. Cale at the time. Anyway, I waited until the club was closed and I took out all their equipment and put it in the parking lot. I didn't want them to lose it 'cause they didn't have it paid for yet. Then I went back in — I had Dayton Stratton with me — and I broke up the pop machine, the beer machine and everything else. The janitor was going crazy, but I told him to get out. Then I put fifteen gallons of gas over everything.

It was at this point that I found out Hollywood has it all wrong. I did it the way they do it in the movies: you know, I ran a line of gas from that honky tonk right out through the back door to the parking lot where I was going to light it. In the movies, you'd light that line and it would roar into the club. What really happens is that when you light it everything goes all at once. You see, the fumes get lit. It all goes, baby.

Shit, it blew me right back through the door. It burned all my eyebrows off. The cops were coming and I couldn't move 'cause I was in shock. But those cops let me go. They said that the owner was an asshole and was always causing all kinds of trouble.

"Shit, boy," they said. "You're doin' us some good. We'll just act like we couldn't find you."

A little later Dayton and Kenny Brooks found where this old booger lived and destroyed his Cadillac right in front of his girlfriend's house. *Then* they went and asked him for the money — and got it. Hell, we probably did him a favor by burning down his club. He probably got the insurance.

It was real wild down there. Up in Canada, things were much better run. In the South, they played rough. They'd take a contract out on you if they wanted to. Sometimes we'd have to go out after them. It wasn't anything like that in Canada. Besides, the scene was happening around Toronto even if people there didn't know it at the time. I was always looking for good, new players and I was beginning to find the ones I wanted.

It was time for me to get a new band. Goddamn, but what a band it turned out to be.

VII

BETTER THAN THE BEATLES

Promising Girls, Thrills, Chills and Still More Girls, the Hawk Puts Together the Greatest Band Rock Has Ever Rolled Out

THESE DAYS RONNIE LIKES TO SAY that they were "better than the Beatles." It's The Band he's talking about, *The* Band; *his* band from the late fifties to 1964; one that left him, ignored him, made the kind of fortune he only dreamed about, fell apart, broke up, broke down, stalled, re-formed, stalled again, then — stopped. At its best, it was the best rock band in the world. At its worst, when everyone was bickering, when the songs weren't coming, it was sad and messy, like a good marriage gone wrong over something said carelessly.

As one of the hundreds of young players around Toronto in the early sixties, I'd sneak into bars to listen to them as the Hawk was piecing his band together, shaping it just the way he wanted it. Like every other young player around, I heard he was looking for a musician and hoped it was a piano player, because that's what I did and I was ready to go. Like most of the others I didn't get the call. I didn't feel any bitterness: they were the best, that's all there was to it. Not making the band was like not making the Yankees' outfield: a pipe-dream not coming true. Besides, this band was the best at a remarkable time, the early sixties, when everything seemed to come alive at once and, for a while, Yonge Street in Toronto was hot and electric with music.

"I came to Canada with Levon Helm, Jimmy Ray Paulman and Will 'Pop' Jones," Ronnie recalls. "I only had the three pieces; the bass player didn't come with us. After the first stop in Canada, I went back and got Jimmy Evans who had played with all the Memphis boys, Conway Twitty and Billy Lee Riley. He was a Memphis session man and he decided to come back with us. That's how we came to Canada. I don't know if Canada was ready."

"God, could they be wild," remembers Harold Kudlets, the Hamilton promoter who first booked the Hawks into Canada. Kudlets had backed into the music business almost by accident in 1946 when he booked the Glen Miller band into a local roller rink to prevent a rival Toronto-based promoter from running shows in his city. Kudlets loved big band music, but being a practical man he went with rock 'n' roll when rock 'n' roll became hot.

"Levon looked about twelve years old when I first saw him," Kudlets says. "Because no one could be in the places they were playing under the age of twenty-one, we had to put dark glasses on him to make him look older. Between sets we had to hide him backstage in case any of the police came by. Then when the band was over for the night, we had to sneak him out.

"The first time they played at the Golden Rail in Hamilton they rehearsed in the afternoon. All the bartenders threatened to quit when they heard what they were playing — and saw what Ronnie was doing. He was into all those backflips at the time. Really wild. But they didn't want to quit after a few days when they saw how much business this band was bringing in. Eventually the Arkansas boys left for different reasons. Like Will 'Pop' Jones. What happened to him is that he had his eyes fixed. He was cross-eyed, you see, but he had them fixed in Toronto and after that he didn't feel insecure any more, so he started liking the girls. That's why he left. The others just got homesick, basically.

"At the time, Roulette Records was spending a lot of money promoting Ronnie and his band," Kudlets continues. "In those days that meant getting people who know. But it never worked for Ronnie for one reason or another. Where he made his money was playing the clubs. They'd work seven days a week, all year, and never once, never, were they late for a job. Ronnie made sure of that. "Right from the start they were hot. They were getting $450 a week for those first jobs. Harold — Conway, I mean — was doing better. He was making from $500 to $750 a week. That was just before he had his first big hit record, 'It's Only Make Believe,' in 1958. But after that the money soared. I wasn't working only for Ronnie and the Hawks, of course. Judd Phillips, Sam Phillips's brother, introduced me to Ray Smith and he did well for me, too. "But it wasn't long before Ronnie and the Hawks were *the* big band. They'd play Toronto, Kingston, London and Kitchener. They played a month each place, twice a year. No club owner ever lost money when Ronnie Hawkins and the Hawks played his place. The only problem Ronnie had was some of his musicians were leaving him."

"All the American boys wanted to go home because they were getting homesick for their ol' ladies," says Ronnie. "Except for Levon. I'd guess he'd seen the ladies up in Canada. I'd seen a lot of Canadian musicians who could really play by then and I decided to start putting Canadian musicians together because they couldn't find work at all back then.

"The clubs would not hire Canadian musicians for some reason. If you were from Buffalo or Detroit that was enough for Canadians in the fifties. It even worked if you were Canadian but said you were American. We changed that a bit, I think.

"I was lucky. I was real lucky that when I arrived in Canada, everything was changing; everything was happening. To a musician, man, it was as if the streets were covered in gold; that's what the late fifties and early sixties were like. It was like the Roaring Twenties in Toronto. There were so many of those damn baby-boom kids coming along right after the war, and they wanted to do things. They wanted to get out and *do something.*"

And where they were doing it was mainly on or near Toronto's Yonge Street. It was not the polite excuse for debauchery it has now become with legit theaters at its lower reaches and upscale knicknackeries at the other end. Christened in 1795 by John Graves Simcoe, the Lieutenant-Governor of Upper Canada, for Sir George Yonge, British secretary of war, Yonge Street evolved after the arrival of horse-drawn streetcars in 1861 into the core byway for Toronto's business. It was not a very pretty place then, as it's not now. One nineteenth-century historian, writing about the area north of Queen and Yonge streets, described it as being thick with wolves and "other wild animals." Talk about back to the future.

By the early 1960s, when the Hawks had arrived, Yonge had begun to rival the sleazy best Montreal could offer as the Canadian epicenter of all that was dubious, naughty, certainly illicit, potentially immoral (we hoped) and possibly illegal. By 1960, Montreal's famous Bellevue Casino was gone, Buffalo's Towne Casino was on its way out and even New York's nightclubbers were limited to the Copa and the Latin Quarter. But not in Toronto-the-Good-going-bad. No way.

"One of the first things I remember thinking about Toronto was that it was the best place for live music outside of Memphis," says Levon Helm. "That's saying something." Now Levon, despite his Memphis excursions, was pretty green at the time when it came to cities. Nevertheless, his instincts were right about what was happening up and down the strip, crowded as always with gawkers on weekends. They wandered wide-eyed in the strip's joints starting with the Brass Rail, then over to the Famous Door for its female impersonators — some of them even female! — passing on to linger over the smorgasbord of strippers at the Zanzibar and Bermuda: the older, cool, professional peelers just in from Quebec, making a few bucks before heading up north to the mining towns where the big dough was found; the others, the scared kids from the suburbs with pale bodies, reddish eyes and runny noses, running away from home with some guy, needing to make some quick cash to finance their dream.

Take it off! And next? Of course — a cocktail or two and the quick striptease at the Westover Hotel or Sterio's Tavern. Sex and more sex, and then? "What about a few laughs, eh? Let's catch Joe King, yeah, the really funny guy. He's *always* at the Brown Derby." And so you went, through the wintery grunge of a Yonge Street Saturday night, cramming as much of it in as you could before the legit joints closed up and you had to search for refreshment elsewhere.

Talk about having a good time. Cities throughout the east were struggling with the first signs of rot from inner urban decay: long stretches of empty store-fronts, the result of haphazard liquor laws, capricious policing, political corruption and ungoverned cabaret licensing which had combined to wipe out night-club action and thus any reason for good honest folk to come downtown. How different it was in Toronto! And everywhere in Ontario. We'd never tasted such freedom.

It was unthinkable that we ever would be left to our own devices. There was no question about it in the minds of the Ontario Liquor Control Board. Without proper controls the citizenry, fueled on spirits, might well run amok. So until 1947, beer — and only beer — sales were limited to hotels where, I suppose the reasoning went, boozed-up patrons could stumble off to bed and be kept off the streets. When the Silver Rail opened its doors on April 2, 1947, as the city's first real live tavern, the line-up of customers stretched down around Yonge Street, east along Shuter Street past Massey Hall, and up Victoria Street. In ten minutes every seat was filled. This fascination lasted "for months," remembers one former Silver Rail bartender. "People would start at the top of the cocktail list and work their way down as far as they could. We used to see tough-looking laborers sipping Pink Ladies. We needed a Brinks armored truck to bring in the change, anywhere from $3,000 to $5,000 in silver and small bills a day." Through the combined efforts of the morality squad and the provincial Liquor Control Board, Toronto always maintained just the right balance of intimidation and repression to make going out at night really exciting. But crackdowns by morality officers on after-hours joints like the Upstairs club or the Juke Box club did little to stamp out our enthusiasm for them.

After all, you were turfed out of the bars and hotels around town shortly after 11:30 P.M., so what else would you do but head over to the Blue Note where little Jackie Shane, Toronto's answer to Little Richard, and one of the best bands on the planet were guaranteed to carry on through to 3 A.M., or the Upstairs club where some equally great r 'n' b was being perpetrated?

What else, indeed. Toronto, the "city of churches," had started staying up late in the early 1960s. You could get a coffee at Ford's Drugs all night, or a sandwich at Lindy's. The quadruple bill at the Biltmore theater might go through to dawn, if you could stand all the gore and bad dialogue. Be around enough nights and you'd get to know everybody on both sides of the law: the hookers back from the hotels, the pool hustlers talking about the fish they'd hooked. Sometimes the undercover cops would try to go from one side to the other, but it didn't work: they always looked like cops.

Yet there was more to it than morality, pasties and rhythm 'n' blues. The Colonial, well down the strip, began a jazz policy in 1960 which kept it fat and jazzy through the rocking sixties. The Towne, a leisurely five-minute walk away, had still more jazz, and lots of desperate characters whispering in its booths. Further uptown were the folk clubs, all very earnest and dingy: the Village Gate and Fifth Peg, the Gate of Cleves (actually much too bright inside), John and Marilyn McHugh's Half Beat, the Jack and Jill and the Cellar club.

But as timely, and even remunerative, as some of these clubs managed to be, they were like ballet classes next to the grunt-and-grind roller derby of downtown Yonge Street where the "wild booger" from Arkansas and one of the greatest bands in rock 'n' roll history were beginning to find their groove.

"A good band," explains Ronnie, "is like a team. You want to have the right balance. It's not always the best people you need, but the right ones for the job, and those boys I was getting for my new band were the right ones for the job. Robbie Robertson was just hanging around, doing things like being a roadie, but I could see he was smart and hungry and when the chance came I knew I had to do something with him. For a while I was looking at having two lead guitars and was thinking of Roy Buchanan and Fred Carter. Both of them were outstanding at that time and Robbie learned a lot from them.

"Then there was Richard Manuel: I'd heard and liked his little group from Stratford called the Rockin' Revols. I financed a little trip for them to Arkansas trying to get them started. But they were wild and they tore up everything, got arrested in Memphis and got into all kinds of problems. But that was Richard all over. Still, I really liked his voice.

"Before Richard I had Scott Cushnie on piano for a while, then we had Stan Szelest. When he left to go back to university, I brought Richard into the band, all the while knowing that he would never be as good as Stan. And the other bass player I was using at the time was Rebel Paine. He was a real good Indian kid.

But he'd gone as far as he wanted. The important thing about this band was that except for Levon, these were young Canadian kids who could really play — or had the potential to really play."

Rock 'n' roll evolves organically. Bands evolve from bands, which in turn come from basement sessions between friends. As much as Ronnie shaped the band, it shaped itself — and its genesis can be traced to a little schooldays outfit put together by three budding rockers: Scott Cushnie, an arrow-straight student at Oakville's Appleby College, Jaime "Robbie" Robertson, a street kid from the suburbs, and Gene MacLellan, whose song "Snowbird" would launch Anne Murray's career into orbit in 1970.

With "Pete the Bear" — his real name was Peter Derimigis — and Pete Traynor, "we started playing with Dave Johnson of CHUM at Saturday dances every week at Merton Hall in Toronto," says Cushnie. "They'd have a live broadcast with a live band. Well, we were the house band. Then we got a gig at Dixie Arena to open for Ronnie Hawkins: we knew he had these records out. We'd heard them on the jukebox, and we thought, this is the greatest sound we've ever heard. We wanted to actually play like that. These guys were great, sort of a combination of Jerry Lee Lewis and Carl Perkins: really clean kind of down-home stuff, exciting, with a lot of dynamics. Thoughtful.

"So we played the gig. The Ronnie went on. And we listened and we thought, fuck, wish we could be like this band."

"This band," says Robbie Robertson, "played the fastest, most violent rock 'n' roll that I've ever heard. It was very exciting and very explosive. I loved the dynamics, the style. Anyway, it was just the way they looked. How young they were. They weren't as young as me but they were pretty young so I could relate to that. And Ronnie was like this animal, lunging around with one arm hanging down, being very neanderthal about it, very primitive about it. I liked it a lot.

"At that point, I was trying to figure out what's the ticket out of town. What's the ticket to this place down the road where I want to go? And that's what I'm doing. I'm weighing all the issues, considering the different bands I'm playing with. I'd been in a band called the Rhythm Chords and one called Robbie and the Robots. That was back when I was pretty young, like fourteen.

"At this time I was playing with Scott Cushnie. But then I finally got to meet the guys in Ronnie's band. I thought they were great guys — and very different: Jimmy Ray Paulman, Levon, Lefty Evans and Willard 'Pop' Jones. Now, the first time, it seemed like they didn't have a bass player, but they came back the next time and they did have one. But I believe they played for a while without a bass — just guitar, drums and piano. And they learned to play like rhythm on the instruments to make up for that. Anyway it was smooth and wicked, I thought. And as I got to know them, I liked their music more, and I liked them, too.

"Levon was the only one even reasonably close to my age — and the icing on the cake. There was another fact, the fact they could play like this and look like they did. They looked *great*, these guys, really terrific. There were beautiful women around.

"Well, with all that I wanted to be the nicest guy they ever knew," says Robbie. "I was trying to do what Ronnie would later phrase as 'swindle' my way in. At the same time, I was trying to get a closer look behind the curtain. Being this very nice guy, I would say things like, 'Do you need anything? I'll go.' If they said, 'I'm getting hungry,' I'd offer, 'I'll go get it if you want.' I was trying to be useful so they wouldn't tell me, 'What are you doing here? You don't belong here.' I didn't want that to happen. I was trying to make myself useful."

"A couple of days later," says Scott, "I was staying at Robbie's house in the Toronto neighborhood of Cabbagetown and we got a call from the Brass Rail in London. It was Ronnie. He said, 'Son, Will "Pop" Jones wants to go home to Arkansas and be with his wife and kids. He's picked you to be his successor in the band. Do you want to come into the band?' I replied, 'Well, I'll come down and talk to you about it.' So me, Robbie and Pete the Bear got out on the highway in the middle of December — it's like zero — and we hitched all the way to London. It felt like days. I marched in with these two other guys and I couldn't understand why Ronnie didn't want to take everybody. He told me, 'No, son, I only want you to play the piano. I don't want these other guys. I've got Levon, I've got a good band here.'

"'I don't know much about the business,' I told him. 'All I know is I started with these guys and I'm with them. If you want me to come with your band, you've got to take Robbie and the Bear.' He said that it was impossible, we'd have to forget it. So we stayed over at the Embassy Hotel, partied with the big boys and hitch-hiked our way back to Toronto.

"We stuck it out on our own for another year." Scott continues. "First we backed up Johnny Rhythm; we had to have a front man to get gigs. His real name was Johnny Rutter; he had been another band's Elvis impersonator. We played the same circuit Ronnie played, but for less money, of course. The Brass Rail in London, places in Hamilton, the Le Coq D'Or. We even played the Brown Derby a lot. That ended when Pete Traynor punched out Johnny Rhythm on the roof of the Embassy Hotel, out in the open, stark naked at two o'clock in the morning.

"So we got another guy, Billy Kent, the 'Singing Milkman' from Maidstone, Kent. It turns out he *was* from Maidstone in Kent, England, where he *had been* a singing milkman. He claimed to have connections with the big producers in England.

"Now by this time, we're all staying in one big room at the Westover and the bill was in my name. Originally Billy Kent had said he'd handle the bill, but then his credit went out the window. He never came up with any money and kept expecting these checks from England. Finally, I ended up going down to the cashier and said, 'Listen, I'm in Ronnie Hawkins's band' — Ronnie *had* asked me — 'and everything's okay. Ronnie's gonna pay this bill as soon as he gets into town.'

"We'd run up a bill of a couple of hundred dollars. We were in the hotel for three months doing nothing. We had the odd gig and the odd practice but basically we were just waiting for this deal with the Singing Milkman to come through. Then Ronnie came back and the shit hit the fan.

"'Here's this huge bill and you're supposed to take care of it, Mr. Hawkins,' said the hotel. He didn't tell them I wasn't really in his band. 'Well, I'll talk to these boys about it,' is all he said. He did talk to me and Robbie, and the next thing I knew I was in Ronnie's band. I went out to London to join them. We finished the gig there at the Brass Rail and we went down to the States, to Fayetteville, Arkansas.

"It was 1959 and Ronnie's record 'Mary Lou' was hitting big. He had already been on 'American Bandstand' with it, and it had sold 750,000 copies. Ronnie said, 'I'm going to England for this "Boy Meets Girl" show and I want you guys to practice. We're all going down to Arkansas,' he says, 'I'll put you up down there. When I come back, Scotty will know all the tunes and we'll be ready to go back on tour.' Well, all the way down there, I was working on Ronnie about Robbie. What had happened was that Ronnie had given Lefty his notice, so I said, 'Ronnie, I've got the perfect bass player for you. Remember Robbie?' He answered, 'Yeah, that boy's got more talent than Jesus Christ. I sure remember him, but he doesn't play the bass, does he?'

"I said, 'Sure, he's *always* played the bass,' — it's not true, of course — 'he can play all that stuff great: "Roll Over Beethoven" and all that stuff with the double-picking bass part.' He said he'd think about it. Of course right after we talked about it I picked up the phone. I called Robbie and instructed him, 'If Ronnie phones you, tell him you play bass, 'cause there's a chance you can get in the band. Tell him you got a gig at the Brown Derby and you can't leave for a week and then borrow Pete Traynor's bass and practice all these tunes. Get the bass parts off the records. It'll be simple for you 'cause you play all this fancy guitar stuff. Take a week and come down and try out for the band.' Sure enough, Ronnie did phone him and the whole thing went down."

Getting Robbie into the band kept him from something much worse — like going to jail. Ronnie saw Robbie scuffling around the city, bound to get into trouble. He knew Robbie's mother, Dolly. He felt she was worried, too. But to Robbie, there's a lot of romanticizing about his days as a delinquent. "What in the world would I have done that I was gonna go to jail?" he says now, incredulously. "I was only fourteen or fifteen years old. I mean, what do you send someone to jail for; what could I have done?

"I think Ronnie may have gotten the idea about me going to jail when we were all staying in that hotel with the Singing Milkman and Ronnie paid whatever it was I owed to the hotel. He helped me out of a jam. Now, you could say maybe they were going to send me to jail; I don't think so. I think I would have figured out something. I was only fifteen but I was hustling pretty good. I could've figured my way out of this without going to fucking jail.

"That story is something like the one about me being a roadie for the band. I never was. I would gladly have been a roadie. 'Hire me,' that's what I was saying. 'I will do anything. I'll walk on a tightrope, I'll be a roadie, I'll play an instrument, I'll write songs,

I'll dance, I'll sing, I'll do anything.' That's the way I felt about it. But the fact is, no one ever did hire me as a roadie. I would've taken it but it wasn't offered to me.

"The main reason I was offered anything was because I wrote a couple of songs that Ronnie liked, 'Someone Like You' and 'Hey Boba Lou.' I wrote those when I was fifteen years old. This is all part of swindling my way, if not into the Hawks necessarily, then into the world. Because I didn't know hanging around the Hawks was going to pan out at this point.

"Well, Ronnie heard these songs and decided to record them. He told me, 'Son, I've got to get more songs. Maybe if you can write these songs, you've got a good ear for songs.'

"So he took me to New York to meet Doc Pomus, Mort Shuman, Leiber and Stoller, Otis Blackwell, Henry Glover, Morris Levy — all of these people. It wasn't like I was going to New York for a week or so to see if anything goes. I was going to New York to look for songs and to meet these great songwriters that I admire. And it was like they're auditioning songs for *me*. There I was, sitting in a room, saying, 'That wasn't bad, you got anything else?' It was amazing that Ronnie put me in this position. I still see Mort Shuman to this day. I still see Leiber and Stoller and they remember this. It was 1959; I was fifteen."

Robbie Robertson pauses while he thinks back: "Everybody was kind of young and innocent. We were a bit like young boys. Nothing demonic was happening to us yet. As I was listening to these songs, Ronnie was going around saying, 'This kid is going to be this and that.' He was always saying good stuff about me, stuff which was convincing me at the same time that he was convincing himself and others. This was very helpful when I was at the crossroads. I was wondering, am I going to reach for the sky or am I going to do some mediocre thing?

"By then I was on a mission to pick up whatever musical knowledge I could; I was definitely on a mission. I remember that everybody around me, all my friends, were saying that this was dreamsville: 'This doesn't happen to people like us. You're gonna end up working down at the thing just like Larry is.' And I replied, 'No, man, you've got to imagine this. You've got to think about what's over there.' I was insisting: I'm going to do this. Everybody thought it was pretty silly.

"By now Ronnie had talked to me about playing bass," continues Robbie. "He said, 'Fred is going to leave 'cause he wants to go to Nashville and settle down with his family. The bass player is leaving, too.' So Ronnie and the rest went back down to Arkansas. I waited. Finally I reached him on the phone at this nightclub, and he said, 'Okay, come down here at such and such a date and I'm going to put you to work. I'm going to put you in training.'

"So I did. I didn't have the money to get down there and he didn't give me any money. I had to hock my Stratocaster, a 1957 Stratocaster. I got on a bus and I trusted them that they knew where they were going. They said, 'Here's what you do. You take a bus from Toronto to Buffalo to Chicago and then you take a train to Springfield and then you take a bus to Fayetteville.' It was one of those deals where I didn't remember the exact route because I was ecstatic, and didn't care where I was going as long as I was going south. But when I got down there they looked at me as if I was a martian. I looked very city-ish — punky, kind of — greasy hair, baggy pants and an overcoat. I was wearing a long overcoat and down there *nobody* owns an overcoat. So they laughed at me and asked, 'Boy, what are we gonna do with him?' Well, Ronnie took me in and had me shaved and made me get a haircut and bought me clothes and all the rest. He took me and cleaned me up and put me into the clothes that all these people wore. New clothes were cool with me. I didn't give a shit what they looked like.

"After we spent some time in Fayetteville, we went down to West Helena to stay while Ronnie and Levon went to England to do the TV show. Carter was to teach me guitar and I was to practice the bass. Well, Fred Carter wasn't overly interested in teaching me anything. I picked up some things from him but not out of the generosity of his heart. There was a good reason for this. He felt it was a free trip for me — that I hadn't earned it.

"I appreciated Fred's reasoning at the time. Later on I thought it was horseshit. I thought, of course, that's what you do at the start. You go here and there and learn from this one and that one. You learn from records. What Fred really did for me was take me with him to Memphis. We went to Sun Records. He was trying to get established as a session guy. I went to Home of the Blues on Beale Street and I spent the first week's money that Ronnie had given me on records. I still have some of the records I bought there. At the time Ronnie was giving me some money to live on. It wasn't a lot. Maybe a hundred dollars, I don't know. But it was plenty for me. It was enough to buy a shitload of blues records. "This was the time I went into full combustion," Robbie remembers. "I was a rocket. I'd seen Fred's attitude. I'd seen the way the thing works. I thought, okay, this is the way it's played, you got it. And I started practicing twelve hours a day. Harder than any man in the world practices. I thought, I'm gonna do this thing.

"Ronnie was good at pumping you up, as a coach would. He put a lot of stuff in my head which was very, very fruitful to use with his kind of mercenary attitude toward music. I stole everything that I could from Fred and off these records; I stole everything. This guy who played with Howlin' Wolf became my hero. I just worked beyond anybody's imagination and when Ronnie and Levon came back, I was making good progress and we started rehearsing. By now I was practicing bass and guitar till my fingers were like rock.

"This went on for a couple of years. I was on this mission. You would meet people like Fred and Roy Buchanan and they would show you a little something, although they didn't want to show you very much. All it did was make you think, okay, all right . . .

"Around this time Ronnie was thinking about what he was going to do with his band. Thinking, 'Maybe I should get Roy Buchanan to play guitar and I'll get Robbie to play bass.' I listened to Roy play this 'Louisiana Hayride' sort of style — like Fred does and like James Burton does but with a different twang to it — and thought he was fantastic. Well, Ronnie was weighing all these possibilities but he could also see that I was a comet at the point, that I had covered in two weeks what other people cover in six months. So he didn't want to gamble against this comet. I knew he was scratching his head at times. Then he was talking about putting Levon on guitar; Levon could play these nice little rhythms and everything, Chuck Berry stuff. He was a great rhythm guitar player."

"After Robbie came down," remembers Scott, "we all went to stay at 'Uncle' Charlie Halbert's place. Uncle Charlie was a friend of Ronnie's, a millionaire with a big mansion on the hill. He had a nice piano in the living room and we practiced there. We met Conway Twitty down there, too.

"Fred Carter called the shots and helped us get everything together. Robbie and Fred seemed to get along fine and Fred ended up showing Robbie a lot of stuff on guitar. Fred played a Telecaster. The two bottom strings were steel banjo strings, a special trick he'd apparently gotten from B.B King or James Burton or both, where you could bend them twice as far as a normal guitar string. It's very bluesy, very black sounding. He passed all that on to Robbie. Robbie was already a good guitar player but he was really young, like sixteen.

"Usually what Robbie played with us was Bo Diddley tunes or other rhythm things. He was always great with rhythm and he always went for the raunchiest, blackest rhythms, like John Lee Hooker and Howlin' Wolf. He played good lead guitar but he wasn't that experienced on it at that point. Robbie and I used to sit down and play all the old Ray Charles tunes on the Wurlitzer electric piano. Robbie would take all the licks Ray Charles played on the piano and transcribe them onto the guitar. That's another thing he picked up, that whole style of funky fourths and thirds that Ray Charles always played. He was good at just absorbing all these things. So anyway, after Ronnie got back from England he tried Robbie out. We all got together in Uncle Charlie's living room and played Ronnie's biggest tunes. They had tricky bass parts, but with Robbie, they were all there. Ronnie said, 'This cat's a genius. Son, you've got the job.'

"Robbie had really been working overtime just teaching himself how the hell to get around this bass," Scott remembers. "He was ripping his hands off; he was desperate to get into the band. Sure enough, we went back to Canada and Robbie was the bass player."

Robertson says, "Maybe I was taken by Roy Buchanan's mystique. Maybe I was influenced by that. I was still so young that I would copy anything in sight. And Roy . . . Roy had a goatee and these eyes, these *strange* eyes. He wouldn't say much and he looked mean. Ronnie was always teaching us that when you play you're having a great time. Now you move up here, now you move over there — it was always like that, show business. Then along came Roy. With him it was, 'Enough of this up and over bullshit. You can be just as effective just by pulling energy out of the music — not moving and all that, not putting on a show.' That shit started to embarrass me. That's like doing leg kicks and stuff in bands. I hated that shit. We didn't see Roy for a while, then about year after he'd left us we were playing in Grand Bend, Ontario, and he came back and stayed with us for a couple of days."

By now Ronnie has heard about Buchanan's "other" identity. "He tells me he's a werewolf who's going to marry a nun," says Ronnie.

"'Jesus, son,' I tell him, 'if you are, we've hit the big time. We're getting out of the goddamn bars, baby. I mean, once a month, when the moon's up, we can do the "Ed Sullivan Show."'

"'No, really,' he says. So it's about the right time of month. And we went out on the beach waiting for the moon. He wasn't stoned. He wasn't on drugs. He said, 'Ronnie, I know you're going to think I'm crazy.' And then I started thinking about how foolish I was standing out on the beach waiting for Roy Buchanan to turn into a wolf."

"About this time," says Robbie, "Ronnie's talking about Levon playing guitar — we could have two guitars. He asked us, 'Do you know how powerful two guitars could be?' Then Roy and I had a showdown in Grand Bend.

"He was still much more advanced than I was," Robbie continues. "I'd been playing at this point a year and a half, two years. He'd been playing many, many years and all over the place. So he had more tricks than I did. But I could play more excitingly at this point. I could scream like hundreds of birds. So that's what it came down to: his more technical thing and all his tricks against this excitement I had. Anyway, we had this out in this showdown and then we never saw one another again until Ronnie took me over to see him one night in Toronto, in 1988, when I was in town to promote my record which had just come out.

"Roy came into the dressing room at the Horseshoe. It was when Rick Danko was playing there. Roy came in and he saw Ronnie and he saw me and he looked at me again and his eyes got all watery. He just looked at me and looked at me. It was just great to see him again. Over the years I've done things for him. I would always talk about Roy. I always wanted to do some nice things for him 'cause he did show me a couple of tricks along the way. People say he taught me how to play guitar, especially the harmonics.

That isn't true. I was a harmonic fool when he came back. It was all excitement and harmonics. Roy would be playing a solo, then he'd do something that'd sound '*booooiiirrrrrooooo*'. I thought, wow, this is like a motorcycle. But I never did it. After seeing him in Toronto I went on to Montreal and I heard him play there too. Then the next thing I heard, he'd died."

Roy Buchanan never did entirely escape his dark vision where werewolves marry nuns. The few times we'd talked over the years revealed little about how he'd come to play guitar so wonderfully — or what it had cost him. Alone, drinking hard late one summer night in 1988, he hanged himself.

But by this time the Hawks were flying. What no outsider could detect was the amazing metamorphosis of the musicians on stage. Ronnie was pushing, pushing, pushing. Then there was Robbie. The kid. His protégé. Something was happening to Robbie. He was driving himself. He developed an insatiable need to learn.

"Right after this showdown with Roy Buchanan I started to read," says Robbie. "When we played dances down South, these cool dances, I thought, there's something missing in my life. I'm getting a whole lot over *here* but there's a space over *there*. I didn't know what it was at first. Finally I realized it was knowledge. So without thinking I knew what to do: I started reading — all kinds of things. I was reading Zen and I was reading Faulkner, Hemingway and just anyone who wrote about the South. I had a view of what that whole situation there was like. It was very enlightening to me.

"Well, Ronnie didn't like this at all. He didn't like this attitude; he didn't like what it represented. To him it was, first you're reading, the next thing, God knows what you're gonna be doing.

"By now, I was feeling that I didn't want to get involved in any of these night charades. I was kind of growing away from the whole thing. It was starting to become embarrassing. What *I* wanted was to up the ante. I was just climbing this ladder. The higher I went on the ladder, the more I wanted to meet the people who were higher on the ladder, too. The rest of the stuff just wasn't working for me anymore. I couldn't do it just to do it. I was starting to feel like saying, 'Just for you guys, I'm going to take this girl back to the hotel. I'll do this just for you guys, so you'll think I'm one of the guys." Well, this was bullshit. What if I hated her? What if she disgusted me? I didn't want that to represent the women in my life. Anyway, that was the kind of thing I was thinking about.

"In the meantime, Levon and I became really close. I thought he was the best guy to me in the world. He had music coming out of his fingertips. He was fun to be with. We were experimenting with life. He and I were meeting more interesting people, more interesting women. We were starting to do things; we bought a Cadillac together, the first car I owned. It was in 1962. But that car started to rule our lives. We thought, God, we're like Cadillac-rich. It was like . . . we're finally getting it. With the band I started at $125 a week, then $150, then $175. By playing on the weekends it might have gone up to $225 a week. If we played on Sundays we made extra money.

"We played Toronto, London and Hamilton. Then we went down South. At first it was Ronnie and Levon and the bunch of us. Then there was Ronnie, Levon and me — and whoever else was playing with us. When we were done playing, we were the three who would get together and do something or talk or date girlfriends or stuff like that. Then it became more Levon and me.

"Eventually the band started replacing guys: Rebel Paine was the bass player, then he was gone. Stan Szelest took over on the piano. Ronnie talked about how he was fighting to get these musicians. What it was, was that Levon and I now were on a mission — a mission to put together a bitch of a band. We had learned a whole bunch of stuff and now we wanted to be able to do some things, and to do them we needed certain players. So we wanted someone who could sing like Richard Manuel and play piano while he was doing it. We wanted someone who could sing like Rick Danko and play bass exactly the way we wanted him to play bass. We wanted someone who could take us further musically. We wanted Garth Hudson. Ronnie was like the daddy of the group. The old guy in the group. We had to convince him."

Rock 'n' roll, like sex or good fiction, is at its best when some danger is involved and a Yonge Street early sixties Saturday night — a sort of wild west movie with a James Brown soundtrack — became the testing ground for an entire generation of Canadian rockers hacking out their style. But a new center of gravity developed after Ronnie Hawkins arrived at the Le Coq D'Or (to purists it was always *the* Le Coq D'Or and never *Le* Coq D'Or), a flash, wonderfully gaudy joint that rocked with rhythm 'n' blues. Soon the Le Coq D'Or was not one of the places you had to check out; it was *the* place.

The rounders found it first. They'd sit around the formica tables with their fancy women and Ronnie, in a special deal with the house which gave him premium brands like Mumms at cost, would buy a bottle of champagne for the table. When that was drained they'd be fighting with each other and ordering buckets of the stuff, not to impress the chicks so much as to impress each other. Next came the musicians: David Clayton Thomas, Dom Troiano, Roy Kenner — all the young, up-and-coming hotshots still too young to drink who would hang around the back where the cruising cops couldn't catch them, to listen to Robbie Robertson. Eventually, everyone else started to notice: kids who'd grown up with early rock radio in the fifties and were now old enough to go witness first-hand the real thing; the small-time cons, pimps, pros and whatnot who figured it was the best place to make the scene; and finally, even the press.

It was with this last group that Ronnie's real genius would emerge. He could hang out with the worst thieves imaginable — "Just as long as you don't tell me anything, boys," he'd say, although he'd eventually get to hear all of their best scams. But he always had a sixth sense about journalists, which amounted to giving them a far better story than they could ever want — or, in some cases, print.

Thus, one cub reporter found himself one night at the Le Coq D'Or getting Hawkins's full-bore champagne treatment, sitting with the master himself after the last show and long after most of the regulars had left. He tried to scribble some notes under the table for a feature he was planning: "The Informal Ronnie Hawkins," something like that. Meanwhile, the informal Ronnie Hawkins was being his most charming. Noticing two women lingering over drinks at a nearby table, Hawkins stuck his face out into the aisle to ask them to join his table.

The women giggled. The Hawk grinned his "come on over" grin. The women giggled. The Hawk grinned some more: "Ladies —

now, please." They giggled some more. They grinned. They shuffled. They adjusted their bras — and started to walk out. The nerve. In front of a reporter! As they passed by, Ronnie snapped, "I guess that a fuck would be completely out of the question then?"

Later in the sixties, when Yorkville was beginning to drag the action away from the strip and Ronnie had become such a fixture that many of us thought of him as the unofficial mayor of downtown Yonge Street, the strip tried to present a softer image. It even had flowergirls. By the late sixties its young vagrants and streetlegends like Alexander Rothschild, the gaunt, bent old guy with lengths of tissue stuffed up his nostrils who prayed over fire hydrants, were part of the great hippie spill-over into the city life. But that came later. Early on, there was nothing soft about it, as Ronnie and the Hawks gave life-lessons in music and mayhem.

"For the young musician there were no other options," says David Clayton Thomas. "Yonge Street was the place you went and Ronnie's was the band you heard. It was that basic, if you wanted to be a musician." Still fronting Blood, Sweat & Tears in those days, the singer saw Yonge Street as his school, and Hawkins as the principal.

"I was fresh out of Burwash, the reform school, and was working at Canada Wire and Cable," he says. "Working at Canada Wire and Cable wasn't what I wanted to do for a living so when I could, which was most nights, I'd go with some friends down to the strip and places like the old Club Blue Note and the Imperial club, down past Queen Street. I'd sit in with the regular house band at the Imperial with people like Steve Kennedy and Doug Riley, who wasn't more than seventeen and was incredible. But Ronnie had *the* band. They were gods to us, particularly Robbie Robertson. He was our idol. We'd go down to the Le Coq D'Or with our Telecasters but because some of us were too young to get in, we'd stand beside the back door. The guys in the band would always make sure the back door was left open a crack; so on any given night you'd always see a dozen fifteen-year-olds, and maybe a twenty-two-year-old like myself, peeking inside watching Robbie Robertson. There'd be Dominic Troiano and George Olliver and Freddie Keeler there with me, watching this incredible band. Watching them made you want all the more to do it, too.

111

"Most of the kids who hung around the band were not as old as I was, so I fell in with the guys in Ronnie's band and became friendly with them much more readily then the younger kids. Back then on Yonge Street they used to have a policy at the Le Coq D'Or, the Edison and other places that would allow underage kids in on the weekends. Ronnie and the band would do a three-show matinee: three forty-five minute sets. And remember, they were doing maybe four or five shows a night; always four a night on Saturday. The club owners arranged it so that in part of the bar they wouldn't serve liquor for these matinees, they'd only serve soft drinks. So any underage would-be musicians would flock to the place. Eventually all those kids turning up, matinee after matinee, would get to know each other, and bands would evolve.

"That's how my first band started," Thomas continues. "Finally I was getting somewhere. After all the watching and practicing and playing in people's basements, I was offered my first paying gig by some tyrannical Greeks who owned a club on Davenport Avenue. So I pulled together some musicians to form a band and told Canada Wire and Cable to shove it. Everybody thought I was nuts. I was probably pulling down three or four hundred bucks a week those days working as second man on the plastics extruder. I made this much money because I worked overtime shifts, night shifts, any hours I could which allowed me to play music. I'd go play till midnight, then work past dawn, then sleep all day so I could play again. Well, the job with the Greeks lasted exactly three nights. And I was between a rock and a hard place. I'd left Canada Wire, there were no gigs, it was winter and about a week before Christmas.

"So I went down to the Le Coq D'Or and asked Ronnie if he knew where I could get a gig. He told me, sure — with him. The next thing I knew he'd put me in his band. I said, 'You've already got a singer' — meaning him. His reply was, 'I'm too busy partying.' So there I was for a time with *the* band. After a while Eugene Smith would come in and sing a couple of tunes with us, a couple of times a week. Ronnie always did his own songs, things like "Forty Days," but we got a chance to a lot of different kinds of music.

"Back then we were all r 'n' b crazy. The early Hawks did stuff like Ben E. King and "Send It Down Home to Me." The only real alternative was country or folk, but not on Yonge Street. On Yonge

Street it was black music. I'd sit and listen to blues all night long. Eventually Ronnie and I got to the point where we diverged musically, especially after I'd first moved to New York and was exposed all the hot new players there, the guys out of Boston's Berklee School of Music or Juilliard. I was listening to music I'd never heard before and it thrilled me to death. After that I could never be the basic rocker I was back in Toronto, although Ronnie wishes to hell that I still was. But there's never been any real parting of ways with us. Even now when I'm in Toronto I don't walk into Ronnie's gig without getting up on stage and singing with him. I love to get down with a band and play boogie and rock; but that's not all I do any more.

"Ronnie's forceful. He's impossible not to like and he's as outrageous as he can be. I know people who hate his guts; I know people who hate mine. But I find it impossible not to like Ronnie. He's forthright with me. He's always straight. He comes right out and says it like it is and doesn't give a shit who minds it or who thinks what. I guess he's hurt himself a couple of times doing that, but that's what he's like. He's also a relentless groupie. He knows everyone in the music business and loves hanging around with them.

"It wasn't just music. We had outrageous parties. We'd close the Le Coq D'Or at one o'clock and go upstairs — the space would later be called the Hawk's Nest — where his office was. He used to hang out with boxers and we'd go upstairs with these guys and go two or three rounds at two o'clock in the morning. And then we'd go back down to the club and start rehearsing.

"The energy Ronnie had. If there was a rehearsal — and there usually was — it would start at one o'clock and go on to about three-thirty. Meanwhile people would start drifting upstairs. There were always chicks hanging about. There was always a party going on around the band. And he was always right in the middle of things.

"Now you can call these parties what you will," Thomas continues. "You want to talk about orgies, well, I've orgies to tell about. But some incidents I just heard about. I do know there was a 'romantic episode' with all five members of the band and an eighty-two-year-old woman in Windsor, Ontario. That's all I know about it. The guys involved, understandably, didn't talk about it too much the next day. By the time the night was over, though, everyone thought she was twenty-one.

"But it'll always be the music I'll remember most. And that band. I love the way Ronnie puts bands together. There's a guiding force in the way he does it, a vision of how a band should sound. A lot of it has to do with the musicians he chooses. He always goes for the same kind of musicians: the right musicians."

"That's why I say that band was better than the Beatles," Ronnie explains. "It was in the way they clicked together. I may be prejudiced, but I don't think so."

Watching Ronnie now remembering The Band — waving his arms, laughing loudly at the memories of all the wild and rocky times they had together — almost lets you forget the pain their leaving once caused him. And the anger, for in its way, it was like children leaving home:

Now, I made 'em work for it, and I tell you they hated it. I used to tell them that everybody is just a cog in a wheel, but once you get the cog exactly right and everybody's pulling in the same direction, the wheel goes round. It's how these different parts fit that makes each band individual. It's always the same old bunch of rock 'n' roll songs they're all doing but each band will sound different because this man will stand out in this band while that man will stand out in that one. There's always a distinctive sound. Well, those Hawks had a *real* distinctive sound.

Levon can play more drums with less licks than any other drummer in the world. He doesn't have to hit everything there is; he just gives the bass drum a kick every now and then and it works. But Garth Hudson was different. He had his own little band playing around western Ontario and as soon as I heard him play keyboards I knew he was exactly what we needed. Garth heard all sorts of weird sounds in his head. I didn't understand what he was doing musically, but it worked. Every band needs someone like Garth. Every band needs a genius musician, the way the Beatles had George Martin as their genius musician-producer to help them out. That's why I hired Garth Hudson. You have to have somebody who's been to school and knows how to do arrangements and all that. You need him to teach the rest of the guys.

Another distinct thing, too, was Ricky Danko's voice, when he sang harmony but with his voice on top of the melody. The Danko boys have really weird ears. Terry Danko, who's playing bass like his brother did in my band right now, can hear harmonies no other human being can. But that's good. That made the sound distinctive. That's what the Beatles had, too: their distinctive voices and the drive they put on it. Likewise, The Band could be really commercial and a lot more.

Then there was Richard Manuel — Beak, we called him — and all the soul stuff he added to The Band. There were better piano players around than Richard, but none had his voice. I've always liked to have two keyboard players. It fills things out in the band. But no matter who's there, they've got to play with feeling. Will "Pop" Jones, my first piano player, would hit a lot of bad notes but what Willard had along with speed and power was the feeling. Richard — who died two years ago, just when things seemed to be going better for him — had that feeling.

Things didn't always go smoothly putting these guys together, just as things didn't go smoothly for them after they left me and were in the big time. Hell, the rest of the guys in my band objected to Robbie Robertson when he first came in. They thought he just didn't know a thing. They were right, I guess. Fred Carter and Roy Buchanan were in the band before him and they were great guitar players. But when Fred Carter went back to be a studio musician in Nashville, Robbie, who'd gone on to playing rhythm behind him, became the guy. I always figure you have two years before you really develop and Robbie back then only knew two or three solos on the guitar. Maybe I forced it on him too quickly, I don't know.

What nobody knows is that Robbie may not have ended up in my band at all. I was looking for a drummer. I thought, I'll bring in a drummer and I'll put Levon on lead guitar. Levon was by far a better guitar player than Robbie — at the time. But Robbie worked and worked and worked.

I really only gave him nine days to learn guitar. And he *had* to learn because he wasn't worth anything when he first took it over. I would have given him more time than that but I wanted to threaten him into doing a good job: after he became good I couldn't threaten him anymore.

There were a lot of kids after his job, too. A lot of kids lived for the day they could cut someone in our band, to show they were better. One guy played with us one night right after Robbie had taken over and he just blew Robbie right off the stage. About nine months later we crossed paths with this guy again and he was bragging how much better he was. But by that time Robbie had learned a lot. Roy Buchanan taught him how to twist that little knob up to bring up the volume. Roy had also taught him a lot of harmonics and other things, about pretending to pop veins in his neck and a lot of other theatrics to make it look a lot harder that what it was.

By then what Robbie was doing was right. What's more, he looked good to the girls. So the next time he crossed paths with this guy he blew him right into the next year. Still, I kept him practicing. He'd play right to one o'clock in the morning and start again at one-thirty or a quarter to two and practice until five.

He only became better and better. I love Eric Clapton's playing, but when Robbie Robertson was rehearsing and playing all the time, in my opinion, Robbie could have blown Eric Clapton into last week. On *The Last Waltz*, where they play together, it's pretty close. Eric Clapton's fans would've voted for him; Robbie's fans would've voted for him. That's how close it was. But at his best, Robbie was the best.

"I started off doing Robbie Robertson licks," remembers John "Ghetto" Gibbard. "Where I grew up, around Stratford, Ontario, rockabilly was really hot. Razor-cut hairstyles were in and a lot of the guys used to wear fedoras and Aquascutum raincoats to dances and super-pointed-toe shoes; Cuban heels, that kind of stuff. A lot of musicians from the area ended up in Ronnie's bands. The first live band I ever saw play had keyboard player Richard Manuel before he was in the Hawks with Ronnie. John Till, a guitar player for Ronnie and then later with Janis Joplin and the Full Tilt Boogie Band, was from Stratford. Kenny Kalmuski, a bass player with Ian and Sylvia for a while, had played with John and Richard Manuel. But to any guitar player, Robbie was the guy to hear. He was the innovator of string bending, in Canada anyhow. He was the Jimi Hendrix of his day in a way, and so there developed a lot of Robbie Robertson imitators and a lot of Robbie Robertson stories.

"He was buying Telecasters at the rate of about one a week, and he'd play them for a while, then sell them, marked up of course. The guy who'd bought one would tell everyone, 'I got Robbie's guitar.' Well, there were more guitar players running around Southern Ontario with Robbie Robertson's Telecaster! And they did have it, too, in a way, because he had played it. Guys were always asking him how he got his sound, not realizing that it all comes down to ability. It's not something that you can do electronically. You either play that way or you learn to play that way.

"Everybody was trying to copy the entire Ronnie Hawkins band, too. That was the only way to go. Ron was my idol. A Hawkins gig was a dance and a concert: there was no sitting down. People would stand in front of the stage and other people would dance. So eventually everybody had some kind of Hawkinism thing going on — or at least, the front men did. Everybody was into wearing mohair suits, something Ronnie started. Before him, it would be red blazers and black pants onstage. Then Ron came along and everybody was into wearing silk, looking a little bit sharper, sort of like the Robert Palmer look. That look was the Hawkins look with the Hawks back in those days."

Early on, though, there was a lot less to this look than met the eye. As Willie Sherman recalls, when "the boys" came to Sherman Custom Tailors, still at 462 College Street in Toronto, "They were after nice suits to wear onstage. But these boys were right from the country. They didn't have any underwear."

"There were quite a few guitar players around who were really good," says Ronnie. "But I always looked for that one who was special. And I'd ask him, 'Do you want to be the goddamn best in the world?' If he did, if I knew he really did, then I knew I'd made the right choice."

To this day, Ronnie puts bands together the way a general manager in hockey assembles a championship team. Raw talent, he figures, is only part of it. There are intangible factors, too:

That's why I took Ricky Danko. I was always looking for those kids with the potential and who had the looks. They had to sing, too. That was Rick. Now Levon and Robbie almost quit when I told them about Rick. He only knew three or four chords, they said. He was really green in other ways, too. I mean, he was from tobacco country, Simcoe, and that's all he thought about. Tobacco. He had a girlfriend — she was this rich farmer's only daughter so she'd inherit the farm one day, and that was enough for Ricky. He was going to settle down with that little ol' girl. To show him there was another side of life, I sent three of my girls to meet him and spend two or three days in bed with him. They were real champions, those. Well, that was that. That was the end of the tobacco farm. He joined us.

It's not that every kid with potential made it. A lot did. Some listened to me, and some didn't have to. But some didn't listen to me when they might've. One kid who had the potential — which I think he blew a bit — was Pat Travers who played with me awhile after Robbie and those others had left me. I almost lost the band I had at the time over him, too. He was one of those young kids who are too wild, one of those kids who just want to play and don't tune exactly as they should. When I told the band about him, they said they didn't want to play with him.

"Listen here boys," I told them, "this is what you don't understand. We're playing for young people. We're in bars. *You* can hear what's out of tune. I know that. But those little ol' girls coming over to the bar to see us every night, the ones who are lifting up their dresses on the side — they don't know he's out of tune. *They're* the ones filling up the club.

"Besides," I told them, "he's going to get in tune. Eventually."

You see, you take one average musician and put him in with four or five really good ones and he's going to be found out a lot quicker. Maybe he's been leader of his own band. Maybe he didn't have to practice. Somewhere along the line he'll get to where he has to be in tune. You can dream about Hollywood and ball parks but you've got to face reality, and one of the realities playing in a rock 'n' roll band is tuning your guitar. I always used to have my boys practice after they finished playing. Why not?

They were used to staying up all night anyway. Their habit was to go to bed about daylight, so why not do something worthwhile? The club opened up at noon, so we would have had to practice before noon, anyhow. Believe me, as hard as it was getting them to practice at night, it was still easier than getting them up in the morning.

Robbie, Levon and those others didn't mind practicing late at first because they knew they were getting good. But they minded when they got really good, of course. But I kept them practicing at night anyway. The way I see it, if you are good, you know you're trying to stay alive playing music, so you've got to work even harder. If you get into a routine of going out to a party every night you lose that edge. Playing all night kept the boys in my band out of trouble. Not playing enough, I think, got The Band into trouble. I think one of the reasons why they finally broke up is because they started making big money and had a lot of time on their hands, and they were partying more than they should have. They should've kept playing and creating. They should have kept themselves to a schedule. They didn't play enough.

Ronnie's Hawks had always been on the road. "Everywhere," says Garth Hudson. "Down in the States, too. Little Rock, Newport, Fayetteville . . . Dallas, Fort Worth, Oklahoma City. We lived in the Silver Moon club in Newport for a month at a time and used to play two or three nights in a row, having a couple of days off intermittently."

"We never stopped," adds Stan Szelest. "We traveled in the same car, slept in the same hotels . . ."

"But things changed," explains Rick Danko, "after Ronnie got married. He had Wanda and that made things different. I think that's when the band started thinking about going out on its own."

VIII

PUKE TWICE AND SHOW YOUR RAZOR

While Bringing Together The Band, Our Hero Learns a Few Tricks from Wanda Nagurski

"IN THE EARLY DAYS OF THE LE COQ D'OR and the Concord I was living in hotels," says Ronnie. "We stayed at the Warwick for two years, then the Westover, then the old Frontenac which later became the Carriage House. I even lived at the Westminster on Jarvis. They were mostly on Jarvis Street because that was the cheapest section of town — without really going to the dead-end joints. Back then we were paying twenty dollars a week for our rooms, but I was making a hundred fifty, so we still had about a hundred dollars to send home. One hundred dollars clear was a lot of money in those days, especially when Canadian money was worth ten or twelve percent more than American money. I was making payments on the stuff back home, my farm and things, which I ended up selling years later to start a club business. I sold everything I had to put ninety grand down on Campbell's Tavern in London, Ontario.

"Now, at the Concord we had had what we called the Coke side — of course that meant Coca-Cola then — where the kids would come in to listen. That's when Dom Troiano, Robbie Lane, David Clayton Thomas and all those kids used to come in and watch Robbie play. 'Cause he was getting good, Robbie was. He was really getting down practicing day and night, and he was just wowing 'em. He was knocking those kids' asses off. So one day, there was Wanda in the Coke section.

"We were there three months at a time before we'd go out on the road, and Wanda and her girlfriend would be there every Saturday, because we were the happening thing in that area, I guess. We were getting airplay. We were getting known, so she and her girlfriend came to watch."

But Wanda Nagurski was getting restless. She was only eighteen, she was pretty, she had lots of boyfriends and she was bored. In June 1960, her dad Walter died. He'd been at the A.V. Roe company, making the ill-fated Avro Arrow fighter plane, and he'd left the family comfortably off. "But being old fashioned and Ukrainian meant that you didn't dance for six months after a family member had died. So I went to a lot of movies," says Wanda. "I went out a lot."

"I met her at an Ontario College of Art costume party," remembers Scott Cushnie. "She was dressed as a black cat. She was a student at the college. I don't know how I ever got to the party except that I was a collegiate type of person in those days. I said to myself that this little cat creature was kind of interesting, and so I started dancing with her. She asked what I did; I told her I played piano for Ronnie Hawkins."

But it was only after a family friend, Bill Avis — who'd later become Ronnie's and then The Band's road manager — took her out one Saturday afternoon to the Concord, that Wanda got to see the guy Scott Cushnie had been talking about.

"Now, I didn't know who this Ronnie Hawkins was," says Wanda. "What's a Hawkins? What's that? I knew some of the songs on the radio. I certainly knew Elvis on the radio. But that was it. I didn't know any Ronnie Hawkins. Bronco Nagurski, the football player, was the closest thing to a celebrity the family ever had, and he's just my third cousin. So I met Ron in September 1960. I was sitting there in the Coca-Cola section of the Concord Tavern where you didn't drink. And it seemed he was singing songs just to me; to me he was just like Elvis. I thought I was in heaven. My heart was gone. Later, Bill Avis brought him over to the table I was at and such a southern gentleman he was, all 'yes ma'am' and 'no ma'am.'

"The truth is, after my dad died, my mother couldn't control me. If my dad had been alive then I'd never ever have met Ronnie Hawkins. He'd never have let me out of the house. But my mom let me out.

"Anyway, they invited me to a party a week later and I made my best friend Marg Harper go with me. The party was at the Frontenac Arms. I didn't know anything about this kind of thing but I always thought Bill Avis would protect me. He was a family friend, after all. So there we were when Ron came in and said, 'Come with me.' I did. I thought he was having another party downstairs so I went with Ron off to his apartment.

"Well, I couldn't be sure of what I was seeing. In his apartment he had that band called the Green Men," says Wanda. "These guys had green hair. Weird. This was my first time out and I didn't know what to make of it. I saw Ron whispering to everybody, and he seemed to be asking them to leave. I was getting nervous. I'd heard about these wild guys. When he shut the door, it was like a movie. I was really scared. I'd already turned down a drink and a cigarette he'd offered me. He knew I didn't drink.

"'Well,' he asked, 'would you like to go into another room?'

"'No thanks,' I replied.

"'Hell, baby,' he said, 'What *do* you do?'

"He got out a bottle of wine. Now, I didn't know what was going on. I'd seen the movies. I thought he'd spiked it. I just took a sip or two — and got light-headed. Then the phone rang. He was over there talking on the phone while I was looking for somewhere to pour the drink. Finally, I poured it in a plastic plant.

"Then he came back and looked at my empty glass and said, 'Oh, boy, you're ready now.'

"He started coming on. I was used to necking with guys. I said to myself, well, okay, I can handle this. Then he got fresh. But I kept resisting. He couldn't believe it. He'd never met anyone who'd act the way I was acting. So he tried more and more — by now he was laughing. 'Well,' he said, 'you're the damnedest woman I ever did see. I think I'm going to pinch you on the titty.'

"'Oh, no, oh, no,' I cried. I was laughing, too, but I was running around the room."

Meanwhile Wanda's friend was coming down the hall. "She heard me yelling so she started pounding on the door. Well, I didn't know what she thought when she finally came into the room. I guess after that I had something of a reputation for being good, or something. Levon would get deliberately fresh with girls just to shock me. He'd go up a girl's skirt, or down her blouse.

"After a while I started seeing a lot of him. Not that he was always around. He was playing the Round Table in New York a lot. He was away in Arkansas a lot. But when he was home he made me feel special. I wasn't his 'girl.' Or anybody's 'girl.' I was just *the* girl.

"There was lots of laughter back then. Lots. Levon and Ron were hysterical in those days. Friday nights were their wild times. Ron had girls coming and going. I remember I walked into a room and saw that every chair, every couch, every*where* had girls waiting for King Perouksi, as I called him — that's after King Farouk — so that they could go into his room where he'd be waiting in bed. But Sundays would be different. They'd be special. On Sunday afternoons they'd play casino, drink Red Cap beer and watch television. It was being-normal time.

"He didn't want to get married. I knew that. He fought it all the way down the aisle. But I also knew back then that he was really old fashioned, that he wanted a wife and a family. I don't think he liked the pretentious kind of women. I'd come there just in my slacks and running shoes. Later on people heard that I'd been a Miss Toronto. That wasn't the case. I was just in the contest.

"But we didn't get married just like that. In fact, I think he married me because he thought I was going to leave him and go to California. And I was, with my brother and one of his friends. I'd written to MGM to get work as a secretary, and they told me I had the job. I had a place to stay, at a girls' rooming house. I'd always wanted to be close to the glamor.

"So he didn't exactly get down on his knees and say, 'Marry me, marry me.' Instead, he remarked, 'Well, I guess we should get married.' My mother had never met him. I didn't care. I didn't know if it was going to happen.

"I said, 'Mom, I'm getting married on Friday' — it was March 10, 1962 — 'if you want to be there, you can.' I introduced her to him on the steps of the church.

"By this time, everyone's thinking I was nuts. I wasn't thinking of marriage at the time. I didn't think of having a guy, a picket fence and all that. When you are young and stupid, you don't think of things like that. I didn't *think* about getting married, or *think* about having kids. I was young; I really didn't even think we were going to get married. I knew that Ronnie had figured that the price of razor blades would go up — that girls would be killing themselves when they heard he was married."

No sooner were the happy couple strolling arm-in-arm out of the church, when who should walk by but a young singer with hopes of joining the Ronnie Hawkins band — Eugene "Jay" Smith.

"Jesus," exclaimed Jay Smith. "You're Ronnie Hawkins, right? You just get married?"

"Me?" said the Hawk. "Naw, it's him," pointing to his best man, Levon. Jay Smith knew better. "And as we were going to dinner," Wanda continues her story, "we heard it on the radio, that Ronnie Hawkins had gotten married. Jay had phoned CHUM. Certainly I hadn't told any more than a few close friends.

"We moved into the Frontenac Arms, where we took over two penthouse apartments. We lived there for a while, then we went out on the road. It was fun. I was really happy."

"I know everybody was surprised I got married," says Ronnie. "Nobody thought I'd do it. I'd always said a musician can't get married because there are too many ups and downs. By the time I'd come to settle in Canada for good, I'd done all that playing in the States. I tried everything. I thought I'd figured out what was going on and I always had in the back of my mind the thought I'd be going back to the States as soon as the bubble broke — and everybody kept telling me it wasn't going to last very long — and take twelve more subjects at the university and end up somewhere teaching high-school science and physical education. I thought I always would have something to fall back on in case the music fell through. And I kept waiting for it to fall through; and I just kept waiting. Here it is, all these years later, and we're still waiting for it to fall through. Damn.

"Anyway, she was just eighteen when she started coming into the club. We got married when she first turned twenty-one. I was getting up there — I was about twenty-seven. After we got married we went on the road the following week and Wanda came with me. We had the weekend at the Concord to finish and when we did that we headed south to Arkansas and Texas. I had a Cadillac and a Ford. Levon drove the Cadillac. Me and Wanda went in the Ford.

"We lived at Wanda's mother's place on High Park Avenue, until I bought the farm in Mississauga. She was going to sell it to somebody, so I said that I'd buy it, because I liked the house. It was a beautiful house, a magnificent house, with walnut and oak and every room inlaid with wood. Later I sold it to Wanda's aunt because Wanda's aunt was into real estate and I needed the money. I didn't sell it other than into the family, because I wanted to get it back some day."

A year after they were married, on March 16, 1962, Ronnie Hawkins, Jr., was born. Their second son, Robin, was also a "High Park baby," born December 24, 1964. By the time daughter Leah, their third child, arrived on July 30, 1969 — she immediately became "the apple of her daddy's eye," explains Wanda — Ronnie had made it clear that he wasn't leaving Canada. He'd told Morris Levy this, and eventually he told Bob Dylan's manager, Albert Grossman, too. Scott Cushnie, watching Ronnie's life at home and on the road, realized that "he really did like the idea of family and belonging and the great American Dream. He liked the security of having a family to go home to every night.

"But," adds Cushnie, "he wanted the total freedom of being the young rock 'n' roll star and being outrageous. So he did both. He managed to pull it off."

By this time, Scott was having mixed feelings about the growing Ronnie Hawkins mythology. For one reason or another he couldn't communicate with Ronnie, with the result that he was now out of the band and Stan Szelest was in.

His "demise" came about weirdly, remembers Cushnie; it happened when he lost his virginity. They'd been in Fayetteville and a guy in the band had picked up a girl at a hamburger joint and had brought her back to where they were all staying. For one reason or another, the young woman was convinced that Scott was indeed the famous Ronnie Hawkins. Scott did little to discourage her in this opinion.

Back in his bedroom Scott asked the woman her name.

"Alberta," she said.

"Alberta?" mused the University of Waterloo drop-out. "That's the name of a province in Canada."

Since this wasn't about to impress her, he did the best he could in another way and in the process lost his virginity. And she *was* impressed, or so he thought. When he went to the bathroom, though, in walked Levon.

Would Scott mind, asked Levon, if he, too, were to chat up Alberta? Cushnie was thunder-struck. Right after him? Yes indeed. As the wild young piano player of the Hawks pretended to snooze, in the bed next to his own Levon and Alberta noisily enjoyed themselves.

An erotic memory wasn't the only thing Alberta left with Scott. "When we got back to Toronto I was beginning to feel tired. I had no life up on stage. I didn't know it at the time, but I had a case of clap. Venereal disease. It saps your energy. But because I didn't go to the doctor for some time, and I didn't tell Ronnie what had happened, he thought something was wrong with me."

Finally, the Hawk decided he needed a new piano player and brought in a hot young kid from Buffalo — Stan Szelest. The night Scott found he was out he sat down at Tops Restaurant, tears streaming down his face, his old buddies around him. No one bothered to tell Ronnie that Scott was not well. He felt he'd been demoted to "the minor leagues."

In time, word got back to Ronnie, and Scott remembers the Hawk giving him some of his older suits as a parting gift. Nor did Ronnie forget Cushnie. Within a few years, Scott ended up working for the newly-formed Hawk Records, and by 1968 he was recording with Hawkins again. But his days with this edition of the Hawks were through.

Not that his replacement, Stan Szelest, lasted all that long. "I started in 1960 but I was only in the band for some months, then I left," remembers the hard-rocking piano player. "I was a kid, just seventeen. I went back to Buffalo, New York, where I was going to university. I was with the Bill Black combo for a while, then I'd be back with the Hawks. I'd stay for maybe six months of the year and then I'd leave again. After I left the first time, Ronnie was really nice to me. He gave me a bonus and he covered what I owed on two mohair suits I'd bought. The next time I came back in and I left I got another bonus. But the third time the bonuses stopped. He finally figured I was quitting just to get the bonus.

"What he wouldn't accept was smoking in his car. We all used to smoke a lot. Levon, me and Robbie would be back there smoking cigarettes in the car. But Ronnie didn't smoke or drink at the time and he was very fussy about this '59 Cadillac he had. He kept it in spotless condition. He offered us each fifty dollars a week more pay to quit smoking. There we were, going down the road in the middle of the night, the windows rolled down, packages of cigarettes flying out of them. So we got to a restaurant and started getting the munchies. Levon got raisins and we started eating those, but the raisins that dropped on the rug of the Cadillac made a mark the size of a quarter. Ronnie then offered us a hundred dollars to quit eating raisins."

For a while, it was all one grand adventure for them all. But to Robbie the excitement was wearing thin. He was tiring of all the parties and sexual escapades, the traveling and the music that was basically all the same, and the tough situations they had to face.

"Situations?" Ronnie grumbles loudly. "They were goddamn tough places back then. They were harder than Japanese arithmetic. We were in one place once where three big old redneck loggers — they were two brothers and a cousin — threw this guy out. He'd been there for some time, and he said something or other. Anyway, they came over to his table, they grabbed him and threw him on the floor. Then *they* sat down at his table. He got up, dusted himself off, went outside. I though he was going after a gun. He wasn't; he was going after a chainsaw.

"Well, he got that ol' chainsaw going and he sawed off half the bar by the time he got back in. At this time, they had the exit doors boarded up, to prevent folks from sneaking in, I guess. Well, with this guy coming at them with a chainsaw, those three fuckers just ripped those ol' boards off those doors and fled to save their lives. These boys had bad reputations, too, for beating up cops and everything. But they wouldn't take on this guy with the chainsaw. We just stopped playing when this happened."

Wanda could see that despite all their good times together, Ronnie and the band were drifting apart. "Those boys were smoking more and more grass and Ronnie was threatening them with fines. They didn't like that. I'd always known Ronnie was an old-fashioned man. Well, he'd didn't want trouble with his band. And when they were smoking so much dope, they were inviting trouble."

But there was more to it than that. Robbie knew, as Ronnie himself knew, that the band was evolving beyond what Ronnie was doing. Musically they were capable of doing more. They'd even changed socially.

"Now there was a kind of pecking order in the band," remembers Robbie. "There was Ronnie, then Levon, then me. I was the youngest one. But when we started hiring these other guys, the band kept getting younger and younger and Ronnie kept getting older and older. After a while, Levon and I had a certain kind of clout. We started relating to certain music that Ronnie didn't connect with. We started going with certain kinds of girls. We started relating to certain kinds of rounders — and it was separating us from the pack a little bit. We almost took it too far at one point. We were alienating people, the other guys in the band and Ronnie.

"The breakup came when there were things going on that we felt were unfair. Well, the whole thing was unfair. The band started to make more money, but we didn't make more money. Then Ronnie said he didn't want Rick bringing somebody to the club. For all of us it was like our human rights were being tread upon. We began to stand up for them and, well, one thing led to another.

"I remember the day we left. I was downstairs at the club on the phone. Levon was going to call Ronnie to tell him how we felt. Well, Ronnie bluffed. Instead of saying, 'Let's go and talk about it,' he put his foot down. He was being rigid. Part of it maybe was the heartbreak of the situation — trying to stand his ground. Anyway, we did leave. The whole reason behind it was this: the band was becoming more knowledgeable about music and the old stuff we were doing was getting on our nerves. We were young and adventurous. We were on a musical journey, and this was the only way to explore it. It may have been partly for business reasons, too, but we really outgrew what we were doing.

"We weren't being mistreated. We just didn't want to feel that we were being taken advantage of. We were getting better and better and growing. And things around us weren't growing as fast as we were. When we met Dylan we didn't know much about him, so we didn't know what we were getting ourselves into. We found out pretty quick. It was amazing period of time."

Two other factors contributed to the split-up: money and music.

By 1964 they'd been joined by sax player Jerry Penfound and by singer Bruce Brono, who filled the role Robbie Lane was to have later, working up the crowd until the Hawk himself arrived on stage. But none of them liked the musical direction in which they were being taken. And none of them liked earning as little money as they were getting.

Then came the day they called Ronnie's bluff. They wanted changes, they said. They wanted to do other kinds of music. They wanted more money. But Ronnie played it cool. He wasn't budging.

"My office was in the Sheraton Hotel in Hamilton," says Harold Kudlets, "and one morning I arrived at nine to find everyone waiting for me in the lobby. They had told me they had left Ronnie and asked whether I would book them. I was an agent so I said, sure. By the time they quit, Ronnie was the best-paid musician in the country. He was making a thousand dollars a week at the Le Coq D'Or and that, in those days, was big money. So I asked them, 'How much do you need to get by? How much have you been getting by on so far?' Well, I couldn't believe it when they told me. They were getting around seventy-five dollars each a week. So I had them traveling through the States — they were the Levon Helm Sextet at the time — and I had them booked into Tony Mart's, a huge place with six stages at Somers Point, New Jersey, when Bob Dylan discovered them. That's when they went to Woodstock. That's when they became The Band."

"The Band did something special," says the Hawk. "To me, 'The Night They Drove Ol' Dixie Down' was a classic the first time I heard it. Robbie and the rest brought it to me when it was still on tape. Now, I always had trouble getting The Band to sound like it might be halfway country. They said they just didn't want to do it. They felt they were too hip for it — at the time. Then I heard that they were doing exactly that on their own. Halfway country . . . If I had to put a name on their music, I'd call it funky country. It had that country feel but it was hip. It had smart lyrics, good harmony and good chord changes sometimes. Robbie picked up that funky country music groove from being down South so many times.

"But they were smart. Even if they did come out with something nobody had heard before it was also something which was commercial. Robbie and the rest had always made musicians' music —

music that people who knew music knew was a little better than everything else. Yet with the stuff they were recording on their own they were also making music people liked; people who don't know anything about music have got to like 'The Night They Drove Old Dixie Down' and 'Rag Momma Rag.' That stuff just *feels* good.

"Some of those great slow songs they did were really good songs, too. Yet some of it was really new, like 'Chest Fever,' where Garth drops those damn big chords on you. I tell you, it's a little better than your average boogie band."

The arrival of The Band in the late sixties came, it seemed, when everyone was beginning to feel a great emptiness. "Against a cult of youth, they felt for a continuity of generations," rock essayist Greil Marcus writes about the appearance of their first album, *Music from Big Pink*. "Against the instant America of the sixties they looked for the traditions that made new things not only possible but valuable; against the flight from roots they set a sense of place. Against the pop scene, all flux and novelty, they set themselves: A band with years behind it and meant to last."

With the release of their second album, *The Band* — arguably one of the greatest albums to appear in pop — they made the cover of *Time* magazine. Photos showed them in beards, wing collars, coats made of solid, heavy cloth: latter-day survivors of the Civil War. Through Levon, modern rock drumming connected with southern juke-joint bands from the fifties. Through Garth Hudson's great open organ chords, modern rock met with the sound and spirit of Sunday morning fundamentalist prayer meetings in that part of western Ontario he came from. They drew into the artificial space of the rock 'n' roll stage the very real sense of the people who made the music in the first place.

Ronnie says that "after leaving me and not doing very well on their own for a while, they ended up backing Bob Dylan. But when Dylan got to where he couldn't play, Albert Grossman, who was Dylan's manager, put the boys on a little retainer which wasn't enough to do much other than save their lives for a while. They didn't have enough to do very much, either, so they rehearsed and practiced — and then they put out *Music from Big Pink*. A lot of other people started liking it and Albert realized that they could do it for real. This was when the whole band worked as a unit, for the most part.

"Later on I think Robbie had to work a lot harder then the rest of them because the rest of them were having too much fun. At the very start, though, Levon was the boss the way John Lennon was the leader of the Beatles. Levon called the shots, but after a while he started having too much fun and so it was left to Robbie to take care of the business. Gradually it became Robbie who ran The Band. But that can mean a lot of pressure. Eventually Robbie became tired of the road. He was tired of the business. It's tough when everybody's not pulling their weight. It's tough when everyone else is having too much fun all the time and people aren't able to go on because they are puking in pianos and fainting and falling offstage. You can't do that if a band is going to survive as a band."

The Band's Last Waltz, back in San Francisco, November 25, 1976, was just that — a grand finale, complete with Bob Dylan, Eric Clapton and a day of nostalgia. An enormous amount of food was consumed: 220 turkeys, 400 gallons of apple juice, 300 pounds of Nova Scotia smoked salmon brought from New York by Bob Dylan, 6,000 bread rolls and 2,000 pounds of peeled yams. Using walkie-talkies to keep the food supply coming regularly, the caterers fed everyone in the five hours before The Band went on. There was the movie, too. Martin Scorsese became involved with The Band when he was shooting *Mean Streets* in New York and went to Woodstock, where The Band was living, for a break from work. They became friends. The choice of the Winterland Ballroom had an historical connection. The Band had made its concert debut here in 1969 — a year after its first album, *Music from Big Pink* and the year before the group appeared on the cover of *Time*. Even in 1969 the group represented the culmination of a lot that had happened in rock — from fifties rock, which they had churned out for eight years with Ronnie, to country, blues and Bob Dylan. So *The Last Waltz* was the crystallization of all these influences.

Everybody who was anybody was there. David Bromberg, Dylan's former accompanist, almost backed into Ringo Starr, who had flown in from Los Angeles in the private jet rented by Neil Diamond. "I'm taking it very easy," said Ringo. Bromberg was otherwise inclined. "On the scale from one to ten," he said to no one in particular, "this concert rates a fifteen." Ronee Blakey, who'd starred in Dylan's Rolling Thunder Revue, for heaven's sake, couldn't even get near the stage.

Walking around largely almost unnoticed was Albert Grossman, Dylan's first manager who, if things had worked out, would have been Ronnie's manager, too. He ended up managing The Band when Dylan left him in 1967 and he wasn't about to admit that the group had quit performing together for good. "It is just not going to happen," he kept saying, shaking his head. But he wasn't aware of who was going to be first up on stage with The Band — Ronnie Hawkins — or he would have understood how completely Robbie, Levon and the boys were going to close the door of their collective past. Reviving the Hawks one last time brought The Band full circle.

"This is the big time, the *big* time," the Hawk kept repeating as he and his former sidemen snapped briskly into one of their old hits, "Who Do You Love?"

After the 5,600 pounds of turkey served in the Winterland Ballroom had finally disappeared and Martin Scorsese's camera crews had packed up and left, The Band's members went their different ways, looking for homes after a life on the road. Robbie Robertson stayed in California for a movie career. Levon went back to Woodstock, where The Band and Bob Dylan recorded what went on to be known as *The Basement Tapes*.

After that — and without Robbie around to dispute the fact — Levon became The Band's boss. But there are those who'd tell you he'd always been the boss, even when they were called the Hawks and were backing Ronnie. Then for years it seemed a reunion was possible. Robbie refused, of course. It had ended when it had ended, he'd say. There was no point in getting together again.

Nevertheless, Rick Danko would go out for a one-nighter somewhere and Levon would show up. Levon played Washington one night and there was Garth. ("So I told him," Levon says, "it's too bad you didn't bring that accordion of yours. I'll be, if he didn't have it.")

And there was Richard Manuel, still writing good songs, they said, and in much better shape. He'd kicked drugs, everyone was told. He was getting back on track. That may have been true, but he had a long way to go and he never made it.

"He was living really hard in those days," I remember Ronnie telling me, not long after Manuel's suicide in 1986 when he was only 42. "But I'd heard he was okay and feeling really good. Still, there are going to be some angels who'll get their feathers clipped when he gets to heaven."

Ronnie remembers how "crazy" Richard could be. Like the time, late one night, when the Hawks were heading into Tulsa for a concert. It was Ronnie's turn to sleep and he curled up in one corner of the back seat. He had a rule that there was to be no smoking in the car but the moment he nodded off, everyone lit up. Manuel, sitting in the front seat, didn't bother to look around to butt out his cigarette in the ashtray in the back. He was grinding it out when Hawkins woke up with a yell. Manuel had been butting out the cigarette on the Hawk's head.

Through The Band's slow decline Robertson, of course, stayed put in Hollywood. He didn't want a reunion. The Band, he felt, had had its time and that was that. Besides, he'd fallen in love with the movies. Ronnie took him down South when he was just a kid, opening his eyes to a world a kid from Southern Ontario might never have known otherwise. But Robbie couldn't take anyone where he wanted to go. "I've spent sixteen years of my life on the road with the same people. It's time we had a change. It had all become like a merry-go-round for us."

As for the rest, they just shrugged when you mentioned that, without Robertson, they were missing a major component. So what? was their attitude. Besides, what could they do?

"After a while they stopped playing in public altogether," says Ronnie. "It put me off that they didn't take care of business better than they did especially after ending up in the big time. Levon could've come back and bought anything — Rockefeller's mountain, anything. And Robbie could've come back and bought all of Cabbagetown. They could've stayed together, too. They owed it to their fans to stay together, damn it.

"I was on their case for years, but of course they wouldn't listen. I saw a lot of money wasted, a lot of money they wish they had now. I think they lost control. They had too much money, too much fun and not enough work. Sometimes now they get mad at Robbie, because he's done all right. But they shouldn't. He took care of business. He was rough and tough when he started out but he was the one who most wanted to learn. I kept pushing Robbie, making him work harder and still harder, because he had the spirit. It's paid off for him. He probably has only one-tenth of what he should have. But still, that's enough."

To get to where The Band ended you have to go to where the sixties ended: Woodstock, New York. I made the trip back with a rented car, and only a few preconceptions.

"Dr. Fido and Dr. Felicia, psychoanimalysts, announce the opening of their joint practice," I read with interest in the *Woodstock Times*. It's next to an ad offering ways to "explore the universe." There's also a sky calendar "of interesting celestial events." I'm munching on something called a bean burger. Incense is in the air. "Your dog is allowed on our couch," Fido and Felicia go on to say. For the moment I have this irresistible urge to put flowers in my hair.

I have time to spare on the drive to Levon's place — actually a recording studio converted into a home — and I realize I'm not far from what was Max Yasgur's 600-acre farm where the Woodstock Festival was held in 1969. A couple, neither one older than twenty-one and both with backpacks, are heading the same way. Perfect. "Years ago, every dropout used to head to Greenwich Village," Rick Danko tells me later. "Now they head up here." Down at the other end of town, past the shop that sells cassettes of "eleven centuries of classical Chinese music," up the country lane and through the huge wooden gate, medieval-looking with its iron bolt-work, Levon Helm is sitting on the edge of his bed, eyes closed real tight, singing songs his daddy taught him.

"Wellll, the poor old dirt farmerrrrrrr . . ."

Levon does this a lot these days. Sometimes he sings downstairs next to that huge flag for Tyson's Chickens, a southern poultry concern much in favor with him and Ronnie. The thought of Don Tyson's chickens is particularly inspiring to Levon, so he sings a bit better. A lot of the time the impulse to go back South is so strong that Levon heads back to his cabin in Arkansas.

He suggests we go upstairs to his bedroom. A tubby little black wood stove sits next to his bed. Several Bloody Marys sit on the wood stove — but not for long. Levon is thinking about going out on the road again, probably back to Arkansas, but mostly he's thinking about obsession. He can look like a rube if he wants to, but when his eyes get silky sweet you know a plan is hatching. "There are some things we can be hooked on," he says, cradling a guitar. "Miners get hooked on mining, particularly coal mining. They can't do without it. That's sort of the same with me and playing on the road.

"I guess that's *my* reason for always going out again with those boys after The Band broke up. Richard was always pretty keen, too. The one who used to surprise us was Garth. We all thought he'd be reluctant because he was busy in the studio. He loves all those machines. But when he heard about it, hell, he was happy as a pig in the sunshine." He nestles the guitar under his arm and tries out something else his daddy, Diamond Helm, taught him. Hudson is somewhere else right now, but in walks Rick Danko, who plops down on the bed.

Levon has aged. Not Danko. Once I said he reminded me of a young and thinner Lou Costello. He didn't like that, I was told. To me, he's sweet, gentle, complicated and cagey all at once. And hurt. His life has had its tragedies: his two sons died when only young men. Whenever Danko says something, his eyes flick sideways as if he's checking out reactions.

Danko sees The Band's future in video: "As old as I am and as dumb as I am," he says, eyes flicking, "I watch the music videos on TV, and that's the best way for anybody to get his name heard." Several more songs are tried out, people wander in and out, the Bloody Marys disappear, others reappear and before anyone knows it, it's late afternoon.

Levon wants to spend more time with his family and Danko wants to show me a little place he knows out back somewhere, which in turn leads to a mad dash in separate cars to nearby Bearsville. "Everyone thought breaking up The Band was a good idea," Danko explains. "At the time," he adds, as we settle in at the little bar, "I was living out in Malibu, but after the years I thought something was missing. It was missing for my kids, too. So we moved back here." He looks around. "There's something about this place that's right. There's something about getting back with everybody that's right, too."

The Band had its moments after Robbie Robertson left it. It wasn't the same, but it wasn't necessarily worse. But after tours and benefits and faced with a shrinking following, it began to fall apart. The Band had had its day, although on occasion someone trotted out the old name and the old songs. So now Levon wants everyone to know he has nothing to do with this thing called The Band. It's all over now. For real.

And the circle will be closed, for Levon is thinking about playing in Ronnie Hawkins's band again.

And so is Rick.

IX

HOW MUCH IS THAT THERE ROLLS?

The Legend Flies High Over Yonge Street, and Learns
What a Rolls Royce Really Costs

WE LOVE OUTLAWS AROUND THESE PARTS. Oh, they'll parade Mounties for us in their nice scarlet uniforms but we love the legend of Bill Miner, our great train robber, a lot more. Watching hockey on a Saturday night, we nod knowingly, not about the apple-cheeked rookie who's a sweetheart of a goal scorer, but about that toothless son of a bitch who knows how to throw an elbow in the corner. All the gloom we must endure brings out the rebel in us. So we've come to love that in others too. Surely it's no accident that our greatest jazz musician, Oscar Peterson, plays like a freight train at full throttle: one enormous, individual, impassioned burst of raw music. Even so, Rompin' Ronnie Hawkins may be the most unlikely hero ever to come down the pike. And it wouldn't have happened if he hadn't gotten "real pissed off" at that most hated of Canadian villains, after politicians — the car salesman.

With his network of clubs waiting for his every visit, with Levon, Robbie and the rest playin' as smoothly as a Maserati's pistons, with the action on Yonge Street beginning to heat up, with all the beautiful women hanging around him all the time, well, damn, life was good for the Hawk. Real good. He'd cut his losses in Arkansas, selling some property. Mentally, he'd moved north — if not for good, at least for the foreseeable future. Even better, he was making money. Big money. He was the big draw wherever he went. Let the teeny boppers listen to the Beatles on CHUM; the folks who paid hard cash in clubs were listening to his band do his music.

Never one to do things in a small way, Ronnie had already settled in a house — a manor house, more to the point — that fit his style. After their marriage, he and Wanda had lived for a year or so at her parents' place at 196 High Park Avenue in Toronto. Before that, he'd lived entirely in hotels. He felt restless. He was used to the open spaces, so he started looking for a "nice little place" (by that he meant a nice *big* place) somewhere out in the country. It wasn't long before he found the one he loved. It was big enough, remote enough, yet within a forty-minute drive of the Le Coq D'Or.

The problem was, Ronnie didn't have anywhere near enough money to buy it. Ronnie remembers: "The man who had it was an old Irishman named McKee. He was a millionaire and was from the old, old school. He wouldn't just sell it to anybody. He wouldn't let any Jews in his house and there were other people who couldn't come up there, too. Anyway, I went up there to talk with him. He was a heavy drinker, real heavy, maybe two bottles a day. So I'd go up there and talk and have a drink or two. He'd already turned down $150,000 for the place so I figured I didn't have a chance. But I got together every penny I could borrow, beg or steal and I was going to offer him $90,000 for it.

"Well, the real estate woman I was dealing with told me to forget it — it wasn't worth her time. She refused to go up there. I decided to take a shot at it anyway. He liked me. I wasn't the drinker he was. I couldn't find my ass with a geiger counter after two or three doubles, but he liked me anyway. I think he gave me the house for about half the price he was asking because he liked me. Now, there was a piece of property right next to mine. It was about ten acres. It had on it the shed that we ended up calling Old Yeller — you know, because of The Band's Big Pink, where they recorded their first album. I was fixing to buy the property so I could join it to what I already had, but a friend of mine got it instead; I ended up just using it as an old house for guests of mine or for the band to rehearse in."

But it was a story, and not his power or his growing empire, which lifted the Hawk's reputation into legendary status. It was the day he bought his first Rolls Royce. By this time in his life, Ronnie was through with driving his Caddy. Having a Caddy may have been impressive once but it wasn't impressive *enough*. Hell, folks were even noticing that Levon and Robbie were driving a Caddy too. Shoot, if the guitar picker and drummer in your band are driving a Caddy — they shared it equally, but which little ol' girl was going to know *that*? — then it was time you moved up to something better. And that meant a Rolls. And that, in turn, meant $18,000 or more. Now, there are many versions of what happened next. Indeed, the Hawk himself is capable of sweetening the story from time to time.

One variant on the basic yarn has Ronnie, rebuffed by the salesman — who assumes that this seedy-looking chap couldn't possibly afford even a windshield wiper for a Rolls — heading out to the bank, stuffing the required $18,500 in a large paper bag and returning to ask for the boss.

"How much is that there Rolls?" the Hawk asks the dumb-founded owner as he fingers a Silver Cloud.

"Why, $18,500 . . . uh, sir," replies the store-owner.

Ronnie starts counting out hundred-dollar bills.

"And how much would that salesman's commission be?" he asks.

"Ten percent."

Ronnie fishes out $1,800 in crisp hundred-dollar bills from the pile on the table.

"Well, goddamn it, there's the money for that car. I'll just keep what *he* would've got."

There are further variations, too, all having one thing in common — they are, sorry to say, not entirely true. The point is, while Ronnie did pay in cash, he wasn't rebuffed. Hell, rebuff the unofficial mayor of Yonge Street? Besides, as anyone who knew anything of Toronto society would have known full well, some of Ronnie's biggest fans — those found at his parties, even — had names that ended in Eaton and Bassett.

With one parked in his drive, Ronnie was on a roll with Rolls and bought his next one the following year from . . . Mrs. Eaton. "It was beautiful," he says. "A Phantom Five, 1960, which I brought up to date. Beautiful." But the Rolls Royce story became one of Yonge Street's better tales — one which best defined who this Ronnie Hawkins was. Style! You bet. Damn, that man had style! If "mortgage manor" in Mississauga had become his Versailles, the Le Coq D'Or was his Elysée Palace. Above the Le Coq D'Or he opened another club, the Hawk's Nest, for a younger crowd. He had his offices. He had his boxing ring. He let rooms to musicians. Ronnie might close Yonge Street on the average night, but that did not mean he himself stopped. No indeedy!

He was doing all right, and everyone who was around at that time remembers the night he whispered in their ear that as soon as he finished his set that night, "there'll be a little party, boys." And there was. The champagne flowed. Some of Ronnie's society friends would show up. There were lots of backslap, bum-pinch and hearty y'all goddamn, because Ronnie was celebrating the first million dollars "I've made in the bars."

Among those at the party were a few folks who had little chance of ever making the society page. Indeed, the only time they'd ever get in the paper would be when Jocko Thomas, for years the Toronto *Star*'s great police reporter, might note that a certain Sid B. or one of the Kleigermans or maybe good old Doc was apprehended for some deed which the police took to be unlawful. Ronnie loved these guys. And they . . . well, they trusted Ronnie. "They knew he was straight, but they knew he was interested in who they were," says John Gilbert, the talk-show host who after meeting the Hawk as a rock promoter in Peterborough made the acquaintance of a number of the same shady characters who later befriended Ronnie.

And why shouldn't they all be friends? Ronnie ran away with rock 'n' roll; Gilbert ran away with a carnival. They ended up knowing all of the same drifters, grafters and guys who knew tricks with dice. They all heard the same stories. They all ended up at the same all-night restaurants. Everybody talked about everybody. Everybody knew about the big games that went down at the King Eddy. They all knew the same old carny tricks. If need be, they could scam anybody. Cards, pool — it was all the same as rock 'n' roll, in a way, a bit of vaudeville with some artistry mixed in. Anyone who'd been to enough shows at the Le Coq D'Or would have been treated to the spectacle of some poor dude, slumping his shoulders, walking slowly up on stage, where Ronnie would put one beefy arm around him to announce, "Folks, you're looking at one of the top criminals in all of Canada . . ."

On a good night, Ronnie could get *really* on a roll this way and point to half a dozen of the most wanted men in Southern Ontario. "Doc!" he'd bellow. "Get up here, Doc!"

And on occasion, if one of these pals liked to take a holiday from "work," he could go on the road with one of Ronnie's bands. Doc Cassidy, one of the greatest "mechanics" of them all, once toured as the band's roadie. Lifting amps and guitar cases was the last thing Doc was interested in doing: he had other business out there in the boondocks. After a few games of cards and dice, Ronnie figures, the good doctor made more than the band did the entire trip. Doc Cassidy is now retired, a fact that has both Gilbert and the Hawk shaking their heads sadly.

"He was one of the great ones," says Gilbert, the afternoon we get together to talk about the naughty old days. The Hawk nods sadly. For the loss of a master mechanic — in gambling terms one who can turn up a King-of-whatever or roll a nine when it's necessary — means the further dissolution of a tradition. And how! When Robbie Robertson filmed the movie *Carny*, he flew Doc to Los Angeles for some background advice.

But there are others — like the guy who smuggled pot across the border in his tie. "His goddamn tie weighed two pounds," Ronnie laughs. And there was Sid Beckerman and his fraudulent chimney repair scheme. There were others, mostly gone now.

Ronnie can get downright melancholy when he starts reminiscing about these guys. Mention a veteran rock 'n' roller who's not the bright star he once was and the Hawk may well launch into a cold analysis of the several faults that brought on his problems. But these old thieves and master criminals — well, they're another matter. He has a real soft spot for them. Like Russian Wally, "a bad, crazy motherfucker," says the Hawk, "who was big and tough, so he protected us." Then there were minor-league hustlers like Howlin' Bony McQueen who would drink everything in sight, and who hung out at the old Warwick Hotel when it was indeed a dangerous place.

"When I used to live there with Levon, they'd have water-gun fights," Ronnie recalls. "One night, Levon filled his water-gun with lighter fluid. Bony's standing there laughing and they're spraying each other in the face. Up until now he's been screaming and going crazy and all that, having a good time. Then he smells it and realizes it's lighter fluid. He sees that Levon has a book of matches and he can imagine himself roasting real quick. He takes off screaming. Now, Levon wasn't going to hit him with the matches but Bony wasn't sure. Levon was crazy, he didn't see the danger.

"As I said, Bony drank. Drank too much, he did. He'd always come to a party hustling booze. Eventually it got to the point where Levon and I decided on a little scheme. By this time we were living at the Frontenac Arms, another hotel that's not around anymore. Levon mixed him three or four heavy drinks and that was it for Bony. He collapsed. So we took all his clothes off, every stitch he had. Then Levon went to work. Bony had black hair and Levon gave him one of those parts down the middle, then slicked it all down. He drew a moustache on him, and sideburns. They took Bony out to the elevator and stuck him on one of those big old ashtrays, buck naked, and punched the lobby button.

"So we were sitting there, waiting for the cops or the manager to come — somebody. Nothing. We never heard a thing all night. Next day Levon was a bit worried because we hadn't seen Bony all day. But that night back at the club, there he was, all dressed, ready to go. He never said one word about what happened — where he'd got to, how they'd found him, who got him out of that lobby. Nothing. We wanted to ask, but if we asked he'd have known who did it. I tell you, that smart-assed booger knew it was better for him to say nothing to drive us nuts."

But not one of Hawk's street friends got closer to him, or was more trusted, than Heavy Andrews. Heavy (his real name, Walter, had been forgotten in the mists of rumor and legend by the time the Hawk got to know him) was even more of a legend on the strip than the Hawk was — for a while. He called everybody "Baby Blue." He'd done a lot of time in jail for an impressive assortment of scams, and he was liked by everyone who knew him well, even some of the cops.

His rise to fame had come from his expertise in the "chimney scam." This later evolved into the roofing scam. Because of his illicit activities, he had managed to come up with both Canadian and American passports, which resulted in his being deported from both countries. But it was around the Pittsburgh area ("lots of suckers," he'd explain) where he refined the chimney scam to the level of impure artistry.

His method lacked violence and had the beauty of simplicity. He'd seek out an old neighborhood of faded elegance. He'd look for a house that showed signs of some disrepair and he'd approach the widow who lived in it, saying that he just happened to be in the neighborhood with his trucks and would be glad to inspect her chimney for free. Of course, this inspection would reveal that the chimney was in terrible shape and needed immediate fixing. He would assure his mark that her insurance would cover the repairs; she would usually sign the contract — and pay. And Heavy and the boys, after a quickie paint job — or no job at all — were out of there.

Ronnie knew that Heavy had done time at a lockup as distinguished as Burwash. That was for one of the oldest scams of them all, the bank inspector fraud. He'd been in the slammer for this one long before, and near the end of his days he'd be back in the slammer for it again — but not before Ronnie had had him driven up to court in his Rolls, accompanied by two gorgeous babes.

When I met Heavy back then — when Heavy had turned his active mind to music and was operating Baby Blue Productions, when not helping out the Hawk with "security problems" such as keeping the world away from John Lennon — he had seemingly given up the game. He was coasting. He had an office near the Hawk's above the Le Coq D'Or and was happily bolstering the Hawk's growing reputation.

"Now, don't tell him I told you this," he said to me one day, "but I remember the time he brought up Miss Toronto, I don't remember which Miss Toronto it was. She was going to be a go-go-er, but I told the Hawk I didn't believe what I was seeing — I mean she had the most incredible build I'd ever seen.

"'Sure she has,' he said, and he whipped down her top to show me it was all real."

If shock tactics didn't work, Ronnie would turn on the charm.

Man, he could be so nice. "He could've been the world's greatest salesman if he hadn't been in music," says a musician who knew him well throughout the sixties. "He'd be downright miserable some days, about himself or the band or whatever, but the second someone walked through the door who was interested in what he was selling — mostly himself, you understand — then, by God, he turned on like a lightbulb. It wasn't fake in any way. He genuinely loved that part of it."

As Duff Roman, a young deejay and promoter around town in the early 1960s, remembers: "You went in the Le Coq D'Or and if you had a radio connection he'd say something like 'Oh my god, it's the king of CHUM or CKEY and his harem.' It was unbelievable. There were times when you actually had to ask him to cut it out.

"Still, everybody ate it up. And you loved it; he just had that knack. You kept coming back. You really didn't expect him to pick up the tab or buy drinks — that was never really part of the deal. You just wanted to be where the fun was. You'd look around his club and you'd see people who would be appearing up and down the street. The Edison and the Friars used to bring in the Beaumarks or Ray Hutchison or The Five MCs and Rockin' Ray Smith. They would run over between sets to be part of the fun and the good time; they'd have a beer or a Coke and then go back and do their show. They had to be where Ronnie was."

Scott Cushnie, though still angry at being fired from Ronnie's band, came back to work for Ronnie at Hawk Records. He was to vet all songs submitted. He watched in amazement how "every goddamn disc jockey who ever worked in Toronto thought he knew Ronnie personally, and thought he was the best guy he'd ever had parties with." These deejays, Cushnie adds, would "do anything for him. He had a genuine thing that everybody reacted to. They remember him forever as being a great guy. Of all the people I've ever known, I have never known anybody who's had his name appear so consistently in the papers over the years and in a lot of cases had done nothing to merit it.

"All of the sudden you'd see he's got this big article in the paper. It isn't because he's really done anything. It's just that all these people love him. It's sort of an Elvis thing. He embodies all of our wild youth on Yonge Street. Yet he's still the same and will always be the same."

Right off, Ronnie understood something basic about the Canadian music industry: that it suffered from a massive inferiority complex. He had met enough club owners who preferred American acts to Canadian just because they were American to know how all the rest of the bands out there felt. He could hear how few Canadian records made the Top 40 charts. He heard all the bitching. So he became a booster. Our own made-in-Arkansas Canuck. Of course, supporting home-grown talent didn't hurt for another reason: he never knew when he would need another young musician or two for his band.

Mel Shaw, the manager of the Stampeders, remembers the Hawk cruising backstage to pep-talk the young Calgary band on their very first date in the east with a major act. "Hell," Hawkins told them, "you just go out there and have a real good time."

"When I started with the Stampeders," says Shaw, "we came to Toronto playing cheap hotels in the summer of '66 and ended up at the El Patio Club. One of the first people who came down to see the band — because we got a terrific review in the newspaper — was David Clayton Thomas. He sat there and watched the six Stampeders play in their bright yellow cowboy outfits with their black cowboy hats.

"'If you guys want to see a good band,' he said, 'see Ronnie Hawkins and then get on a plane and fly back home to Calgary.' So when the time came for the Stampeders to play their first gig with Ronnie, in Guelph on a Sunday night, the guys were very excited about finally getting in that upper echelon. They still hadn't had record success — that was years to come. When Ronnie arrived he said, 'Let's not worry about this one-act-on, one-act-off stuff. You go out and play as long as you need to, then I'll just finish up the show. We don't have to go back and forth.' Whatever Ronnie said went.

"Yet when it came to his band, he could be tough. Jay Smith, his singer, was late. There was Ronnie, so casual and fun-loving with the Stampeders, when his man came in late. 'You are half an hour late,' he said. 'You're docked twenty-five dollars. I don't want to hear a word out of you and tomorrow you're rehearsing until nine in the morning.'

"That was it. The guy didn't say a word. We were all jolted into seeing another side of Ronnie which was more professional — a side more for toeing the line."

It had to do with professional loyalties, figures Jay Smith, who sang with Ronnie for four and a half years up through 1968. "If someone who'd only been in the band for four or five months decided to leave, well, Ronnie would throw this really nice party. There'd be champagne. It'd be really pleasant. But if someone who'd been with him for a couple of years decided to leave, that would be a different thing. There'd be no party. Instead, there'd be bad feelings. It was as if he felt you were deserting him."

For by now, Hawkins had developed a typical distinction. There was his world, and there was the world out there. His world was his band, his family, his friends and all those who wanted to party like his friends. For these he'd do anything, reveal anything, admit anything. What the rest of the world found was the Ronnie Hawkins legend, carefully polished, like the hood of one of his Rolls cars.

"They'd set up camp in the Frontenac Arms," remembers Duff Roman, "they had parties that went on and on. They were on the second or third floor and they pretty much had the run of the place. You'd get a special invitation to go. Sometimes it was well after two in the morning before the band showed up. Everybody was there. Well, at these parties, Ronnie always gave fair warning. I remember one night when he said, 'Okay, those of you who are staying should get on with the party. Those of you who don't want to party, it's time to leave.'

"It really was his way of weeding out the younger ones and the people who really weren't into it. It was saying: 'It's okay, we've done our P.R. bit — we've chitchatted and we've been good people and good boys. Now it might get a little hairy.' So you'd see one of the girls clutching her purse not wanting to go and her friend saying, 'Maybe we'd better catch the last bus.' That was the Frontenac Arms in those days. He was daddy. He really was."

Playing or partying with the Hawk became a rite of passage. He was the major leagues. Hell, he was even developing his own farm system, as David Clayton Thomas, Jay Smith or Robbie Lane knew. First you heard the Hawk; later you got invited up on stage by him. Then, *maybe* you got the big call.

"For instance," says Robbie Lane. "I started as a fan of Ronnie and his band, and being a fan was the thing that brought us together. You always have to have someone that you look up to.

"I'd put my own band, a seven-piece group, together in high school and we did everything the Hawks were doing musically. We started going to see them at the Concord Tavern in 1962. We were all about fourteen, but we could go on Saturday afternoons when they had an underage section. On those Saturday afternoons you could see a lot of Toronto bands. You'd meet a lot of people who ended up in different bands in the sixties and seventies. As time went on, a friend of mine introduced himself to Hawkins and told him that there was a young band out in the audience. Would he get us up to play a few numbers? Well, it would've been too difficult to get the whole band up, but I knew most of the songs so I did two songs with the Hawks. I guess Ronnie saw something in me because from that day forward we kept in contact.

"Eventually he used our band as an opening act for different one-nighters around Ontario," Lane remembers. "It was during the summer in the mid-sixties. What was funny about being his opening act was that we opened with the exactly the same material he played when he came on. We didn't know that at first. We didn't think about it.

"The summer I turned seventeen, his group, the Hawks, decided to leave Ronnie and go to New York where they met Bob Dylan. Hawkins called me and told me what was going on.

"'So, what are you doing for the summer?' he asked finally.

"'Some one-nighters,' I replied.

"'How would you like to come and back me up?' he continued. 'You and your band — come back me up at the Le Coq D'Or. Okay, everyone knows you're all underaged. But we can get away with you playing there because it's a licensed dining room. And it would just be the weekends.'

"From that point it became Ronnie Hawkins with Robbie Lane and the Disciples. He loved watching how we reacted to things at that age — things we very definitely had never seen before. Like that night in Port Dover, Ontario. We were still just an opening act for him and he phoned me saying that he would like us to come down to the Summer Gardens in Port Dover.

"'I'll provide you with accommodation and food,' he said. 'It'll be a great weekend.'

"So, fine. We thought we were getting rooms. In fact we ended

147

up in a room with him — one room. There were seven of us sleeping all over the floor. Because I was the leader of my band, Ron said to me, 'You and I'll sleep on the bed.' So, there we were, the two of us.

"The next thing I knew," Lane remembers, "a girl came into the room very late at night. She was naked by the time I noticed she was there and she stayed most of the night doing all kinds of strange things. A lot of us pretended to be asleep because we didn't know what else to do. We were embarrassed. We didn't know how to react or what to say.

"At this point in our lives we were very naïve. But rock 'n' roll was very naïve in those days, too. Nobody trashed rooms. There wasn't a lot of drugs going on, other than alcohol. By today's standards, Ronnie would be considered very tame. But in those days we thought that was just incredibly wild and rockin'.

"Of course, we'd heard all about Hawkins the myth before we met Hawkins the man. So this only reinforced everything we'd ever heard. Yet he always kept things under control. He had, and still does have, an incredible way of being able to control a situation that might become stupid or silly or crazy . . . or even out of hand. He never really lets it get that far. He has fun with it but if things get carried away, he knows how to control it."

Robbie Lane pauses to think back to those early days, then goes on: "But there were a lot of changes in the year and a half we were with him at the Le Coq D'Or. He started his own record label, Hawk Records. We were the only other act on the label beside him. This led to problems between us. He'd paid Fred Carter to come up from Nashville to write material for us. Fred did and we went into the studio — the studio Ronnie paid for — and recorded eleven songs. Two of them were released as singles and did reasonably well in Ontario and some parts of Canada.

"The rest of the material was just sitting there. At this time Ronnie was still under contract in the U.S. to Roulette Records and for various reasons he couldn't release anything in the U.S. for another two or three years. So he came up with a plan to make as much money as he could with our material. He suggested that he record "Blue Birds Over the Mountain" and release it in Canada. Then I would take the same basic track — remember, we both used my band — and record my voice on it. That's the version which would be released in the States. So he offered me a record deal, but the royalty he offered was the lowest imaginable. There were reasons he had to do it that way, although at the time we didn't know them: his operating costs were really high, record sales were nowhere and he was losing money. At the time, though, we were thoroughly disgusted and insulted. And we told him so.

"But after we'd turned down his offer," recalls Lane, "he took our band track and recorded someone else's voice on it, a singer named Buddy Carleton. Buddy had the Stratatones at the time, a Toronto-area band which was fairly well known. They were good people and Ron liked them very much. I guess Ron was already thinking that if we left he'd have somebody else there with a voice for those tracks. I found out all about this at a Christmas party when Buddy got drunk and played me the tape.

"I confronted Hawkins with what I knew. At first he denied it but eventually he admitted it. That's when we gave our notice. We gave him lots of time to find another band and when he asked for an extension we gave it to him. When we finally did leave, I thought it was on fairly good terms. I mean, there's been nobody in my life who's had the effect on me in the music business that he had. He was my mentor. We learned in that year and a half with him what it would have taken five or ten years to learn on our own.

"But then we ran into a problem. You see, we landed a television show about six months after leaving him: a network show too, on CTV. And that was something Ron always wanted to have. The show had already been on the air the first time I went to see him with my drummer Kirk Shearer. Ron and I had agreed to see each other after six or eight months. So as we went up to Ron's office on the third floor of the Le Coq D'Or, over on Yonge Street, I thought he'd be proud of us. In fact, he was absolutely furious. Ron called us every name possible and chased us out of the office with a broom.

"I was absolutely petrified. Ron is a big guy and when a big guy is running after you screaming obscenity with a broom over his head, whipping it around, you move pretty quickly. And we did. We didn't see much of each other for a couple of years but I think we've grown a little bit closer together since then. We laugh about those things now."

149

"Sure I was furious with them being so cocky about getting the TV show," Ronnie remembers. "But Robbie forgets that I had been wining and dining the Bassetts to maneuvre Robbie Lane and the Disciples into a position to get that show. Plus I had a contract. But, as Fred Foster says, artists want to get big enough to fire their management — to be able to say they made it on their own."

"I only saw his temper a couple of times," Robbie continues, "and it was usually when someone was infringing on his territory, like this guy, Joe Somebody, who used to hang around the Le Coq D'Or. Joe kind of fancied himself as a gangster type. He would come in and tell the waiter to fill up the table with shots of rye. They had small tables at the Le Coq D'Or, round cocktail tables. So the waiter and the bartender came over and completely covered the top of the table with bar-shots of rye. Then Joe would demand the entire band sit down and drink these. He got very pushy and mean. He used to say he'd killed people, and although he probably hadn't you believed him. He got off on scaring the hell out of everybody.

"But one time he pushed us a little too far and Ron stepped in. I'd never seen anyone move so fast in my life as Ron did that night. All he was doing was kicking Joe out, but boy it scared the hell out of me, the power of that man when he was mad. You got out of his way. Although we'd heard about a lot of the brawls Ron had been in before we were with him, we never saw any of them. We didn't see any blood that night, we just saw his temper — and how powerful he really was. He used to tell us about the Brass Rail in London where it was all brass knuckles and combat boots. But we played there a month with him and there was no problem at all.

"Ron was a remarkable musician," Lane says fondly. "He could hear things that no one else could, even schooled musicians. Ron would say, 'I don't know what it is, boy, but this country ear of mine tells me something's wrong.' And he was right every time.

"The best way to describe what he does is this: he can take any kind of song and reduce it to its gut level. That's what he's trying to appeal to, the gut level. He wants every Joe on the street to understand what kind of music he's doing. Every band before us and every band after us he schooled in exactly the way he schooled us. That's why he told us to stay at the Le Coq D'Or and to keep going over and over the songs on his albums. For a year and a half — and for four nights out of seven every week for those eighteen months — we rehearsed and rehearsed the same old stuff over and over again.

"But it worked. If it weren't for that we couldn't have done the TV show every week where we had to learn ten or fifteen new songs. Without Ronnie's training it would've been impossible to learn that much in that time. That's exactly the high level he got us to.

"The Hawk's way is the right way to teach bands. He always said, 'Don't play for yourself.' The first time I saw The Band after they left him was when they were playing just down the way at the Friars. We were playing with Ron at the Le Coq D'Or but they were still our idols so we went running down the street on our break to see them. They were still brilliant musicians but something had happened to them: they were starting to play for themselves. Even though the place was packed they were turning around on stage and looking at each other — and this was before they'd had any major record success so they couldn't get away with it. They were completely ignoring the audience.

"Of course, within a year and a half they had one of the biggest albums in the world," Lane remembers. "And Ron wasn't happy about that at all. The same feeling that made him chase us down the stairs with a broom because we'd gotten a television show came out when The Band made it big. He was jealous — and bitter. But I don't think that's unusual or a flaw in his character. That's a natural reaction, until time passes and you can look back on it without bitterness."

Ronnie was realizing that he always had to be on the lookout for new musicians.

"When The Band left me I had Robbie Lane and the Disciples and in the bars they actually out-drew The Band. I had them doing the Beatles and the Rolling Stones, even if they didn't like the Beatles and the Rolling Stones. I didn't like the Beatles or the Stones either — at first. I'd heard all that shit done better, I thought. Bubblegum music, that's what I called it. But it was selling records. Record companies may like me the best in the world and they may hate Michael Jackson but they're going to pay Michael Jackson because he sells records. It all comes down to money. But that's how things were back then. There were certain places, like the old Club Blue Note in Toronto, which had a rhythm 'n' blues crowd and liked heavier music. Maybe you could play r 'n' b for a week in a regular bar, but forget it if you wanted to stay some place for three months. Then you had to play that commercial shit.

"In my opinion, the best band I ever had was the band which came *after* The Band, and after Robbie Lane. I had Jay Smith singing. He was great — and I'm talking about real quality singing. Levon and I both knew we weren't exactly Mario Lanzas. That was all right, though. Everybody's got a style and having a style is important. But Jay Smith was something else. He had an eery voice; he could hit *all* the notes; he had soul. He was one of the top talents. In the end it didn't work out with him because he didn't know what he was doing and didn't believe anybody. But he was great.

"And we had John Till. He ended up playing lead guitar for Janis Joplin's Full Tilt Boogie Band. He had just hit his peak. There was Rick Bell, the son of the famous conductor, Dr. Leslie Bell, on one piano. And we had this kid named Gordie Flemming, whose father was a big-band arranger, on the other keyboards. He had learned everything from his dad so he knew all the old standards. The way he pumped those bass pedals on the organ, he was like Garth Hudson. He knew what to put in and when to leave something out. Most of the young organ players just play all the time. They play it like a piano. But an organ isn't a piano. And it takes most keyboard players a long time to realize that. Hell, it takes a long time to learn to play tambourine and maracas. They were all good players. They all went on to do something."

"I keep hearing about all these people who've gone on out from under the Hawk's wing," says Robbie Lane, "people who've gone on to make a name for themselves and become huge stars. The truth is, no one has been better at creating a name for himself than Hawkins himself has. A lot of people have come and gone, but his legend still keeps growing. And it doesn't matter where you go or what age group you're talking to. They all know him."

"The thing about Ronnie," says Jay Smith, "is that he'd always be going around listening to the bands around the city. You might not know he was there, but he would be. And when he heard Robbie Lane was going to leave him, he was out listening.

"I started listening to Ronnie like every kid did. We'd go to the
Concord for fries with gravy and Cokes. All the singers and all the
guitar players would be there watching. For us, no other bar group
came close. His band was *the* band. Well, he got to know the
musicians sitting in the audience. He knew I sang. He knew Dom
Troiano played guitar. And eventually we'd get up on stage to sing.

"I had started some bands, but the first money-making band was
J. Smith and the Majestics. I was eighteen. When Robbie Lane
finally left, Ronnie took a couple of musicians from my band.
Ronnie called to ask me, too, but I said no. I was making good
money — I was a foreman at a fiberglass factory. I made the first
Johnny on the Spot portable johns in the country. But one day I
poisoned myself; not wanting to go through that again I phoned
him up and asked him if the job was still open and what the pay
was. 'Son, it's fifty dollars a week and all the booze, pills and girls
you want,' he told me.

"His offer was okay. Maybe I could make fifty dollars a weekend
with the Majestics, but this was Ronnie Hawkins. The fifty dollars
a week was for a sort of training period. Afterwards we made about
$150 a week. In the four and a half years I was with him, the most
I earned was $200. At the same time I joined the band he hired
another singer, Bobby Ray. He wanted him to do the uptown songs,
like Frank Sinatra or Bobby Darin. The problem for Bobby Ray
was, the downtown life got to him, so he lasted only six months.
Ronnie got him a job with Joe King and the Zaniacs.

"Next, Ronnie hired Bob McBride, who ended up singing with
Lighthouse," Jay Smith continues. "Back then if you closed your
eyes McBride sounded like Johnny Mathis. He only lasted four
months. Then Bill Bullicon, who owned the Le Coq D'Or, wanted
David Clayton Thomas because he was hot, but *he* was with us for
only a couple of weeks. Next came Jackie Gabriel, who was with
us for two years. I think people left because they got bored. Even
Ronnie used to say, 'Boys, Ah'm tired of singin' "Forty Days" night
after night.'

"Besides, the nightlife was rough. There was lots of speed, LSD
and marijuana around then. I could never understand why people
got screwed up doing marijuana but they did. And they wouldn't
stop there. It was really easy to get the stuff. And Ronnie had his
parties — it was fun. And there were a lot of celebrities who came

into the club. Frankie Avalon came in one night and got up and played the trumpet with us. Henry Mancini and Andy Williams showed up. I met all the boxers. I met Joe Lewis, Ernie Terrell, George Chuvalo. Jim Brown, the football player, came into the club the night Muhammad Ali — he was still Cassius Clay then — fought Chuvalo at Maple Leaf Gardens.

"By now I was doing Ray Charles stuff, Bobby Bland stuff. Then Ronnie decided he'd take the band on a little tour through Arkansas, Oklahoma and Tennessee. I had decided I wasn't going to go because it was not long after all the race problems down there. I'd already run into some prejudice in Toronto. We were the only black family when I was a kid living in Mimico. I was the only black kid in public school and high school. Still, the prejudice wasn't as blatant as I knew it was going to be down South. But Ronnie told me, 'Son, you don't have to worry.' And so we took the Rolls Royce and I played the chauffeur. For a while, doing that bothered me — but only for a while. There were other things to think about.

"Like the time we were playing in Eldorado, Arkansas, at a concert hall sort of like Toronto's O'Keefe Centre but a bit smaller. They had scheduled four bands, a guest speaker, then Ronnie Hawkins and the Hawks. We went into the dressing room as the guest speaker was just finishing, so I decided to get a look at him. As I watched through the curtains I couldn't believe it. He was up there yelling away about keeping Jews and niggers out and asking everyone to join the Ku Klux Klan.

"'Holy shit,' I said. 'Ronnie, you know who that guest speaker is? He's talking about killing niggers and Jews.'

"'Well, son,' was Ronnie's response, 'you don't have to worry about a thing. Everything will be all right.'

"By this time the band was nervous, but they talked me into going out there. Just before the curtain went up, Ronnie came up: 'Son, you're singing the first tune!'

"'What? I don't want to be out there.'

"'Do "Georgia on My Mind,"' he said.

"They started up the intro. I was petrified. I just froze. I stood there holding the mike in my hand. So Dave Lewis did *tap tap tap* on the snare drum and I came out of the trance I was in — and they loved it.

"After that we carried on with the shows. Then came Bald Knob Arkansas. The other guys in the band got there before Ronnie and I did. It wasn't until the job was over that I found out what had gone down. John Till, the guitar player, told me that the owner had come up and asked, 'You boys with Ronnie Hawkins? I hear you boys got a nigger with you.'

"'Yeah, we got a nigger,' they told him.

"'So what's he going to be doin'?' asked the owner.

"'Well,' they said, 'he's not really in the band. He drives the Rolls, helps with our equipment — and sometimes we let him get up to sing.'

"When we got back to Toronto, I kissed the ground. All my relations had told me I was nuts. Ronnie protected me, though. He would make some racial jokes in the Le Coq D'Or, if he had friends at a table. They'd all laugh and I was supposed to find it funny, too. I didn't. But when we were down South he'd protect me. Sometimes I drove him around in Toronto, but it wasn't the case of me being his chauffeur. I was just the one he could count on. He couldn't count on anybody else.

"After he got back, Ronnie hired Jackie Gabriel back into the band — she'd sung with it a little earlier — but the band didn't want her. They felt she hated the guys. She got pissed off if they made any mistakes and of course that made them make even more mistakes.

"'Boys,' Ronnie told us one day, 'I'm having a meeting. I've decided to hire Jackie back into the band. I want you boys to think about it.' We didn't want that. 'Well, boys,' he responded, 'I may not always be right but I *am* the boss.'

"I lasted two more weeks. It just wasn't working out so one night I came up to him and said I wanted to leave the band. As it turned out, I stayed away for a year, then came back for about six months before I left again. I didn't leave on good terms, although they've improved over the years.

"I think because Ronnie had been with Levon and the others for such a long time, he was trying to recapture that situation. The reason I stayed with him was because I couldn't see anywhere else where I would be exposed to better musicians. There was an electricity that was going on in downtown Toronto then. We'd start at eight-thirty at night and finish at one o'clock in the

155

morning and the place would be jammed all night. Ronnie had the Hawk's Nest going upstairs, where he had a teenage dance with rhythm 'n' blues. People were coming from all over suburbia. When he had a party there were stock brokers and cops and musicians and everybody. The band could go if they wanted to. I'd leave, then come back with the Rolls to pick up his friends. I'd go upstairs to the gym and see bodies lying all over the place. What got me, these same people would come back the next night looking for more. Old Toronto families were there.

"I think after our band broke up, when John Till and Rick Bell went to play with Janis Joplin, Ronnie was looking around again. It's ironic. He'd go around and pull other musicians away from other bands. But when it happened to him, he hated it. He became a terror."

Ronnie's parties were the stuff of legend, although he was discovering that these new "young" bands he had weren't up to partying the way Levon and the Hawks had been.

"All right, folks," he'd cackle up on stage, "it's midnight. Just an hour to orgy time. You never know what you'll be doing later on so girls, take your pills, and boys, remember, you can't knock 'em up with spit."

But Robbie Lane didn't hang out much. "Jay Smith tried, but he wasn't the type either," says Scott Cushnie. "Me? I was never able to keep up with Ronnie in any way. For these parties could become orgies. They'd get these chicks from the bar, take them upstairs and start partying in the offices. Not even the guys in Robbie Lane's band who were around would be into it. Just Ronnie and Heavy and a few of Ronnie's cronies. After a while, I just didn't know how to deal with it so I'd sort of hide.

"I remember one woman phoning up the offices and saying, 'I want to find out what happened last night. I went to a party last night totally innocent; today I woke up and I want to learn what happened.' She was very upset. I was the only one there in the office so I met her in a restaurant and sat with her the whole afternoon trying to calm her down. Eventually she gave up the whole thing and went home.

"Ronnie was able to get around these chicks when they found out what happened and came after him. He could talk his way out of anything. Sure there were incidents where the women were willing. And there were incidents where Ronnie or his buddies would get some chick up at the party and have a wild time with her. Then her mother would come and complain and Ronnie would end up with her mother."

The Band's soaring success, with a *Time* magazine cover story, and the expiration of his ten-year deal with Roulette Records, led to an unexpected and unprecedented break for Ronnie: in 1968 he signed a two-record deal with Atlantic Records, for its new Cotillion label. Atlantic! thought Ronnie. It was the label he wanted most. The home of rhythm 'n' blues.

"He was very excited at this stage," Cushnie remembers. "It was his biggest deal. Atlantic Records — Ray Charles and all that. He figured this was it. His biggest chance: 'I'm going to make it back into the big time for once and always.'"

The modest little airport at Muscle Shoals serves four tiny Alabama cities: Florence, Tuscumbia, Sheffield and Muscle Shoals itself. Muscle Shoals has had its share of great singles and albums recorded. The great r 'n' b producer, Jerry Wexler, salvaged Wilson Pickett's career by recording "Land of a Thousand Dances" in Shoals's studio which has some extra psychic advantage in being situated directly opposite a Civil War cemetery. Wexler brought Aretha Franklin there to rescue her career. And back in the summer of 1968, he brought in Ronnie Hawkins. At the time, only a few flights a day passed through the small and efficient airport. When there weren't any flights, the airport, which had little more than a fifteen-foot ticket counter inside, was shut. To this day Tom Dowd considers this fortunate.

The airport in this part of the Bible belt was officially closed when the Hawk squeezed out through the door of his specially chartered Cessna, to be followed by one of the most striking women the men around those parts had ever seen.

Wexler greeted Ronnie enthusiastically. A couple of still pho-tographers tried to get in some shots.

"How ya doin,'" grinned the Hawk. "I brought the pot and the pussy."

Tom Dowd was horrified. "If the airport had been open, we'd all have gone to Muscle Shoals jail."

In the weeks that followed, Dowd, who served as the floor

producer of the first album (and the main producer of the second one recorded more than a year later), would find himself awestruck by the Hawkins approach. With Wexler up in the control booth, Dowd worked the floor with the musicians: "I was carried away with some of the insanity. Dale Hawkins was there. That made things crazier. Unlike Ronnie, who was a roughshod cowboy Marshall Tucker kind of guy, Dale was walking around like a dude: hiney shoes — with a vest.

"And the two of them were telling story after story after story, mostly about someone they both knew called Crazy Don Nix. It seems Dale and Crazy Don were coming out of some gig in South Texas one night and they had to stop at a truck stop. Crazy Don had shoulder-length hair so he figured they'd get killed in this place, with all those old truck drivers sitting there. So what did Don do but crawl in through the door on his hands and knees, stick his finger in his mouth, and crawl over to a gun rack, saying, 'Dale, wanna buy me one of these?' The place emptied in seconds. They figured they had a real sicko on their hands."

Between stories, Wexler and Dowd worked the Hawk hard. "We just sang him out," recalls Dowd. "We were taskmasters, so we just wasted him. We had to take a break from the session and take him to Florida. Wexler was living in Muscle Shoals. He took Ronnie to a studio in Florida while I was doing other things."

To further work out the kinks, Wexler and the Hawk took in a little deep-sea fishing aboard Atlantic's forty-seven-foot yacht, *The Big A*, run by Captain Randy Lacey whom Dowd describes as a very "vertical" — that is, straight — Floridian. After an hour or two with only a few small fish they didn't bother keeping, they managed to land a pair of sharks.

"Well," thought Ronnie, "here at last is a trophy."

As Captain Lacey began washing down the sharks, he asked: "How do you want them mounted?"

"Son, I don't want them mounted," said Ronnie. "I want them shaking hands."

If Wexler thought it might end there, he had another thing coming. Some time later, after they had returned to Wexler's luxury condo, Ronnie was passing the time having a beer in the sunroom. Wexler's wife came up with a deli tray of cold cuts.

"May I offer you a little tongue?" she asked sweetly. Ronnie looked around. "Do you think we should be doing that with Jerry here?"

Meanwhile, Dowd was back listening to the tapes. "I thought we had captured the era all over again," he says. "I didn't know if we were timely in doing it, though. There are lots of times you can make a great album, but when you release it you find the public has headed in another direction. Capturing Ronnie's spontaneity — that's the thing. The spontaneity and the spirit of the thing. When Ronnie does a show there's a vibe going on and one thing leads to another. For the second album, Ronnie was more sensitive to having to deliver on the spot in the studio."

"We were there for the first album for two weeks," remembers Cushnie, who came down to play some piano on the tracks. "Ronnie lost his voice after a while so I had to do ghost tracks for all the vocals: sing a track in the key that he would sing it in so we could make the record later. The piano player on the session had a heart murmur and had to drop out so I had to take over on the piano even though I wasn't slated to.

"At that time, in 1968, I was only person in Alabama with any grass. Wexler wouldn't go for anything else — and there was no smoking dope in the studios. Nobody in that rhythm session had any dope or any booze that I saw. So Duane Allman, who also played on the album, hung out with me. At night when we finished recording we would go for a walk or out to eat. He was in good shape, a real gentleman, really modest. A terrific player.

"Ronnie and I have always had a failure to communicate, and it happened again at this point. Ronnie said, 'I'm going to go down to Miami and get my voice back and rest up in the sun, and I'll see you back in Canada.' Well, he didn't come back for about a month. So we had to wait. As soon as we finished the session, we got in the car and drove all the way back up to Toronto.

"We'd expected to make good money and we were finished but we hadn't been paid a cent," Cushnie remembers ruefully. "We had no idea what we were supposed to make. We hadn't spoken to anybody about it. We figured with all these wonderful people involved, they'd have us covered. So we got back up to Canada and Ronnie didn't show. It may have been a month, but I think it was three months before I saw Ronnie again. When I first played with Ronnie I was eighteen and anything went. I idolized the guy and his band and just wanted to be with him. I didn't worry about money. But by this time, I was much older, thirty, and money was very important to pay the rent.

"In order to survive till Ronnie got back to Canada, I had to start my own band and get some gigs. When he came back to Toronto I was actually rehearsing my own little band in Ronnie's studios above the Le Coq D'Or. He listened to the band and remarked, 'That's a good little band but I'm back now and I want you to play with me.'

"I told him no, we already had jobs. Well, we didn't get very many and we didn't make a lot of money. We struggled, getting by for a few months and then I had to find another band. So I missed out on being with Ronnie Hawkins's next band: Crowbar.

"To get the money from the recording session, I had to phone Jerry Wexler at his office in New York. I said, 'I'm gonna get thrown out of my room here because I can't pay the rent. I never got paid for that recording session.' Jerry was amazed. 'What? you never got paid? I thought Ronnie paid you guys.' He said that I was owed $299, for two weeks, I think — and he sent it up. So again I was pissed off at Ronnie.

"But not for all that long. So many people have played with Ronnie that whenever I run into one of them we end up laughing and going into the corner somewhere and just telling stories. He always had something to say when you came to him, like, 'Its just bologna money for now, but stay with me and we'll be farting through silk in no time.' He has so many contradictions. One minute, it's 'We're gonna go all the way together!' Next thing you know, it's as if you don't exist. It's a shock. I don't think he realizes he does things this way. But he does have this way of hooking you in."

Ronnie began the sixties hustling and rocking just to live. He ended the era looming larger than life. He was the king of mainstreet Canada, not just Yonge Street in Toronto. He was *the* Act. He had *the* band. *His* club was where you had to be. The Legend had taken off. Now all that was needed was for the rest of the world to catch up.

That was to happen, soon enough.

X

THE JOHN & YOKO
PEACE FESTIVAL BLUES

> *Where a Famous Beatle Almost Saves the World in the*
> *Legend's Living Room and Redecorates Wanda's Ceiling*
> *in the Process*

WHEN YOU LEFT "MORTGAGE MANOR" in Mississauga on any of the cold December nights in 1969, you went along the driveway past a guard or two at Ronnie's gate before you were out on Streetsville Road, which then wound south past St. Peter's Anglican Church in Erindale, then along the Credit River before it met up with the highway back into Toronto. And I remember feeling mildly depressed the several times I passed through those gates; as if I were leaving something as charmed and special as a kids' party which would be all over before I could ever come back. I'd turn around each time and watch. And most times, way back past the big white house, snowmobile headlights burned holes in the night. John Lennon was having a ball. Giving peace a chance.

In the grand scheme of things, John Lennon's stay with the Hawkinses probably left little lasting impact on either party — except for the $16,000 phone bill the Lennons stuck the Hawkinses with. As any two families in a single house might, the two couples staked out their own turf: the Lennons in the living room surrounded by phones, flunkies and famous visitors; the

Hawkinses in the kitchen where Wanda whipped up food for the family alongside the Lennons' imported macrobiotic chefs who cooked for their bosses. For the most part the Hawkinses left the Lennons alone while the Lennons attended to saving the world. Before long, though, Ronnie started thinking about being alone with the family again, Beatle or no Beatle.

"Jesus," he thought to himself just before Lennons caught a special train for Montreal, "as soon as they're gone I'm gonna lock my gates, clear out the trash, and start living normally again. Goddamn."

Odd couples they were. Lennon wasn't prepared for "the legend in his own mind." The Legend wasn't prepared for Lennon, either. Or his wife. All he knew about John was what he'd gleaned from the press which, with the magical Beatle years fresh in memory, had come near to sanctifying John.

Ronnie wasn't ready for the pragmatic, business-savvy guy he met. Damn, but John would get on the phone and worry about his goddamn records. Ronnie liked that. At times he even felt a kind of Arkansas blood kinship for Lennon — that is, whenever he could get close to him. But that wasn't possible for a reason Ronnie found absolutely amazing — John Lennon was henpecked. He couldn't leave the room without Yoko. He couldn't get a bite to eat without Yoko. Damn, they even went to the bathroom together. No sir, Ronnie certainly wasn't ready for Yoko.

What did John see in her, Ronnie started wondering to himself, when Lennon could have anybody — bodaceous teen queens, lusty movie stars, *anybody* — swarming around him like flies around honey? Maybe it was something private. Whenever the press asked, Ronnie was "understanding" when it came to Yoko. She had "some highly creative ideas," he ventured. Hmm, yes. Highly creative. She was real intelligent, too. Real intelligent. But before the happy couple had jetted back to London, the Legend was calling them "John and Loco."

For a city which can brag of few moments of true show-business importance, Toronto can make at least one claim. It saw the beginning of the end of the Beatles. Not that it wouldn't have happened without Toronto. But Hogtown just happened to be the right place at the wrong time; or, more to the point, it was about as close to the American border, and the even more important

American media, as John Ono Lennon could get in those days.

In the flurry of rumors, stories and books that followed Yoko's arrival in John's life, two basic facts consistently emerged: the other Beatles, although they kept surprisingly silent about it, didn't like her; then again, she energized John as much as she had stalled the band. Not that hard-core Beatles fans wanted to know that. They thought she was wrecking things.

John, working on an enormous variety of projects with Yoko, was increasingly desperate to get out of the band. He changed his name from John Winston Lennon to John Ono Lennon; he and Yoko formed Bag Productions — an offshoot of "baggism" and their "bag events" in which they appeared in public covered in large canvas bags; they recorded abstract "sound-scapes"; they shot experimental 16-mm film; they took drugs.

As Paul, reluctantly with the help of agent Allen Klein, was pruning back Apple Corp., the band's wonky effort at communal capitalism, because it had become a financial drain on the Beatles' empire, John and Yoko formed Zapple Records to release their collaborative musical autobiography, *Unfinished Music No.2 — Life with the Lions.* Their life had become their work — and public property. The release of "The Ballad of John and Yoko" furthered the story of their misadventures and caused some new ones on its own, being banned on various radio stations, particularly in the American South, for its refrain blaspheming Christ. And it *was* getting harder all the time. But it was their spur-of-the-moment decision to sail with Ringo and George and their wives Maureen and Pattie that set off the series of events bringing them to Wanda Hawkins's kitchen.

Ringo was coming to America to shoot scenes for *The Magic Christian*, the movie that was going to cash him in as a movie star, and John and Yoko were coming for peace, planning to stage a bed-in in New York. But the United States was having none of the newly radical John Lennon and blocked his application for a temporary visa because of his 1969 drug conviction. Angry but now even more determined to start their peace campaign, John and Yoko went immediately to Heathrow Airport and flew directly to Bahamas, where John, as a British citizen, would be allowed in. What they soon realized was that the American press wouldn't jet to the Bahamas to listen to the World's Most Famous Couple in bed, so after only two days they headed someplace where the press *would* come — Toronto.

At first the Beatles hadn't impressed the Hawk at all, no matter how many of their tunes Robbie Lane might do. More than that, Ronnie was beginning to get a sense that all was not harmonious with peace and love. He'd seen too many of the drug casualties, the freaked-out and the frauds. So while the world around him was pleasantly bemused by the hours the couple spent in bed in their suite at the King Edward Hotel in Toronto, Ronnie saw something odd about it. This was how you started world peace? From the Lennons' point of view it was meant to be a media blitz and the media certainly blitzed, along with more and more celebrities. Everyone waited in line down the somber old hallway of the King Eddy to be shepherded in by the Beatles' press secretary, Derek Taylor, for an audience with the King and Queen of Bag.

Now, no musician — famous, infamous or somewhere in between — ever passes through *his* town without the Hawk giving some thought to having him down to the club for a set. But Lennon left Toronto before his invitation could be extended.

In Montreal, John and Yoko spent ten days in bed at the Queen Elizabeth Hotel, a widely covered media event that peaked with a singalong with Timothy Leary and Tommy Smothers, before they headed back to England. By now, though, a kind of momentum had been established with the Lennons leading the way. With a Beatle, a *real* Beatle near enough to reach, everything seemed possible. Anything could happen. Even Woodstock didn't have the Beatles, and the festival was seen as rock's finest moment. So how much bigger could the plans and expectations be if for the next mega-event, a Beatle was actually involved?

And no one planned bigger than John Brower, a Toronto rock promoter with a hustler's easy smile and absolutely no fear of the famous. Knowing the Lennons were now accessible in a way the Beatles had never been, Brower phoned John to invite him to attend the promoter's Rock and Roll Revival show in Toronto's Varsity Stadium, on the University of Toronto campus. Brower, who'd flown over Woodstock in a private plane and dreamed of topping it, only wanted John and Yoko to be part of the crowd. Lennon, smarting from Paul McCartney's rejection of his song

"Cold Turkey" as part of the Beatles' new *Abbey Road* album, immediately upped the ante. Sure they'd come, if they could get up on stage. Brower couldn't believe his ears. For a few first-class plane tickets he was about to land the biggest name in rock 'n' roll. Lennon couldn't believe what he'd just said, either. He had no songs planned, no band, no rehearsals — and no time. A few quick phone calls lined up what in other circumstances could be a dream band, led by Eric Clapton and old Beatles cohort Klaus Voormann. Subsequent reports about what happened late that summer's day tend to appear as what *might* have happened or what *should* have happened. The Lennons' appearance on stage did not cause "a near-riot in the stadium," as several books have remarked. For one thing the unrehearsed performance of "Cold Turkey" and a number of oldies like "Blue Suede Shoes" was not the great blast of Beatles magic everyone was waiting for. For yet another, there was Yoko, stepping out from a canvas bag, to wail her very own howling microtonal ululation. Give peace a chance, indeed! As hip as everyone there tried to be, Yoko was too much. "Get the fuck off of the stage," people started to scream. John tried to comfort her immediately.

But John was excited. He'd done it! He'd done it! He proven to everyone — and most of all to himself — that he could do whatever he wanted to do on his own. And again there was John Brower with just the idea John wanted. A peace festival.

In the months to come, Ronnie, getting close to Lennon, would detect all the anger building up in the now ex-Beatle: the anger and frustration, skewed by drugs, which would not long after lead to a near-total collapse and a hermetic existence inside the Dakota apartment building in New York. But outsiders saw the opposite. They saw his returning his MBE medal to the Queen as a further sign of his deepening commitment to peace. And this vision was strengthened when Lennon announced from London that they'd be coming back to Toronto to "pursue" peace. That is, to hold a peace festival. To Brower and Ritchie Yorke, the *Globe and Mail* rock critic, the pursuit was going to lead to a mammoth rock festival, bigger than Woodstock, which would be free, or nearly free, and climax with the appearances of the Beatles and Elvis — maybe more! The site would be Mosport, the racetrack east of the city with grounds large enough to hold a crowd of as many as one

million fans. Or two million. Or a zillion. With John Lennon, lots
of hype and lots of money, the promoters saw no end to the
possibilities.

And they weren't alone. Yorke, who'd written a long profile of
Ronnie for *Rolling Stone*, maneuvered Jann Wenner, the
magazine's publisher, to get behind the effort. Everything was
falling into place. Soon after Brower returned to Canada from
spending five days with the Lennons at their home near
Weybridge, Surrey, the first rumblings of peace were heard.

"War is over!" proclaimed the handbills and posters that turned
up in newspaper ads and on posters around Toronto that December. Then in smaller type we read: "If you want it. Happy Christmas from John and Yoko." What they wanted, Lennon and Ono
said, was "complete public understanding. And Canada, we
found, is a good place to announce it from. Its proximity to the
United States is helpful. And its general attitude is conducive to
what we want to do."

Meanwhile, Brower and Yorke were looking about for a place
close enough to the city, but safe enough for Lennon to plan his
peace festival, and they thought of Yorke's pal, Ronnie Hawkins.
Yorke knew that was the Streetsville mansion was big enough for
John and Yoko. He also knew that Ronnie would dig playing host.
Ronnie always did feel better when the Rich and the famous were
on his turf, particularly the rich and famous from rock 'n' roll. He
was one of the granddaddies of rock 'n' roll, wasn't he? Besides,
as Anthony Fawcett, Lennon's factotum, said, it'd be great publicity, and sure enough the Hawk was not one to turn great publicity
down when it walked through his door.

To make sure the security was really secure, Hawk had his old pal,
Heavy Andrews, man the gates. Heavy may have looked like a
grizzled old rubbie to the hot-shot reporters who eventually came
snooping around but he had a punch like a mule's kick and he had
occasion to use it.

Certainly, Lennon's retreat would have been discovered soon
enough: Streetsville was then a small town of retired farmers and
genteel first-generation suburbanites who were happy to be away
from Toronto's growing clatter. In this milieu, the great rolling ball
of hoopla that followed wherever John Lennon went would have

stuck out like a holy-rolling Baptist in a decorous Anglican service. But ironically it was John Brower, the man most obsessed with guarding Lennon's privacy, who turned it into a media circus. All three dailies had assigned reporters to cover John and Yoko's arrival at Toronto International Airport, only to find that the couple were not going to go through customs inside, but were being processed on the runway and driven away from there. Marci McDonald, the Toronto *Star* reporter, noticed that beside the pair of black limos waiting for the couple was a big, fat, white Rolls Royce. Only one man around town had a Rolls like that. "That's Ronnie Hawkins," she said to Frank Lennon, the *Star's* photographer. The two raced to his nearby Dodge and followed the limos and the big fat Rolls west along the highway. Soon after they drove down Streetsville Road the two limos turned into a little plaza, letting the Rolls rush ahead. The *Star's* team followed the limos only to find themselves confronted by an absolutely enraged Brower screaming at them. Brower then ducked into the limo hoping he'd scared the reporters away. At least he hoped he'd given the Hawkins car time to get their guests safely down the road.

But no. Frank and Marci, figuring they might get a scoop, followed the fleeing limos, although by the time they arrived at the Hawkins place only one limo was near the road. No sooner had they closed the doors on their car when Frank Lennon found himself confronted by an even angrier Brower telling him to "fuck off," then giving him a push.

"Push me again," said Frank, himself enraged, "and I'm going to jam this camera down your throat."

But the next thing he knew, the photographer was reeling from a good sock in the jaw he'd been given from behind.

"Who did that?" he yelled, turning around to come face to face with Heavy Andrews. Frank had boxed enough as a kid to realize that Heavy, at one time a heavyweight fighter, had held back his punch. Heavy was being cool, but Frank now broke out into a sweat realizing how easily the old man could have taken his head off.

"Should we get a shot of this?" he asked Marci.

Before anyone could think, though, Brower ran up and hit him from behind, and then started to kick him. Marci began to yell and

Brower was quickly pulled off the photographer.

Unbelievable! Photographer and reporter glanced at each other. Here's John Lennon coming to Toronto for a peace festival and a media blitz and it begins with a brawl. It would not be the last, although Lennon was furious when he finally heard what happened.

"God, what an amazing thing to do," Ronnie told me later. "You know, John Brower put Heavy in charge of security at the front because he was a gangster, right? But then Heavy slugged the guy, he whipped the goddamn newspaper man. Knocked him plumb on his ass, trying to climb over the fence. What a thing to do right off, like that. Eventually Heavy even got sued and had to go to court. God! And that story, not John Lennon, was coming out in the papers. Now you *know* what the press can do with something like that. It was 'Security Guard Knocks Journalist Out' or something like that."

More and more, Ronnie was beginning to see the dangers in all these grandiose schemes. Still, he kept them to himself. Stop worrying. Goddamn, he had the pre-eminent Beatle in his house and that had to count for something, didn't it? And did Lennon ever have pull. "Now, you know how hard it is at *any* time to have even one ol' phone installed," Ronnie warned Wanda. But with John Lennon ready to make long, *long* world-wide calls, the phone company pulled up on a Sunday to install *racks* of phones.

At first Wanda thought Yoko was "very sincere." She liked her openness, but Wanda said later, after hearing some of her bizarre anecdotes, "I don't know how to handle things like that. I didn't know what to ask or not, you know. And John and Yoko weren't the first people we entertained. But Ron was always good at it. He always felt good when people were around, putting everyone at ease and making everybody feel that they were just like regular people, which is exactly what he did with John and Yoko. He also did that for me because I didn't know you're supposed to act in front of people like them. So whatever he did, I just followed suit, and everybody just relaxed and everything was fine."

Well, to a degree. Wanda was all ready to whip up great dinners of pinto beans, steaks, potatoes, great heapings of Arkansas vittles but Yoko reacted as if she were trying to poison them. Steaks? Meat? Not on your bean curd, my dear. In a flash, a phone call was made to New York and within hours two women chefs, Yoko's own Zen macrobiotic cooking specialists, were jetting to Streetsville.

At first Ronnie couldn't figure out why *two* Zen macrobiotic chefs were needed, since what the two women were concocting was for only John and Yoko. His curiosity was satisfied when he came upon them making love. This whole thing, he started to think, was getting weirder and weirder. He tried to explain things to Wanda: that Yoko was different, that they had to understand her. Damn, she was John Lennon's woman, wasn't she? But his patience was wearing thin.

"After a while it seemed to me she was into playing games with everybody," maintains Ronnie. "There was a lot of real silly shit going on."

Ronnie was willing to be impressed by Yoko. World peace? He could dig that. It was her style that began to get under his skin. "After the first two or three days they had all their yes-men around them and it felt as if everybody was laughing at us so we just kept away. Shit, there were enough problems there without all those yes-men running around. And you could tell they were just telling John all the good stuff he wanted to hear. They were leaving a lot of the negative stuff out. When he asked me what was happening with the peace festival organization — hell, it went bankrupt in the end — I'd say, 'Well, this is going wrong, that's going wrong, that's going wrong and that ain't right.' Then he'd call his man in and check it out but they wouldn't tell him anything wasn't right.

"The whole thing was a power trip for Yoko, in my opinion — that she was big enough to chew up the leader of the Beatles in public and get away with it. That gave her strength. John Lennon and the Beatles were the biggest act in the world and for Yoko to talk to him like she did in front of the press — well, if I'd been John I'd have broken her goddamn nose. But he told her that she was cleverer than he was; that it was okay that she wanted to take over and that he was going to let her. Maybe that was his way of behaving so he wouldn't have to deal with her. Christ, it got so that even Paul McCartney could not get through all the yes-men to speak to her or Lennon. And this was a long time before it was announced the Beatles were splitting up and John and Paul weren't speaking. So John and Paul handled their business through Yoko or through one of the agents or yes-men. The guy in the middle took the messages from both sides and put it together.

"As I understood it then, the rest of the Beatles would not let John come in with Yoko and record with them. He'd have to come in by himself. Paul McCartney would not show up for any session that Yoko was at. John wanted Yoko to become the fifth Beatle.

"But Yoko sing? I don't know if you'd call what she did singing, but goddamn it, it was different. One morning we were sleeping and all of a sudden we heard this . . . *sound*. Damn. Someone was getting murdered, for sure. We jumped up and ran around. We didn't know what the hell it was. I was looking for guns and every goddamn thing. But it was just Yoko. She was in her room singing.

"Now, I've always believed you can't criticize what you don't understand so when John asked me, 'What do you think about her singing, Ron?', I said, 'I've always believed that you don't want to criticize what you don't understand. And I don't understand what she's doing.' I'm not musical enough to figure that kind of singing out, I told him. It didn't sound like any music I've ever heard."

"Then I heard Ron talking later how awful it was," says Wanda. "So I said, 'Tell him the truth. If you don't think it's any good, tell him.'"

"It was a power trip for her," says the Hawk. "Staying in bed for weeks across Canada, getting all that publicity — they were trying to outdo Elizabeth Taylor and Richard Burton. Burton and Elizabeth and John and Yoko were the two big couples who got all the press for a few years. They were on the phones all the time they were with us. They had phones all over. There were several phones in the family room and at one moment she was talking to someone in Japan, then she'd say, 'Just a minute,' and then she'd talk to someone in England or Switzerland, 'Hello Peter? Peter Sellers?' she'd be saying. It was like that. Then she'd talk to somebody else and she'd go back to the person in Tokyo. And all these lines were going and she'd be talking to all these different people and it was not real. They were in a big fancy world and they were having some fun."

Reverence was the tone of the day. The entire city had adopted a tone of High Seriousness over the prospects of a peace festival, as if anyone who questioned the organization was questioning the Lennons' intent — questioning peace itself. If John Lennon had been discovered walking across Lake Ontario it wouldn't have surprised any of the rock stations. Reporters were meant to spread the word. What the Lennons were offering as they talked from "Hawkins central" to radio stations as far-flung as Luxembourg and Melbourne, San Diego and Tokyo, were not interviews but propaganda.

Ronnie had told me that the Lennons were never apart — if Yoko could help it — and indeed, as I sat on the couch next to John — I was interviewing him for the *Toronto Telegram* — Yoko was on the other side of the room talking to Rabbi Abraham Feinberg. Dick Gregory, I was told, was wandering around somewhere. No doubt he was lost in the crowd, for several dozen people ambled in and out of the room while I was there. To me, it had tone of a rock 'n' roll tour — without the concerts coming up, without the music. An in-house photographer shot everything John or Yoko did, even when that only amounted to sitting absolutely still. All this history would not go unrecorded. On occasion, one of the Hawkins children would appear. Wanda had trouble keeping them from seeing Lennon's sexually graphic lithographs he was now signing.

And endlessly the phones would ring. "Belgium," someone would say, and John would get up to repeat what had become the standard line. "Yes, the festival could be expensive. But that will be cheaper than a life." Upstairs, Ronnie was looking over papers on his huge, black desk. He was feeling a bit better about the whole thing because he'd finally found some common ground with Lennon: snowmobiles and Amphicats. John loved them. He'd been racing around with the ones Ronnie had on his place, and then he'd gone to the local dealer to get one for himself.

But again, Yoko had gotten in the way. She hated being apart from John, particularly, Ronnie realized, when John was having a blast of a good time on his own. Yoko had gone for a spin with John on one of the snowmobiles and had been scared stiff. After that, John didn't ride as often as before. Besides, he had business to attend to.

"What we're doing this week is having strategy meetings," Lennon told me between phone calls. We'd managed to get alone — well, almost alone — for a half hour or so. "We keep

171

trying to plan things in advance. And after all that, we talk about every person we met, about every conversation we had."

He retained the cuttingly cynical tone of voice that I remembered from the times we'd talked over the years. Just how seriously was he taking this? I wondered. They'd received a letter from Cesar Chavez, wanting John and Yoko to fly down to California to join his boycott of California grapes.

"Yeah," said John, "I've got the badge on." He then looked straight at me. "I was pretty cynical as a Beatle. I was a full-time cynic, you know. Now there's some direction to things. Peace is the 'must thing' in the future thousands of years — and not just for the next generation. Too many people have got hooked on material things. That's why we've got drop-outs and hippies. What good is it to me if I can watch twenty TVs with twenty suits and have twenty cars? I mean, these are what other people consider success."

I looked around at the thousands and thousands of dollars worth of phones, consoles and assorted electronic gewgaws winking, blinking and buzzing in the room, and wondered exactly what his idea of austerity was. Suddenly I had my answer. John Lennon was asking me to do some digging around for him.

"Listen," he said in the very tone he'd used when talking about world peace, "I want you to find out how our record is doing. That song, 'Cold Turkey,' is just dying. Tell the people, tell the record people here, to get off their asses."

"Cold Turkey" was written after it was discovered that Yoko was pregnant and the couple had decided to kick their heroin habits by going cold turkey and not taking drugs. Graphic in its description of the pains of withdrawal, its lackluster performance on the pop charts had proven McCartney's Top 40 instincts were intact in rejecting it from the positive-sounding *Abbey Road* album.

He asked someone to get Capital Records, the local distributors of "Cold Turkey," on the line. He wanted to check out the chart action. Feeling a little bit more at ease with him, I wondered how at a time like this he could worry about something so mundane as a single.

"Listen," said John Lennon. His eyes were bright and hard — no irony here. "I have to worry about records and things still. How else would I make me money, eh? How else?"

Still, here in the sanctum sanctorum of peace, with herbal tea being served to multi-millionaires as Mexico City phoned up for an interview, it was decidedly heartening to hear crass talk about commercial records. This was the John Lennon Ronnie could get through to.

Yes, he was a good guy, this Ronnie Hawkins, Lennon said. He was sure he'd seen him on television in England "long before there was a Beatles." It was on one of those package rock 'n' roll shows. "But I know I heard his early stuff. It's strange about those old songs. I know that if I tried I couldn't remember a lot of the Beatles songs. But I know I could do 'Blue Suede Shoes.' I'd know it right off. It'd be interesting to try something like that with Ronnie."

That's what Ronnie was figuring, too. Something told him that Lennon would like the chance to jam for a while. Well, damn, Ronnie thought, that would be easy to arrange. His band was rehearsing out at Sarnia. Why not have them come up here and just happen to be rehearsing when John Lennon whizzed by on a snowmobile?

"We were still rehearsing when Ronnie asked us to come to Mississauga," remembers John "Ghetto" Gibbard. "So we moved all our equipment into 'Old Yeller,' the farmhouse in front of his property in Streetsville. We'd rounded out the band. Kelly Jay was a backup vocalist. There was Richard Newell — King Biscuit Boy — on harmonica. We needed a bass player and we needed another guitar player. So Kelly brought in Rheal Lanthier and Roly Greenway, people he'd played with in the Ascot Review. We had Larry Atamniuk playing drums. Rick Bell played keyboards. Johnny Rutter, who was going by the name of Johnny Rhythm, joined up. He could sing. We had three singers, which was more than necessary, but it meant that when Ron was not there we could play any club because we had all the bases covered. We were just billed as the Hawks.

"To make a bit of money we played the Guildwood Inn in Toronto at night and rehearsed during the day. We rehearsed for twelve hours a day and jammed for two or three after that. There was no place to go. There was no money. There was nothing to do but practice and we practiced hard.

"Ron, of course, loved that," remembers Gibbard. "'Boys,' he'd say, 'I want this band to be tighter that a gnat's ass over a rain barrel.' So the band got *real* tight. So this day Ron showed up and said, 'Boys, John Lennon is staying here, and I'd like you boys to come back and set up and I'm going to see if I can get John to come out and jam with you boys.'

"He thought that would be fun. 'Maybe you can get something pressworthy out of it,' he went on. 'You never know.'

"'Boys,' said Ron, 'just set up the equipment and start practicing and then I'll try and get old John on a snowmobile and I'll drive him out by Old Yeller and I'll see if I can talk him into coming in. If you boys are playing, it'll just seem natural. It won't seem like we're setting him up for anything.'

"Great. So we were jamming and jamming away for what seemed like hours and doing some pretty good stuff. All of a sudden, Kelly decided that because we were doing the Guildwood Inn, and it's a supper-club place, and because we were playing to middle-of-the-road, upper-middle-class audiences, we should work on something that would appeal to them, like 'Raindrops Keep Falling on My Head,' which was popular because *Butch Cassidy and the Sundance Kid* was out. 'Besides,' he said, 'Lennon's not going to show up, come on.'

"Nobody was really into 'Raindrops Keep Falling on My Head,' but we started. So there's Kelly singing, and who pulled up on the snowmobile right then but John Lennon with Ronnie. And there we were doing 'Raindrops.' The skidoo just pulled away and we never got the chance to jam with John Lennon. Gone.

"Ron sure had some comments to make about that: 'What the hell were you guys doing in there?' he yelled. 'What are you doing playing music like that for? We got a rock 'n' roller here. He's not interested in listening to that.'

"So, we blew it."

The peace festival took silvery sleek new offices on Toronto's Avenue Road, and plans and dreams bubbled bigger and bigger. For his part, Ronnie maintained — for any inquiring reporter at least — that he was behind the festival. But he was sure that John had understood his skepticism.

"Yeah," Lennon had told him, "it's just a dream. But sometimes dreams can become real." Ronnie bought that part, certainly. He knew that Lennon had the clout and the money to carry it off. What he wasn't sure of was the other aspect of it — the weird, pie-in-the-sky stuff he kept hearing. Like Yoko's Land of Bag. Now, to Yoko, this was not an imaginary country as much as some future state established after Year One A.P., which would gain admittance to the United Nations. And she was being serious; at least Ronnie thought she was. In her vision, the Land of Bag would be a cross between Disneyland and King Arthur's court. John had even announced that Ronnie would be Bag's first knight.

"He called me Sir Ronald, the Good Knight," Ronnie told his band at the Le Coq D'Or awhile later, with not a little pride. "I even had to get down on my knees, the whole bit. It was like being in Olde England."

Again, Ronnie wasn't sure how far to let his natural skepticism about the other-worldly aspects of Lennon's festival take over. The Lennons seemed to be okay. They smoked some dope — a bit of pot maybe, some hash, but that was about it, he thought. But what was going on during all those long hours they spent alone in their room, he wondered.

Late one night, unable to sleep, Ronnie got up, walked the dog and was heading back to the house when he saw a light on in the kitchen. Coming up to the window, he peeked in to catch John and Yoko wolfing down ham sandwiches, salami, anything in the fridge they could get their hands on. Zen macrobiotics indeed! Dope hunger, he suspected.

A little later he had further confirmation that they were doing a lot of drugs. The couple had gone to their room and run a bath but had fallen asleep, letting the bath overflow. Downstairs the Hawkinses noticed that something weird was happening to the ceiling in their living room, the *new* ceiling in their living room. Bits of it were falling down. There were drops of water.

Hawkins asked Tony Fawcett to go up and check what was going on, but knock as hard as he could, Fawcett couldn't get them out of bed. The only thing they could think of was to have Wanda go out their bedroom window, along the ledge on the roof and in through the John and Yoko's window. Wanda wasn't too sure about that. What if some of the guards out there had guns? Nevertheless, she crept around to the window, and climbed in to turn off the taps. Sure enough, there they were, out cold on their bed.

By now Ronnie was merely trying to survive the burdens of his new-found fame by making sure life went on as normal:

You know, the way I figure it would work out was this: I was going to play at the club and do what I had to do and John and Yoko had all kinds of things to keep them busy. I figured everything would work out in the end. Everytime they set something on fire or burned something or broke something, why, someone would come up and say that they'd cover us — that they'd pay for the damage or for whatever was wrong. Besides, they'd say how much money we were going to get from this whole thing so we didn't have to worry about it.

When you get as big as John and Yoko were, I guess you don't realize the responsibility you have for what you owe or for what you have. Everybody always seems to be doing things for you so I guess you're not aware of what is happening. Originally, so I understood, the whole idea behind John and Yoko staying with us was that there'd never be more than one or two people there to look after them. All of their business was going to be done downtown. They wouldn't be around much. But as more things went wrong — things getting broken or whatever — they kept telling us, "Don't worry about it, we'll remodel the whole house. We'll do everything. We'll rebuild it. Don't worry, there's going to be millions."

Then they left and we had those phones and all the phone bills. Who was going to pay for all those calls? John said, "Don't worry, Ronnie, we'll take care of that." He also told *Rolling Stone* magazine that. Don't worry. I didn't. But I still got the bill for goddamn sixteen thousand dollars. They didn't pay a dime, not a dime.

We had to pay it off. Those phones didn't have anything to do with us. *We* didn't put down the deposit. *We* didn't ask Bell Telephone to put those phones in my house. Somebody else signed for them. But when the bill didn't get paid, Bell Telephone came straight to us. "It doesn't make any difference who did what," they said. "It's your house, the calls were made there, they're your responsibility."

So I said, "If that's the law, then I'm going to take myself and my band and we're going to set up in the yard of somebody who's rich. And even though they may not want us or like us we're going to play and then give them a goddamn bill. It seems as if it's the same thing to me. I'll give this rich person a forty thousand dollar bill for playing for them even though they didn't want it."

Mother Bell is powerful and boy, they can do whatever they want to. You can sue them for five years but in the meantime you haven't got a phone. So we had to pay that bill over the next year. And all the time we kept hearing in the news John saying that he was going to take care of all the bills.

Well, that hope ended when he announced to the world that he wasn't having anything to do with the peace festival. We ended up having to fix everything that had been damaged. And we never got anything back for it. It took us a year or two to get out of debt after that because nothing was paid for. The house was wrecked, the garage was burnt and no one was going to pay for that. We'd been promised millions. We thought we were in the big time there for a week or two.

There is one small irony in all this. One of John and Yoko's lasting disappointments was not being able to reach Elvis Presley. Actually, they *did* get through to his office. It was just that ol' Elvis didn't give a fast flying doodley squat about phoning back the World's Most Famous Couple. It drove John and Yoko bananas. But after they left, Elvis responded. And it seemed he was more interested in the Lennons' host than in Lennon himself.

Wanda remembers: "I got a phone call — now, let me explain that I'm the biggest Elvis Presley fan that you ever saw in your life — and this man says, 'I'm Elvis Presley's business manager.' Well, as soon as he said 'Elvis Presley' I was delirious. I was so excited when he said that Elvis knew of Ron and that he wanted to get some things happening with him. I told him, 'Well, Ron's not here.' The manager said that Elvis couldn't call because he was at an airport or something so I should have Ron call him back later on. I wrote the number down and I phoned Ron. Ron of course didn't believe it, but the call was genuine. Elvis, according to several friends around him at the last, listened to Ronnie's old records all the time.

"When Ronnie finally took the message seriously, he discovered that the phone number was wrong. I'd written it down backwards," Wanda continues. "So I tried all these different number combinations to find out what it could have been, but they didn't work. A month or so later I checked it all out and this person who phoned was in fact Elvis Presley's business manager. I guess they didn't want to phone back so I felt we blew it. Or *I* blew it."

But this wasn't the only lost opportunity. With John and Yoko gone, the organizers of the peace festival somehow had to drum up interest, commitments from other musicians and, more important, money — and they had to do this without their best salesman.

For a while everything seemed to roll their way. Brower, after his earlier scrappiness, became the soul of charm. The mainstream Canadian media may not have lost their cynicism, but the underground press was warming to the idea of the festival. And why not? Woodstock was still in everyone's mind and Lennon's peace festival would be, in its way, an extension of it. It would be free, or almost free, or "free for a dollar."

Unknown to everyone, though, the festival was beginning to come apart just as its various pieces were being assembled. Brower and Yorke had an early run-in with John over ticket prices. They'd followed the Lennons to Aalborg, Denmark, where Yoko's ex-husband, Tony Cox, lived with their daughter, Kyoko, and his new American wife, Melinda Kendall. They arrived to find that Cox had put the Lennons through a psychological wringer. He wanted to keep Kyoko and was ordering John and Yoko around like a pair of kids themselves. The promoters from Canada found John and Yoko, their hair shorn to the scalp, hollow-eyed and bristling with anger. The festival would be free, Lennon insisted. Absolutely free. And he wasn't going to lend his name to it until he could be assured that it would be free. Get corporate donations to finance it. Get the government to help. Wasn't Trudeau on their side?

Brower, battered by the intensity of Lennon's anger but not beaten, returned home to begin drumming up support. Lennon, back in England, began rethinking his commitment. Meanwhile Ritchie Yorke, knowing he still had a good story to promote, headed out on a whirlwind world tour which just happened to coincide with Ronnie's trip to England to push his new single, "Down in the Alley."

Brower knew things were going seriously wrong with the peace festival when Tony Fawcett, on the phone from London, played him the song Brower had hoped might be the festival's signature piece. Karma Productions was the name Brower had give the festival's production company and here, said Fawcett, was John's new piece, "Instant Karma." But instead of the expected anthem, "Instant Karma" was a warning — to all those who seemed to be cashing in on peace, like rock promoters. Later on, *Rolling Stone* took Lennon's side, giving him space to explain why he'd backed out of the festival. But many festival watchers didn't need to wait for the dream to explode. They knew it was too heavy with self-importance to ever get off the ground.

A call one afternoon from one of Brower's subordinates took me up to Karma's Avenue Road offices, nearly empty at the time. Brower was in Los Angeles, I was told, Yorke was in Australia with Ronnie, but the festival looked as though it was going to be even bigger than they had imagined.

"Bigger?" I asked, starting to scribble in my note pad, "You mean the Beatles are coming, then?"

I was given a conspiratorial look, "Better," he said. "A space-ship."

Christ, they're talking little green men, now, I thought.

He smiled. No, it wasn't like that. We weren't talking about extraterrestrial visitors. We were talking about John and Yoko arriving in a spaceship at the very peak of the festival.

"The spaceship will be powered by the psychic energy waves coming from the crowd. Isn't that something?"

"When promoters started saying flying saucers, and Elvis and the Beatles and the Rolling Stones and everyone, playing at the same thing, I guess I knew something was wrong," says the Hawk. "As I told John Brower, 'Goddamn, if you don't deliver, you're definitely in trouble.' And I knew the promoters weren't going to deliver *that* package. Damn! A flying saucer? Man. When you tell the press that, you're going to end up with some press all right — the wrong kind of press.

Later, on his world-wide publicity tour publicizing his new album and single, *Down in the Alley*, for Cotillion Records, as well as the peace festival, Hawkins was a bit more cautious about Lennon during a talk he had with Richard Green of *New Musical Express* in London.

"He's a strange person," Ronnie confided. "He changes from one day to the next and I couldn't tell exactly what he was thinking about or thinking of doing. He and Yoko spent all their time together and I didn't see him about the house most of the time. I really can't say if I think his peace project will work — most people believe in peace, but . . ."

Wanda concludes the story of her enigmatic house guests: "John and Yoko didn't completely forget us. They sent us a pair of white love doves for Christmas. We kept them in a beautiful cage and we strung it up high where nothing could bother them. But somehow or other the weasels got them."

XI

IF THIS IS CHINA,
WE'RE IN TROUBLE

*Typhooned in Tahiti, Hassled in Hong Kong, the Hawk
Circles the Globe in Search of Peace, Publicity and the
Perfect Party Surprise*

JOHN LENNON LEFT RONNIE WITH MORE than watersoaked ceilings
and unpaid phone bills. Lennon also left him with the biggest
publicity coup in his life when John recorded a little blurb for
radio stations hustling Ronnie's comeback single, "Down in the
Alley." Now, John Lennon certainly wasn't unaware of the value
his name had. He was still a Beatle. He knew that if he pushed
anything at all it was going to get noticed. What he'd also liked
about promoting Ronnie's single was that it was his own idea.
Ronnie hadn't tried to sell John on the record; quite the opposite.
John had been sitting signing autographs the day he first heard the
album; at first he didn't know it was Ronnie who was singing.

"I was the only person he didn't talk to about it," Lennon said
later. "He listened to my new album again and again," Hawkins
remembers, "and by the time night rolled around, he was so heated
about one song, 'Down in the Alley,' the remake of the old Clovers
hit, that he phoned Jerry Wexler. Bring out that song, John told
Wexler, and you'll have a smash hit."

Lennon admitted that his commercial instincts weren't perfect;

nevertheless, he was sure this single had it. So when the world heard the tape by John Lennon saying how much he dug Ronnie's hot new single, the world was going to take notice. And that's how high they all set their sights in those heady days when they drank herbal tea in Mississauga and planned for peace. Everything was falling into place, it seemed. Everything John did was getting publicized; they couldn't let the momentum stop. But when the Lennons had to rush to Europe to sort out their lives and John Brower had to sell the festival to sponsors, that left just Ritchie Yorke and Ronnie Hawkins.

"Well, the peace festival folks got together and decided they were going to send me around the world to promote the festival for John Lennon," says Ronnie. "Everyone involved thought it was a really good idea: the people at *Rolling Stone*, everybody.

"'Hell, I'll go,' I told them. 'I can promote the peace festival and at the same time I can promote the Cotillion album. 'Cause I want to promote this album everywhere.'"

So with the local media scrambling to follow up on the barrage of peace plans, Hawkins and Yorke headed east for the first leg of the 55,000 mile, round-the-world-junket — and into their own barrage of trouble. Says Ronnie, "We had trouble everywhere we went. In Tahiti there was a typhoon out of season. In Tokyo I had one of those baths I've always been reading about with geisha girls but I must've expected too much because that's all I had — a bath.

"It was just like a James Bond movie in Japan because of Yoko's power over there," Ronnie adds. "They took us into a warehouse which had a brick wall that opened up — just like in the movies. Behind that brick wall there was an illegal radio, manned by deserters from the American army. They wanted to play my record. Great, I thought. So I started telling them what I was doing there.

"'No,' they said, 'that's not it. That's not what we want.'

"They wanted me to say something against the Vietnam War. But how did I know who they were? Were they deserters? Or did they kill someone getting out of the stockade? They wanted me to get on the radio and say, 'Come home,' and 'no more war,' and all that.

"'Baby,' I said, 'I ain't saying nothing on any illegal radio. In fact I'd like to get back to the hotel.'

"Then came Hong Kong, where I was nearly arrested in

mainland China. It made the front page of nine papers, including the communist papers. At that time the only thing separating Hong Kong from the mainland was a traffic barrier. We'll, Ritchie Yorke was looking for some free publicity for the peace thing. You know how these journalists are, they're crazy. The harder a story is to get the more they want to get it. That's where the trouble started."

"BEATLE POSTERS AT HK BORDER," blared the headline of the *China Mail* the day Hawkins and Yorke set off to cross the border into China, providing the Red Chinese guards with the full details of the least secret peace initiative ever taken. Ronnie was described as a "cigar-smoking singer," and "leader of the Plastic Ono Band." The poster he carried said "WAR IS OVER — if you want it."

"We'd like to cross the border if we can," Hawkins told reporters bravely. "And we're not afraid of the Chinese shooting at us. We have to get our peace message across."

So off they drove to Lokmachau in their mini-bus. "Remember that barrier I was telling you about? The one you stop at? Well, we didn't stop at it," Ronnie remembers. "We just drove through the barrier. I tell you, I'd have jumped out then if I knew what the driver was doing. Because that's when there was some trouble. You know, it looked like there was an uprising with Mao himself and lots of young cats, those young Red Guards. They surrounded us. They looked like fifteen- or sixteen-year-old kids. So I brought out the pictures of who I was. That didn't work. Then I tried to crack a few jokes but those buggers weren't laughing. They didn't even smile. Well, it was too late for me to go back now. I found out then that we were in a commune. So they took all these pictures and grabbed everybody and they left me in the car. I told the officer I flunked English and I sure couldn't speak Chinese. That didn't matter, as he could speak English. In fifteen minutes they knew more about me than I knew about myself.

"They were looking for spies, I guess, or something like that. I don't know. What I *do* know is that anybody would be crazy to go through that barrier. As it turned out, they actually blamed the cat in charge of the border crossing because there wasn't anybody there guarding it. Then again, nobody had ever been stupid enough to drive through that barrier into mainland China before. Anyway, they let us go. I guess ignorance sometimes works as an excuse."

Well, almost. Hawkins and Yorke's next move was to try cross-ing into China farther down the border. This time both British and Chinese rushed at them, the Chinese making angry gestures, the British insisting that they couldn't protect them if the Chinese took it beyond the gesturing stage. "Anyway," says Ronnie, "we finally left. The next day it was in all the papers again. I wanted to get out of Hong Kong, I tell you. I couldn't tell who was communist and who wasn't."

Ritchie Yorke knew instantly what a publicity coup this was. As soon as he could, he phoned Lennon in Ascot, England, to tell him all about it. Lennon thought it was "great." Within days, papers back in North America were running pictures of Ronnie Hawkins standing in a barren landscape, holding a peace poster. He didn't look happy.

The Bangkok *Post*, forewarned about the arrival of "Ronald" Hawkins in Thailand, announced, "Peace-Tripper Arrives." But it took only a few minutes for the Hawk to announce his own priorities. "I'm not on this peace thing myself," he informed reporters who'd heard about the famous "Chinese border inci-dent." He added that he was really just a "country boy who's been singing rock 'n' roll for the past eighteen years and this is the first vacation I've had that whole time."

He looked around a bit, particularly at the women who crowded around him. Hmmm. "From what I've heard," he said diplomati-cally, "the Thai girls are supposed to be the prettiest little things anywhere, so we'd like to go out to some places where they have nice girls."

Australia, on the other hand, was a perfect territory for their pitch. And it soon became a prime market for the Hawkins mythology. Yorke was born there and had solid media contacts. Even better, the Hawk wasn't exactly an unknown himself. Rock-abilly. Arkansas. Yeah, the rock press had heard about him. But they hadn't heard *from* him. Within days he'd spun enough stories to make the local press sit up and notice. And why not? Canada, after all, seemed so remote, so . . . romantic, so farfetched. Perfect for your basic larger-than-life rockabilly hero legend. Who could resist believing the tales that the Hawk spun?

Like the one about the time "we were doing a gig in the north," as Ronnie told Greg Quill, the Australian writer at *Go-Set*, who later immigrated to Canada to appear as a Toronto *Star* columnist, "and Levon had to go to a town which was about twenty miles away from where we were staying." Hawkins looked at Quill, cocking his cigar. "Levon had been driving for three days without sleep in the band's truck, so I gave him three pills to make sure he'd get back that night. Three days later the truck pulled up outside, steaming and about to fall apart. Levon was glued to the wheel, his eyes fixed to the windshield. He said to me, 'Man, those five pills were out of this world. I just didn't want to stop drivin'.' And I said to him, 'What five pills? I only gave you three.' When we looked in the glove compartment where we'd put them, he'd eaten two ten-amp fuses out of the amplifiers. Any man who can get high on fuses is a good man to have in your band."

From that story on, nothing was going to stop Quill from finding out more about Hawkins, peace festival or not. And what he found excited the Hawk the most was the unlikely opportunity of meeting an old Hawkins buddy, Roy Orbison, about to start a week's gig in the main room of Sydney's Chevron Hotel.

Meeting Orbison was important for Ronnie. The "peace thing" had been all right, but what was nagging his mind was his single. That's what he wanted to get from this global jaunt, a hit single. What he also needed to know was if others thought it was as good as he thought it was — others like Roy. After all, it was Orbison who'd helped him with one of his first hits, "Mary Lou." What would he think of this? Well, it turned out, Roy hadn't heard "Down in the Alley."

He hadn't seen Ronnie in years. There was something that needed straightening out, something that started the night he'd sat down on Ronnie's porch at 519 West Maple back in Fayetteville, seemingly a million miles away, and started playing guitar. In the twilight, he'd run over the chords of a old song he'd picked up along the way, something Ronnie had taken a sudden shine to because it was in a minor key. Ronnie remembered he'd heard something like it before. Roy sang something, Ronnie added a bit, and the song had slowly grown as the evening itself grew darker.

That night was forgotten until the day a few years later when Roy happened to be listening to the radio in his car. There he was, out in the middle of nowhere, still making the rounds of the clubs, looking for that new hit to keep his career alive, when he heard it — the song he was after, the very song he'd played to Ronnie that night.

"Out of the blue I heard this old song I used to sing," Roy told Ronnie, "and when it was finished the deejay said it was by Ronnie Hawkins. I nearly drove off the road.

It was "Mary Lou." The two good ol' boys smiled at each other. Perhaps the story had been staged for Quill. Orbison knew he'd been following Hawkins around.

"I could've killed you, Ronnie," said Orbison as he reached out and put his pale hand behind Hawk's neck for a friendly squeeze.

By the time Hawkins and Yorke reached London in late February, the final stop on their "mission," Ronnie was in full stride. The peace mission had become an adjunct to his own personal mission to spread the word about himself and his single. And this was exactly what his hard-core British fans were waiting for.

In fact the British passion for his music startled Ronnie. The only time he'd been there was in 1960, for an appearance on the "Boy Meets Girl" pop TV show. But that was all it took, for some. The English, ever given to clubs, cliques and discreet cabals devoted exclusively to such subjects as Gilbert and Sullivan, Charles Dickens or ferrets, ended up with the most tight-knit fan club ever devoted to Ronnie Hawkins.

It started in the early sixties with Wild Little Willie Jeffery and continues to this day, although it no longer has a formal organization. It's still led by the very same Wild Willie along with Ian Wallis, the owner of an insurance company in Kent by day and columnist for the *England Country Music News* whenever else he can find the time. Wild Willie is such a Hawkins fan that he has spent time with him in Canada, getting as close to the legend as he could. Although Ronnie is loath to admit it, Wild Willie has in some ways out-Hawkinsed the Hawk himself. Wild Willie's Playboy mansion girlie show was so outrageous that even the Romper was caught by surprise. More recently, when Ronnie played in England in October 1981, it was Wild Willie who introduced him on the live album recorded at Dingwall's. But by common consensus, the most die-hard Hawkins fan of them all was Brian J. Simmons, or "Screamin' Brian" as everyone knew him, who died of a heart attack at only thirty-nine years on New Year's day, 1985.

Screamin' Brian was the first new member of the fan club — he answered Wild Willie's ad the day after it appeared in the paper — and he was by far the most fanatic. After spending several days with Ronnie in Canada and hearing how the Hawk wasn't getting any royalties from Roulette Records he grew so incensed that he flew down to New York and stomped up to the Roulette offices demanding the money, there and then. For his trouble he was heaved right out into the street.

It was Screamin' Brian who published the *Camel Walk-Er Magazine*, the typographically adventurous "publication of the friend's of Ronnie Hawkins club (*sic*)," which boasted such articles as: Ronniw (*sic*) Hawkins Strikes Again." One reading of the *Camel Walk-Er* prompted Cliff White in the *New Musical Express* to declare it "proof positive that British eccentricity is alive and well." After listing its contents — each and every article written by the very same author, Screamin' Brian — White confessed, "I love every stupefying line of it."

And why not? Screamin' Brian lived his entire life for Rompin' Ronnie and his era. Oh, he might have also listened to Screamin' Lord Sutch and Screamin' Jay Hawkins, and he also loved Jack Scott although he *didn't* scream, but his heart belonged to the Hawk. "He was the number one Ronnie Hawkins fan in the world," says Ian Wallis.

"He was a total fanatic. You couldn't have a conversation for ten minutes on anything without ending up talking about Ronnie Hawkins. He was unmarried, lived with his mother and had a vast record collection, complete with everything Ronnie had done. He had a massive collection of memorabilia. He was an uneducated man, he had a poor job — he worked in a warehouse, just stacking furniture and stuff — and he earned very poor wages. Yet he'd spend all the money he'd got on Ronnie Hawkins. He would have gone without a meal if it would have done anything for Ronnie's career."

But Screamin' Brian's obsession with the Hawk peaked when Ronnie finally arrived in his own backyard. Forget John Lennon. Forget the peace festival. Brian had a zillion things to do and ask. More than anything, he had a zillion people to convince of Ronnie Hawkins's stupendousness. Along with Wild Willie he made sure the right folks got to speak to the Hawk. If they wouldn't bother coming out well, hell, he'd just go to them with the story. And it wasn't long before they had another story about Hawkins to tell.

"Now, some folks heard some stories about that little party I threw in London," says Ronnie dryly. "It was written up in *Rolling Stone* and to everyone it sounded really weird. Like, there were supposed to be midgets jumping out of walls and all that. Well, that's not what happened at all. But it was still wild."

And why not? Wasn't he already known in the United Kingdom as "the wild man from Arkansas"? Besides, maybe he could show John and Yoko something about making an impact:

It started when John and Yoko threw a little party for me. They'd provided me with the penthouse pad at the Playboy mansion in London. They'd already stayed there. That's when Playboy was going full-tilt with gambling. What a reputation that place had! This suite must've been used only for orgies and all because it was high-tech, push-button, five bedrooms, four bathrooms. It was the heaviest thing they had at the Playboy mansion and only celebrities took it. And they rented it for me. The phone rang every five minutes with somebody wanting to know if there was any action. Making money.

Now, I was pretty busy at the time. I had that Cotillion album I made in Muscle Shoals with Duane Allman and all the rest on it, and I was still associated with the peace festival. Ritchie and I had been around the world. Everything was happening so here we are, going to the Playboy Club for a major-league party, and — nothing! Everybody was sitting around looking at everybody else. Not a damn thing was happening. You see, everybody there was from the Beatles' company, Apple Corp., and it was in a real mess, I tell you. It was not my kind of party at all. Finally I couldn't take it.

"Folks, let me tell you something," I said. "This is the about the dullest goddamn party I've ever seen in my life."

Hell, I got up and made a real speech. "I thought John and Yoko would throw better parties than this," I said, "so here's what I'm going to do. I'm going to throw one tomorrow night: all you same people come back. I'll show you what a party *is*."

The next day I called up Wild Willie and I said, "Willie, call up your connection. I want three or four little girls that look like they're about fifteen, although they're of age, and who will put on a show for me. I don't want anybody to know that they're together, that it's planned that they're borrowed or paid for."

So they arrived and I told them: "I want you to circulate through the audience for a little while till I go into my little coochy-coochy act. When I go into it, I want you to scream and jump and start ripping one another's clothes off and start eating pussy right there in the middle of the floor."

John and Yoko weren't there, although they heard about it later. I'd already had Yoko figured out by then. I knew where she was at. She was playing heavy head games then and John was just a victim of these head games. That's why they weren't there. So I just waited for everybody to have several drinks, several tokes and several of everything else.

Then all of a sudden I got up. I announced: "Look at all the women here. I feel horny. I think I'll cast a spell, and . . ."

Hell. No one knew what to think. There even was a guy with me who was doing a story for *Playboy*. I don't know if he knew what to think. So I said, "Okay folks, I'll stir this thing up. It's getting started like last night. I'm not going to allow that again."

I went out and said, "Girls, I'm putting the spell on you. I looked at the four girls: "You're getting horny." I did a little abracadabra shit.

All of a sudden these four little girls start moving around in the audience in four different areas of the room. Each one jumped down right in the middle of things and started tearing off her clothes. These girls are going, "Oh stop it, Ronnie, stop it, stop it . . . " Hell, Bette Davis and Katharine Hepburn couldn't have put on as good an acting job. Well, they put on a thirty-minute show and not one person left the room. You could tell everyone enjoyed themselves. Three different guys got divorced because of this party. Because, you see, their wives were there but they just forgot them watching those girls.

True to form, Ronnie wasn't about to let a perfectly good orgy, especially one that upstaged Yoko Ono, go to waste. So he had made sure he'd invited the key press folks — like Ray Connolly, the *Evening Standard* columnist, Stanley Booth and Richard Green from *New Musical Express*.

"They told me that Ronnie Hawkins used to hold parties that Nero would have been ashamed to attend," wrote Connolly later, "so when the invitation came late one night I didn't need any arm-twisting.

"It was quite a party," Connolly went on. "They never had them like like that in Ormskirk. God knows who all the people were: record company employees, girl friends and pick ups I imagine. There was a lot of drink around too. And some really dirty picture books from Sweden (and I mean *dirty*) for those who had no one to talk to, and a lot of low, behind-the-barn Deep South humor. And sitting there right in the middle of it all was Ronnie Hawkins, the host, alternating the shapes of his lips to take sips of brandy, puffs on his cigar and drags on a weedy little home-made cigarette that had a funny smell . . . this is Ronnie Hawkins in his element. Boasting, bragging, telling stories, the center of the party, the man with nothing but friends. Get him going and neither he nor you want him to stop."

Ronnie laid it on thick for the folks, letting them have his best stories. "Hard livin'? Why son, you ain't heard *nothin'* yet . . . ."

But why not enjoy myself? Ronnie was thinking. Hell, it's the first real vacation I've had in years. Since this was the last stop before heading back into the Canadian winter, a new band and what seemed to be an entirely new phase in his career, why not sit back and take it all in?

London had been good to him even if it was getting weirder than weird, with all the skinheads around. He had friends there, fans — but he had to go back to Canada. He had his band waiting. "I've put them on the skid-row circuit to see if they can go without me," he said. And he had to get back into training himself, to head back out on the road.

"I've got go to home," he thought to himself, looking around the Playboy suite, "lose some weight and start playing. I've got to."

And he had to start making some money. The more he kept hearing about the peace festival the less likely its chances seemed. Meanwhile, his stock was rising. The festival, plus Lennon's stay at his place, plus the band's increasing fame, had made him a hot commodity again. "All the big companies came offering me money like I'd never heard of," he told a friend at the party. "One even flew me out to Hollywood and offered me a quarter of a million dollars front money to sign for them, and they'd never even heard me sing a note. For all they knew, I might not have even been able to carry a tune." He was aware how out of hand his association with Lennon had become. "They're wanting me to walk on the water," he kidded Peter Cole from the *Evening News.* "I want to have some nice boots on when I do that."

"What about the family?" someone interrupted one of Ronnie's stories. For all the wild stories about him, his reputation as a family man was also part of his mythology, even though the fact of a wife and three children "didn't deter him from telling every interviewer he met of the wild times he's had," thought Connolly later. "Wanda?" said Ronnie. "Luckiest girl in the world. Well, she knows how I am. I've always been this way, I suspect maybe she thinks it's just me bragging and showing off and not really meaning any of it. She's a good woman. But to tell the truth, I'm getting so old that I can't go chasing the girls like I used to. And if I do chase them, when I catch them I'm fit for nothing. You know those oysters that are supposed to make you passionate. Well, I'm so old that if I take half a dozen, only five of them work."

Taking all this in was Wild Willie himself. Until Ronnie had come along with "Down in the Alley," Hawkins's British fanatics had to be content with nostalgia and whatever news they'd get about each new band he was forming. But now he was back, living up to his legend with a fourteen-inch cigar, drawling his stories about the good ol' days; and he had brought them a song which, if not exactly vintage rockabilly, had a kind of authentic bluesy drag to it.

Like their idol, Hawkins's British fans were spectacular. To Peter Cole, meeting Willie was like meeting "an old-style English rocker, black drain-pipe trousers and all, who forgot to stop rocking." But Willie's passion had paid off in one way, at least. He convinced Roulette Records to release what they titled *Arkansas Rock Pile*, a collection of vintage Hawkins songs. Both the Roulette and Cotillion albums were just hitting as Ronnie passed their way.

The way Roulette executives figured it, if the Cotillion album was going to offer such oldies as "Matchbox," "Who Do You Love" and "Forty Days" — as well as the old country gospel piece, "Will the Circle Be Unbroken" — then they should remind rock fans that they had put out most of this stuff first. And to hard-core fans the old record was a godsend.

After checking out the facts with Wild Little Willie, *Record Buyer* columnist Max Needham publicly went bananas over *Arkansas Rock Pile*: "The Hawkins style — trademarked by Ronnie's driving vocals — negates any minus marks he may have. I suspect you think, at least vaguely, his hair is caked with Brylcreem, eyes red and close together, nose crooked and legs like pillars of oak. Far from it. Take a shufti at a mugshot and see what I mean. A cool cat whose philosophy is to live fast, love hard, die young and leave a beautiful memory — wild man, wild! As for the tracks, Ronnie chants superbly and caters for all tastes, with an assemblage of medium pacers and wild uptempo ditties such as 'Dizzy Miss Lizzie,' 'My Gal is Red Hot,' 'Forty Days,' 'Odessa,' 'Horace,' and 'Bo Diddley.' A strong enough boodlebag to make leg-shakers (in drainpipe trousers, string ties and luminous pink socks) augment the Arkansas music with rootee-tootee handclapping, stomping and hipbumping contortions. This package is a rewarding souvenir of just how exciting Ronnie Hawkins and the Hawks were in the Long Ago of pop music."

Even the new Cotillion album was getting solid reviews. To the *New Musical Express* critic it was "not unlike Creedence Clearwater Revival," that is, "naturally up-dated but raw and basic with just a hint of country. Connoisseurs of early rock and roll and heavy rock groups like Creedence, Rolling Stones and Led Zeppelin, will be pleasantly surprised by the new-found Ronnie Hawkins magic."

Ronnie liked that. He liked the idea of being rediscovered and when he arrived in Canada, he figured finally everything was going to go smoothly.

The Hawk was in for a surprise.

XII

BOY, THERE'S TOO MANY NOTES IN THAT BO DIDDLEY

Showdown at the Le Coq D'Or or Our Hero Meets the New Generation of Rock 'n' Roll and Shows It How It's Done

"I WAS BURNING WHEN I GOT BACK FROM ENGLAND — burning hot," remembers Ronnie. "And I wanted to stay hot because I thought I had a chance to get a big hit. The timing was right for the kind of album I'd recorded. This was early 1970 and Creedence Clearwater Revival was big, city kids were rediscovering more basic rock 'n' roll and baby, there's no more basic a rock 'n' roller than me. Because of the album, Jerry Wexler and his folks were helping us get booked in a lot of places. The Fillmore East, places like that, with big names. It was the big time. Now, we weren't going to make all that much money. You know how the big boys in the record business operate. They get away with whatever they can. They *knew* we'd get to those shows even if we had to hitchhike. But I knew ways we could survive. I knew that when we were in New York, I could put the band up at my sister Winnifred's place out on Long Island. I could pay her ten dollars a day for each man in the band. That was instead of the forty or fifty dollars a day it would've cost for each man in a hotel room. But even with me being away, I knew we were ready. I had that band of mine busy."

"Rehearsing," says John "Ghetto" Gibbard, "that's all we were doing, and playing wherever we could, when word came down that Ron was coming back. Some gigs had been booked and one of them was the Fillmore East in New York City. Now, the first full gig we did with Ron, our debut so to speak, was at the Hawk's Nest. Gordie Lightfoot, Ian Tyson — numerous people from the music business were there. Because we had a little spending money that night we all went to the Edison down the street and started drinking draft. Maybe we got a little drunker than we should have but we were still playing well when we got back. It was just the way the band operated. It was a good-time, bluesy, knock-down have-fun type band.

"Then the weekend before we played at the Fillmore we played the Fergus, Ontario, high school by ourselves, without Ron. We went from Fergus to the Fillmore East as the warm-up for Joe Cocker and the Mad Dogs and Englishmen tour. It was such a strange thing to be playing at a small-town high school and then it seemed the next minute we were driving to New York City in Ron's Rolls Royce. But he wanted to do the tour that way. He only wanted to work weekends. He didn't want to get out and do a night-by-night grind across the United States. So the idea was to do a weekend in New York, do a weekend in Boston, driving home in between.

"Mostly, there weren't any hassles," remembers Gibbard. "Traveling with Ron we had no problems getting across the border. They knew who he was and they didn't make any problems for us. He had all the equipment manifested. The paperwork was in order so they just let us go through. What a world of extremes it all was, though. One week we couldn't afford to buy a hot dog, next thing we're staying at his sister's mansion on Long Island. Two nights at the Fillmore, March 27 and 28, 1970, were even stranger.

"Two nights: terribly drunk, ridiculously high. Joe Cocker's band had been put together on a moment's notice but it was a good band for its size and considering the little time they had to practice. We sounded good, too. We drew really good reactions. As a matter of fact we had calls for a second encore on the Sunday night and Joe wouldn't let us take it because they were concerned that we were making it a little tough for them. They were recording a live album and they wanted the audience to still be hot for them.

"We had a very strange band, a really weird mix of music," Gibbard continues. "There was Ron's stuff, King Biscuit Boy's stuff — which was bluesy — and we had John Rutter who was doing la-la songs, for want of a better expression. But they worked. One of the tunes which got the crowd going was more like a kid's tune. There we were, playing in New York City with all these people out there we thought were super-hip and we're doing this tune that had a chorus that went 'la, la, la, la, la, la, la, la, la, laaaa, la.' That's all there was to it and all these people were going 'Yeah!' They were nuts. They thought it was great. I guess it was just because it was different. It was crazy. They couldn't believe that anybody would get up and do this kind of stuff on the Filmore stage. At one point this hippie father handed up his kid to Kelly Jay on stage.

"He said, 'Here man, I want my kid to be on stage with you guys 'cause you're great, man.'

It was a good experience. We got good press — *really* good press. We were reviewed in the New York papers. That was amazing in its way, too. And strange.

"You see, Cocker — or someone connected with his band — sent down a few joints for everybody in our band," Gibbard says. "It turned out to be angel dust. I don't know who did it. I do know we were all wiped out. John Rutter was the guy who lit up the first joint. He took one pull on it and it started to go around the room. There were a lot of other people there, not just the band — visitors and such. Mickey Dolenz from the Monkees was there. Michael J. Pollard, the guy in *Bonnie and Clyde*, was there. So John Rutter took a toke on that joint and passed it down the line but before it got to the second person he warned, 'Hey, everybody, go easy on this.' That's how fast it hit him. It was really bad, heavy stuff. We got through the set but I don't really know how we did it. I think Cocker's band was smoking the same thing. I don't think they were trying to do our band in, in any way. I just think that they were acclimatized to the stuff or they were just into it. There's a line on one of the tunes in the *Mad Dogs and Englishmen* album where Cocker says something about moondust, angel dust and every other kind of dust.

"I think Ron was pretty well gone that night, too," Ghetto Gibbard figures. "I think we all were. But we got through the night and did real well. We managed to get through because we were on automatic: we could play the tunes inside out and backwards.

"I remember at one point Biscuit playing harp. Biscuit is not a drug person; he drinks. Well, he was doing this wild harp solo and he went crazy at the end. He started flailing all over the place and jumped backwards — he jumped right into Larry Atamniuk's drum kit. Larry's drums were going everywhere and he had a look of sheer terror on his face. There he was, trying to hold this heavy funky rhythm together and all of a sudden his drum kit was not there anymore. Somehow he managed to do it. He was hitting drums and kicking his bass drum and pulling cymbals up while he played, all the time with a look of abject horror.

"I looked over," says Gibbard, "and there was Ronnie, standing off to the side. He looked as if he was probably saying to himself, I don't know. These guys are nuts. What am I doing with these boys? But we got through the night.

"Now, Ron had a 1950 Mercury at the time. We used the Merc and the Rolls to travel in but he was just scared to death about both of them. He loved those cars. They were both really nice cars and here he'd got all these weirdos in them. He had a guy named Patrick to drive the Rolls but Ron let the members of the band drive the Merc. It was a beautiful car, in mint condition, a fantastic automobile.

"We drove it down to Boston to play a club called the Boston Tea Party," Gibbard recalls. "Ron got himself a room and wanted some of us to stay and protect the equipment 'cause this club was in a horrible, dangerous part of Boston. Most of those clubs were, in those days. He wanted someone in the band to stay near the club overnight and sleep in the Rolls. He got a room in a Quality Court Hotel, which was the only nice place near this club. He left it up to us to find our own accommodation. Ron didn't want to spend the money on it for us. There wasn't a lot of money to be made in these gigs. There was fifteen hundred bucks, or something like that, in it. It was more promotion than anything else. The main deal was catch as catch can: you did what you could to get by. So we pooled our money and got a hotel room. We took the Merc with us. But we knew someone had to be with the Rolls."

"So I was the one to sleep in the Rolls Royce that night," explains Rheal Lanthier, the band's other guitarist. "We parked it behind the Boston Tea Party and Ron put a loaded .38 revolver under the back seat. 'Here's your sleeping bag, son,' he said. 'Take care of my wheels.'

"I was scared. There was people running up and down the alley all night long. The Rolls was okay. But they broke a window out of that black Mercury we had at the hotel.

"Ron wanted us to stay at the club. He didn't want us to drive to the hotel in the first place," adds Ghetto Gibbard. "'It's free, boys,' he kept saying. 'Just hang around the club.'

"The guy who ran the Boston Tea Party was going to rig up somewhere we could sleep inside the club, but we didn't want to do that. We'd just finished playing all night. We wanted to find a bed to sleep in. So what happens? We come out in the morning and the car is gone. Holy shit! A couple of guys in the band went racing around the streets looking and finally they found the car. Somebody had broken a window but they hadn't driven it. They couldn't get it started so they just pushed it around the corner. We raced to some auto-glass place and they put in a new window. I don't know whether Ron ever noticed that it had been broken. I don't think anybody ever mentioned it.

"The Boston Tea Party gig was a lot of fun because I got to jam with Johnny Winter," Gibbard continues. "It was sort of like a factory — a very hard-edged place with huge galvanized tin pipes. A large place. I remember walking in and Mountain, the band headlining the show, was doing a sound check. It just about ripped off my head, they were so loud. It hurt — because of all those metallic surfaces. It was just excruciating. Johnny Winter had been doing a gig somewhere else in Boston and came over to jam with Leslie West, the guitarist with Mountain, but Leslie had left as soon the gig was over. Anyway, Winter got up and wanted to jam with whoever was there. So I got to play with him.

"After we went back to Toronto again, the next gig was the East Town Theater in Detroit — a lot of these places were old movie theaters — where we played with Lee Michaels headlining. We had a good reaction there, too.

"All this time I was getting to know Ron a bit better," Gibbard feels, "but we didn't hang out together. Maybe it was because of the respect I had for him. I never thought of him as being like a buddy. I never related to him on that level. He was always a tutor, somebody I respected highly. He was the boss.

"After we played the East Town all hell started to break loose. Ron had made a comment at the Fillmore about Albert Grossman. You've got to understand that Ron was always putting together these great bands and Albert who, managed The Band and Dylan, would come along, talk to one or another of the musicians in these bands, then grab him to put in some other band he had. And Ron would be back to square one again.

"So this one night he was very drunk at the Fillmore," Gibbard remembers. "The dressing room was full of strange people — we didn't know any of them. Ron pulled Albert's pigtail and said, 'I'll whip enough piss out of you to scald a hog.' Well, despite the fact that the reviews were good at every gig we played, and the crowd reaction was good, all of a sudden all the concert dates dried up. Maybe Grossman said something to all the promoters who were booking Ron like, 'You want to book Ron in, that's fine, but don't expect to book any of my groups anymore. I'll give them to your competition.' The tour just collapsed and we were stuck. Ron put us into a place called the Grange Hotel in Hamilton."

"The problem was," says Ronnie, "nobody had ever talked to Albert Grossman that way. Maybe I was a bit drunk, but I sure meant it. I mean, there he was again, hanging around my newest band, one I was just breaking in. Finally I had to say something.

"'Albert,' I said, 'what am I? The Albert Grossman farm club? Listen, I've just brought you another band. If you want 'em, take 'em goddamn it. You've done that before.'

"I was pissed off. He'd taken John Till from me, and Ricky Bell, and put them in the Full Tilt Boogie Band backing Janis Joplin. I'd just get the kinks worked out of these bands. They weren't very good when they first came to me. It was the practicing and hard work that did that — playing every night six nights a week, sometimes seven. Six months, seven or nine months of that and they'd be good. And Albert would come in and take them from me. Damn it, but it was pissing me off."

A message for mankind: the Hawk and Ritchie Yorke on the border between Hong Kong and Red China. (ANNE YORKE)

With geisha girls in 1971: not exactly what the Hawk expected. (RITCHIE YORKE)

Ronnie moves into Ye Olde City Hall in London, Ontario. (LONDON FREE PRESS)

Elephant group, April 1974. *Clockwise from center:* Bev D'Angelo, Al Brisco, Nancy Kr Jim Atkinson, Joe Ambrosia, Bert Hermisto Usher, Don Harriss, Mike Turnpenny and Sa Carrothers.

Dynamic trio: Carl Perkins *(left)*, Ronnie and Kris Kristofferson. (TORONTO STAR)

"He's my idol," said Bob Dylan *(left)* when he visited Ronnie in Toronto. (ART USHERSON)

The Hawk joins Bob Dylan's Rolling Thunder Review at Maple Leaf Gardens
in Toronto. (ART USHERSON)

Ronnie with pianist Peter
Goddard at the Royal York's
Imperial Room, 1982. (TORONTO
STAR)

Ronnie feelin' the blues with
an old buddy, James Cotton, at
the Club House in 1979. (BARRY
THOMSON)

Watching over guitarist
Robbie Robertson in 1960
and 1982.

David Clayton Thomas flanked by Ronnie *(right)* and Ronnie's manager, Steve Thomson. (BARRY

Bass guitarist Rick Danko of The Band fame with Ronnie in 1988. (BARRY THOMSON)

Even before The Band had landed in his backyard, Grossman had heard about Ronnie's talent as a talent-spotter. At one time he had wanted the Hawk to work for him.

"Ronnie," Albert offered, "how would you like to make $3,500 a night?"

"Is a fifteen-pound robin fat?" asked Ronnie. But he hadn't heard the entire deal.

Although Ronnie turned down the offer, the two remained friendly. This time, though, he felt he was being taken advantage of, so he didn't care who he offended. Even rock's leading manager. Screw him, Ronnie thought. Grossman must've figured he was dumb. Trying to steal another band like that. Shit!

And he knew how good they could get, because *this* band had given him a chance to play with the best of the big time bands. To Ronnie, "you can always learn from just about everything you hear. It's always fun being on stage with friends like Kris Kristofferson, particularly when you can tell some stories together. Conway Twitty used to play for me at the Rockwood and I would get up on stage with him. But the band that Joe Cocker had — the one Leon Russell had put together for him — that was a great band. That kind of band, with horns and everything, was always my dream band. That's the kind of band I'd have if I could ever get the budget where I could afford that many musicians. That one and Levon's RCO All Stars, which he had when he was on his own, were probably the two best bands I'd ever heard. Levon's band — it was named after where some of it was recorded at the RCO Studio in Woodstock — that had Robbie and some of The Band on it, as well as Dr. John on piano, Fred Carter and Steve Cropper on guitar, plus a lot of other good'uns. Putting a good band together is like putting a team together. You have to have all the right ingredients. Levon had it with the All Stars. I was getting close to it with the band I had taken to New York.

"We were working real hard, going in and out of Canada, and then goddamn it, one night as we were coming into Windsor from Detroit I found a bit of dope hidden in the back seat of my Rolls. Imagine smuggling stuff across the border, and after all my lecturing and threatening, too! I fired them on the spot. I mean, you have to be able to trust your own band.

"You can just imagine what customs would have done at the border if they'd found any dope in the back seat of the Rolls. They'd've confiscated the car. Hell, we were the perfect subjects. A bunch of long-haired guys, right out of the film *Deliverance.* 'Deliverances,' I called those guys. That's what we looked like. Hell, with a bunch like that somebody's just got to suspect *something.* They'd give us the shake down at the border just to be smart. So that was it. And I was out of a band. And just when we were promoting the Cotillion album."

Ronnie tried to recruit Biscuit Boy and Atamniuk for a new band he was scrambling to get together. But they'd been through five different versions of the Hawks in only a few months, and they decided to stick with the castoff crew. Besides, after the Fillmore East the boys in the band were beginning to think about their own independence. Crowbar was out on its own: their belated parting gift from Ronnie was their name.

"Those boys," he told a friend one day in frustration, after thinking of his latest ex-band, "could fuck up a crowbar in fifteen seconds."

Within months Richard Newell had recorded his own solo album, *Official Music,* for Daffodil Records, the label Ronnie had set up with Frank Davies and Ritchie Yorke. With or without Ronnie, it seemed at first that Crowbar had a real chance of making it. It had been shaped with The Band in mind: a collection of soloists, personalities and characters which, somehow, would coalesce around a central notion. The only problem with Crowbar, aside from mixed critical reaction, was that while the collection of individuals was certainly in place (although like Heraclitus' river, Crowbar was permanently in flux), there was no real focus, aside from Newell's driving blues. "Corrina, Corrina," the band's first single, was a solid hit across Canada. For a while the missing focus didn't matter, as Crowbar soared along on lots of great publicity, piano-player Kelly Jay's innate ebullience and Newell's hard-edged harp playing. But when Larry Atamniuk thought he'd have a better chance of making it with the much-hyped American band, Seatrain, Newell — by nature a soloist and not a boss — was given the job of making Crowbar work. It was a job he didn't want. He left Crowbar and settled, as The Band did before him, in

Woodstock. Ironically, it seemed for a while that Ronnie might have been instrumental in creating yet another band, the Full Tilt Boogie Band. After Janis Joplin's fatal drug overdose, her band had returned to Woodstock and was looking around for a singer. The thought was that the Biscuit Boy might be it. Again, Albert Grossman was on the scene, as Ronnie knew he'd be, trying to get Biscuit to sign with him. Instead, Newell came back to Toronto to record on his own.

Ronnie's decision not to sign earlier with Grossman, like his decision to fire Crowbar, and like so many key decisions to turn down a promising offer at exactly the moment when the elusive big time was close, led several of Ronnie's closest friends to worry that in fact he might be frightened by success.

"Every time he's had the big chance, he's avoided it," one of the Hawk's pals told me in the early spring of 1970. "He tells everyone it's because of his kids. Or Wanda. But I don't think that's it. I know what everyone thinks — that despite all his big talk, he can't handle it. I don't know. There may be something in that. But I've watched him. I don't think that's it at all. I think he's so goddamn ornery, or single-minded, or whatever you want to call it, he'll only do it his way. Shit, he's seen it all. He doesn't want to gamble on it. He wants success guaranteed, and until that comes along he's going to do what he *wants* to do."

The Le Coq D'Or was Hawkins's home throughout most of the sixties. Bill Bullicon, the bright, young club manager running the Le Coq D'Or for his parents, decided to bring in black rhythm 'n' blues bands to attract a harder-drinking audience. Ronnie warned him that he would "get all the big-time pimps and hookers from Detroit." Ronnie insisted, "I'm not prejudiced, but that's what's going to happen. You know the way whores like to drink together. You're gonna find you've got more stabbing and knifing than you know what to do with." Nevertheless, Bullicon persisted, and in May 1970 Ronnie was out of the very club which he'd nurtured and which for a decade in turn had nurtured him along with some of rock's best bands. Finding a new place wasn't hard. He simply marched down the street to the Friars, managed by Gord Joste, one of the Le Coq's former managers. Josie was only too happy to open up the unused loft over the Friars for the biggest draw in the city.

So Ronnie had a new home. The Nickelodeon, it was called. But it would not be as long lasting for him as the Le Coq D'Or had been.

It was a time of remarkable change for Hawkins, and intense pressure. Each piece of good news came with news that was bad. For every new direction taken he'd heard of one he *should* have taken. A few friends noticed he was drinking more and eating more. His weight was beginning to soar. Still, he was the Hawk. Rich, cigar-chompin', Rolls-drivin', woman-lovin' — the Hawk. Worry about Ronnie? Hell, if ever there was a man who could take care of himself, it was the Hawk, right? More and more he seemed to be the center of attention, Gordon Lightfoot's buddy, and Kris Kristofferson's. Everybody coming through town either stayed at Ronnie's or, failing that prestigious invitation, jammed with him at a club.

What outsiders couldn't see were all the pressures on him. The bills were coming in from the peace festival promotion, and for the $10,000 he spent on his round-the-world tour. Yorke's passage had been handled by the peace festival foundation via a Toronto travel office. But Ronnie had to pitch in some of his own money. The peace festival had become a disaster. Yorke had resigned a week after the two had returned home. And although Ronnie was never officially part of it, he kept getting questioned about its growing problems. Lennon, who'd supported his single so lavishly, had since renounced everything to do with the festival. Jann Wenner at *Rolling Stone* had also backed out.

Then there was his album. Its sales had stalled, although everyone around him was absolutely convinced it was the best thing he'd ever recorded. Ritchie Yorke, who'd become "an unofficial publicist," as Yorke put it, was absolutely certain that all Ronnie needed was one hit single. One American hit. "Imagine what he'd be like on the Carson show," Yorke would think, looking forward to the day he could become the Hawk's full-time press agent. "All those stories he could tell. Think about it. All we need is that one hit single."

But the timing wasn't right. The year 1970 saw the most remarkable period of Canadian pop music in history before the late 1980s — a blossoming foreseen by *Rolling Stone*, whose plans for a Canadian issue the year before had led to Yorke's piece on

Hawkins. The Guess Who dominated pop's Top 40 charts with "American Woman," "Hand Me Down World" and "No Time." Anne Murray had "Snowbird," and Gordon Lightfoot could be heard with "If You Could Read My Mind." There was even a string of one-hit wonders such as Edward Bear's "You, Me and Mexico," the Poppy Family's "Which Way You Goin' Billy" and Mashmakhan's "As the Years Go By." Blood, Sweat & Tears, Joni Mitchell and Neil Young all had hit albums, too. But with the possible exception of Blood, Sweat & Tears, these hits were decidedly "white" sounding, in direct contrast to the funkiness of Ronnie's "Down in the Alley." It seemed he had the right record, but at the wrong time.

This didn't keep GRT, a hustling new Canadian label, from wanting a part of the Ronnie Hawkins legend, however. It leased the album from Ronnie's own company, which had the Canadian rights, gave it a different cover and included two additional tracks. Ross Reynolds, GRT's young president, knew that almost every other Canadian label had had a shot at selling the Hawk, but this album looked as if it might provide the breakthrough the earlier ones had not. Like everyone else, Reynolds was disappointed when it didn't take off.

And Ronnie began to brood about it. What he needed, he started thinking, was someone he could build an entirely new band around. In the past few years he'd been using up musicians the way a skyscraper goes through lightbulbs. In a way, he'd become his own worst enemy. As soon as any one group was good enough they started thinking that, hey, they're the next Band, and they'd split. So he'd have to start again, with an entirely new set of players.

But where could he find a new focus? He remembered someone he'd met when he was with his old buddy Keith James, the deejay out at station CHED in Edmonton — Tommy Banks. Banks was a one-man show around Alberta: an arranger, bandleader, local hero. He had a bit of a rep for finding good musicians. So Ronnie flew out to Edmonton and told Banks he was looking for "another Garth Hudson" type. The name David Foster came up — the keyboard genius who was working with Banks.

These days, to get to David Foster, you must make the appropriate appointments with the appropriate public relations folks. Although he's thinking more and more about the movie business, he's been, as one critic described him, "the dominant commercial producer of the 1980s."

Foster has always had a remarkably keen sixth sense for grabbing the main chance — for doing exactly what should be done. When Ronnie showed up in Edmonton, talking to Tommy Banks about forming a new band, David Foster knew what he had to do, and made himself available.

"It all happened so fast," Foster says. "Ronnie blew through town and kind of zeroed in on me. He always needed that guy who knew too much, so that Ronnie could get what he needed from him then eventually fire him because he knew too much. That's exactly what happened to me. But at the time he turned up I was looking to further my career. I thought that moving to Toronto with Ronnie Hawkins would be a good move."

"Ronnie actually went to Edmonton to get a band called Privilege to be the next Hawks," says B.J. Cook, the Vancouver singer who was to end up in his band. Ronnie heard that band for five minutes and realized it would be a big mistake. So David Foster — being an opportunist and a pretty smart cookie — started thinking this was his chance: that Ronnie was going to go a lot further than Tommy Banks at that time. The irony is that David was a complete jazz freak who dabbled in contemporary music. He produced the band Chicago because they were jazz-oriented. So David and Ronnie struck up a deal and David headed back to Vancouver."

To Ronnie, Foster was going to be his next Garth Hudson, his resident Musical Genius.

"The way I figured it, I would let David choose the musicians for my new band according to their musical ability, while I would go by their personalities and how they looked and what they could do. You've got to put a team together that can get along, so you need the cats who can handle it. Music may be the main thing, but right behind it are the personalities of the people playing. 'Cause you've got to mix with your audience. I've taken less great pickers because they had better personalities than the cats who were really musical but were really weird with people. So with David, we started auditioning — I must've auditioned about four or five black singers — and doing the same old bit I've always done with the Hawks. All of my bands. It started coming together really good, too, but it was coming together really uptown. David could write great harmonies and these cats could really sing but, shit, it was a long, long way from good old rock 'n' roll or rockabilly. Still, it was coming together really good. It sounded really good. We just needed a few more ingredients."

But as much as he tried, he was finding it increasingly difficult to work with David. "Play it simple, son," he kept saying. "Simple, goddamn it, not too many notes." But it was impossible for David Foster *not* to play notes, *not* to want to stretch it out. Finally, out of frustration, Ronnie gave him one of Chuck Berry's collections of greatest hits so he could hear how Johnny Johnson, the pianist on Berry's great sessions, did it. To Ronnie, all great rock 'n' roll piano playing could be traced back to the kind of boogie woogie Fats Waller played. To Ronnie's ears, Johnny Johnson was an extension of that. That how he wanted all of his piano players — Will "Pop" Jones, Scott Cushnie, Stan Szelest, Richard Manuel, everyone — to play it.

"What they were doing was good music, with all those close harmonies and shit," says Ronnie. "I liked the music, and we tried it out, but it wasn't working for the people. I can tell by looking at an audience if something's going over or not and no matter how good this stuff was it wasn't going over. So I went and bought that goddamn Jerry Lee Lewis record and said, 'David, listen to this!'

"Well, he listened and came back, saying 'This is primitive. It's like first-grade piano.'

"'Well, do you think you can go back to the first grade and copy this son of a bitch note-for-note in a month?'

"He said, 'I can do it in a night.'

"Well, when David came back he said that it was more physical than musical but he finally got into it and realized that it was saying something. Still, he couldn't do it. That's when I realized we needed another piano player as well and we went out and got Dwayne Ford. Ford wasn't exactly the piano player we needed but he was closer to it than David."

Although originally from Edmonton, Ford was in Vancouver playing with bassist Steve Pugsley when right in the middle of a set, Pugsley got a phone call from Foster asking him if he'd like to play for the Hawk. "Green with envy," Ford said goodbye to his buddy and caught the bus back to Edmonton, thinking from there he'd try to get into the Berklee music school in Boston which had helped shape so many pop arrangers and composers. So he was in Edmonton, mulling over his future, when he, too, got the call from Foster.

"When I was twenty years old and hadn't been exposed to too many famous people, well, the Hawk was *the* name," Ford remembers. "He was a monster. I was so young and impressionable at the time; he really did a number on me."

Unaware of what was going on, B.J. Cook was cooling her heels but desperate to go on to something new. "Now I was back in Vancouver working at a place called Diamond Jim's. When I worked a bar I always knew who came in and where they sat. So I was on stage checking out everybody when I saw David Foster come in and sit at the band's table. I wondered what he was doing there.

"'Looking for a girl singer,' he told me. He was going to Toronto to put a band together for Ronnie Hawkins. 'Do you know one?' he asked.

"'What about me?' I asked.

"'Yeah, sure,' he said.

"But that's not all there was to it. You see, at this time I was having this weird thing about Ronnie Hawkins. Ronnie Hawkins had started to appear to me in dreams. I didn't even know what the guy looked like. But I was so in tune with the Beatles at that point that I thought this guy must be pretty amazing to have one of the Beatles stay at his house.

"So when Foster asked me to join Ronnie's new band there was no question in my mind. I took the job. Well, David told Ronnie he'd got a pistol, the perfect woman for him. She'd had an illegitimate child — my daughter, born in 1959, was in Victoria at the time, with my parents — she was a real slut. 'We call her Bonnie Banger in Victoria,' David told him. 'You'll like her for sure.'"

B.J. — Bonnie Jean, although no one ever calls her that — was a find for Ronnie. She could sing. She looked good. Better, she was downright earthy. "They met me at the Edmonton airport," B.J. remembers, "and right off Ronnie said, 'You can move in with this long-peckered piano player or you can come and stay with me in the trailer.'

"Well, I took one look at this mountain of a man standing there. I said, 'No thanks, I'll go with David Foster.' "David was terrified. He was twenty years old. I had just had my twenty-eighth birthday. So I moved in with David where I knew I was safe. We were not on a dating basis at this point, we were just friends.

"The day after, Ronnie had a rehearsal. Now you have to understand I didn't know his music or anything about this guy except that he was somewhat of a legend. I knew the The Band's *Big Pink* album but I didn't know about Ronnie's song, 'Forty Days.'

"We rehearsed at the Embers in Edmonton. The band consisted of Dwayne Ford, Hugh Brockie, a guitarist, a drummer named Reno who never made it, Steve Pugsley, David Foster, Ronnie Hawkins and me. I did a couple of rock 'n' roll numbers — Aretha Franklin's 'Baby I Love You,' and 'Good Golly Miss Molly' — to prove to Ronnie that I was qualified. He loved it and I was in. He thought I was a hip broad and he liked me.

"Now it was his turn to sing. I was going to hear the legend for the first time. So I sat back. Ronnie kicked in with 'Old Man from the Forest.' Within one second, he'd got his pants right off, down to the ankles. I fell on the floor laughing, of course. There he was, the legend. Balls to the breeze, singing away, everybody laughing.

"'I thought I'd better show you this big bugger right off the bat so you know what you're getting yourself into,' he said. 'If you're going to come on the road you got to be prepared.'

"He does everything to test you right from the beginning," B.J. says with a deep laugh. "If I had screamed and run out of the room, I'd have been gone in two minutes. That would have been the end of it.

"We had six weeks of rehearsal in Edmonton, warming up for Toronto, and in those six weeks Ronnie was the instigator in getting Keith James, Terry Tyler Pitts and others to try to get me away from David. Ronnie doesn't like when you're with someone else. He wanted me to be a free agent. To be qualified to hang out with him meant I shouldn't be involved with a band member. It gave me no freedom.

"But by then, I was in love for the first time in my life, really, really in love. David was the only thing I could think of, I crawled into the sack with this beautiful young boy every night but he wouldn't sleep with me. I was singing with a legend, going on the road. I was twenty-eight years old and I looked good. I had the world by the ass, ready to go.

"But then Ronnie had this incredible party," remembers B.J. "He came to David and me — and although we were a couple by this time, Ronnie was still trying real hard to break us up — and said that he wanted us to come to the party and that no one else in the band was invited. We thought we were privileged characters.

"All kinds of people were at the party, sitting around drinking cocktails. Ronnie even had a Japanese houseboy serving lobster. It was the birthday of his lawyer friend, John Finlay. So when we walked into this party we saw all kinds of people who'd been at the club in Edmonton, about thirty in all, but people we knew really well. It's all very proper. About an hour or so into it a joint went around. I even talked David, who was the world's straightest guy, into taking a couple of tokes off this huge joint. We were sitting on the couch by the stereo, grooving on the music, being real social, talking to everybody.

"All of a sudden, Ronnie left the room. He came back a minute later back wearing a towel. He said, 'There's a rumor going around that this friend of mine has a bigger dick than me. Girls, I want you all to line up on this side of the room and we're going to have you judge the contest.'

"We were all laughing and like little obedient girls we stood against a wall and watched for what we thought was going to be a hilarious floor show — and of course it turned out to be just that.

"Ronnie walked out with this big towel wrapped around him," B.J. remembers vividly. "Behind him came this young guy, a kind of hunched over, nondescript kind of guy, a Terry Tyler Pitts protégé or something, also wearing a towel.

"Ronnie said, 'On the count of three we'll pull off the towels and girls, I want you to let me know who's got the biggest dick here.'

"I was laughing, high, roaring. After 'one-two-three' Ronnie ripped his towel off. The kid still had his towel on — kind of shy kind of embarrassed. And of course, with Ronnie there was this huge bush of hair, an enormous set of balls and a soft average-sized penis — a little small penis poking out from this huge bush. O course, I laughed. The next thing I knew Ronnie was turning around to this kid saying, 'Come on, son, you challenged me, let's see.' The kid whipped off his towel and there was the world's largest penis hanging between this boy's legs. I mean, it was like a donkey's. Unreal.

"I thought this was the end of it. I was on the floor in a fit of laughter thinking this was the funniest thing I'd ever seen. Ronnie put on a strobe light and started dancing. He'd had too much to drink, I think — although maybe he wasn't drinking then because he had that little houseboy feeding him fish and he was exercising and very health-conscious — and he came to sit beside me.

"I was terrified," says B.J. quietly. "At this point, I knew something was happening. I had one man sitting near me who'd offered me thirty-five thousand dollars for I don't know what. Another guy had offered me a brand new Jag. All these men in all the weeks I'd been with David Foster were offering me anything to get away from him. They could not understand why I was with this twenty-year-old piano player.

"Now Ronnie had also brought a couple of hookers to the party, who were being very sweet and nice until he clapped his hands twice. Then they ripped their clothes off and started going down on each other and feeling each other up, sucking each other's tits.

"I'd never done this or seen it before in my life. I was this little broad from Victoria. And there's David, having smoked marijuana for the second time in his life, going 'heh, heh, heh.'

"I said to him at this point, 'Whatever you do, don't remove your clothes, because if you do you'll watch me being gang banged by everyone in here.' As the party progressed, people started taking off their clothes and getting into it. David, John Finlay and I had our clothes on but everyone else was naked. Ronnie walked up to a guy who had passed out and waved his penis in front of him to make sure he was asleep. He kept saying that he could make these people do anything. 'It's like a circus and I'm the ringmaster. Watch this.' And he'd yell out instructions for someone to do something to do someone and they would do it. I just felt I'd been set up. I was angry and scared. Really scared. But Ronnie kept coming over to reassure me, 'I can do anything.'

The strobe light went back on. Ronnie continued to dance and everybody was clapping. Next thing I knew, he was on his hands and knees crawling towards me. I had big bell-bottom pants on and boots with zippers up the inside. He reached up and started pulling down a zipper. At that point I didn't care who I was dealing with. I grabbed Ronnie's hand and said, 'Listen, you fat fuck, the only time I ever perform for you is onstage, so go fuck yourself.'

"He jumped up, turned on the lights and went into the bedroom. He was just furious with me."

"Anyhow, the day came when we had to get to Toronto. David Foster said he could drive the bus. Well, Ronnie went to sleep and eight hours later David still hadn't got the bus turned around. He went into a ditch. He was terrified that Ronnie would wake up and find out we hadn't gotten anywhere. He wasn't even out of the driveway."

To Foster, being with the Hawk, like driving the bus, was one great adventure — until reality set in. "When we arrived in Toronto, Ronnie told us he had a contract with the Le Coq D'Or, and that's where we would be staying, too. We had to pay some rent even though the rooms had no heat in them. As I recall, we made $2,500 a week for the entire band. Ronnie took half. The rest of us got the other half."

Dwayne Ford, however, was awed by Hawkins: "Ronnie kept saying, 'Don't worry, we've got plenty of room for you to stay in boys, plenty of room.' Well, that plenty of room was above the club where the offices and the gym were. We slept in the boxing ring, But so what? At that age it's like an adventure. It wasn't that bad. Of course, we bitched and grumbled a little bit. But the excitement of the whole thing was incredible."

"Ronnie had told *me* that we were going to live in luxury apartments right on Yonge Street," B.J. says. "As it turned out these 'luxury apartments' were the Le Coq D'Or offices. My neighbor was Heavy Andrews." This was Ronnie's triumphant return to his old stomping grounds. He didn't have a name yet for this latest group, so he called them the Fayetteville University Collegiate Klan (F.U.C.K.). Their opening night was classic Hawkins. Champagne, laughs and good times for everyone. *This* band, Ronnie kept telling everyone who'd listen, *this* band was going to be the next great one. Better than The Band, bigger than the

Beatles. 'To get the group I've got now,' he told me, 'I auditioned thousands of kids, just thousands.'"

Yes sir, he was in fine form. Atlantic Records had picked up the option for a second album. Maybe the combination of John Lennon and "Down in the Alley" hadn't worked, but there was still the promise of the big time just down the road; and sometimes, for him, the promise was as good as the real thing.

Better than that, he was being noticed again. "Ronnie Hawkins back at Le Coq D'Or with style," ran the page-wide headline in the Toronto *Telegram*. By then the band was getting into the entire Hawkins mythology. If he could be larger than life, well, shoot, they could be too. B.J. in particular went for it. With David Foster never far from her side, she could be her own version of the Hawk.

"Well, honey," she asked me breathlessly after the first night I'd heard her. "Did that get it up for you?"

Ronnie thought David was a genius, B.J. recalls. "Ronnie can charm the pants off anyone and David wasn't immune to that. Ronnie stroked him and said all the right things to him. I loved it. I watched Ronnie manage David at that time. But David had definite ideas about what he wanted, where he was going and what he was doing with his life. He was very rebellious. He didn't want to play 'Forty Days.'"

Foster admits that he thought he knew it all back then. "When you're a kid you can't be told anything and it makes it difficult for anybody you work for. Now that I'm a full-fledged adult I understand that. I didn't then. Now I do what he did then. When I get someone for studio work, I want someone I can work with. That's the most important thing.

"I had my classical music training up until I was sixteen years old, but then I started playing rock 'n' roll. Ronnie wasn't the first basic rocker I'd played for. I'd been with Chuck Berry, too. I hated Chuck Berry's music then. It's taken me all these years to really understand what it was all about and to understand what Ronnie's music was all about. To a trained musician, Chuck's music all sounds the same. Every single song sounds the same. And they *do* sound the same. Yet in a way they aren't the same."

The problem was, the Hawk didn't know what to do with his resident genius. "David was driving me crazy but I could see he was going to be somebody. I told B.J., 'You'd better get knocked up and marry this cat 'cause he's going to make some money some day.' But they didn't know that I was getting ready to fire his ass. I'd given up on this band. I play for the people, and this band wasn't playing for the people."

Music wasn't the only problem: control was a problem as well. More and more, B.J. and David were running the show — Ronnie's show. More and more, Ronnie felt he was losing control. In Ronnie's vision of things, a band had only one leader.

Dwayne Ford could see how the power struggle was beginning to pull the band apart. "By this time B.J. and David were stronger together as a unit then Ronnie was. And I think Ronnie might have felt threatened by that. So one night he chewed David and B.J. out for something. He made them feel really small. He can do that to you. As I watched I felt sorry for David; I don't feel sorry for him now, but I did then. I think he was bored with the whole thing by then. It was exciting at the beginning for him to put the band together and to rehearse it, but he was a jazz musician and rockabilly just didn't challenge him enough. It was one-chord songs or two-chord songs. There never was a thing like a flat fifth. We'd be on up stage, maybe doing a duet on the piano in the middle of a song. He'd be playing the bass and I'd be playing the top and he'd look at me and say how unexciting the music was. To the audience it was probably very exciting, but not to him."

"So one day," B.J. remembers, "we had a meeting at the Le Coq D'Or gym and Ronnie said, 'Listen, son, you might play like Beethoven but you look like a cadaver on stage.' David left. He had just been fired. Then Ronnie turned to me and said, 'David Foster wants your knowledge and he loves the fact that you are a great fuck, but if you go with this long-peckered piano player you'll never be a singer. He doesn't give a shit about you. But if you stay with me I'll make sure you're a singer.' But I was in love so I chose David Foster.

"As for David, he went berserk. He'd never been unemployed before. I called Doug Riley, the jingle king. I called everyone I knew in this town, because he couldn't get work. David was all set to get a day job and we were lying in bed thinking about this when we decided, 'Fuck 'em, let's put our own band together.' The group was Skylark and it was the start for David Foster.

"Ronnie was very gracious to me, though," B.J. continues. "The hardest thing I've ever had to do was tell him I was leaving because we'd always loved each other so much — from day one, we'd always been connected. It was very painful to leave him. I don't know if we were in love with each other or just loved each other. It was difficult because I'd never connected as well with anybody in my life. We saw and understood things the same way. I've never met anyone like that. We stayed in touch with Ronnie, but Skylark had a hit and we moved to Los Angeles."

Without B.J., Ronnie figures, David Foster might still be in Vancouver. "Well, that B.J., she's a yapper, you know. A talker. David was as green as Ricky Danko when he came to my band but she's got him out to Los Angeles and she's on the phone about him twenty hours a day and she got his ass going. And how."

What B.J. and Foster both found out later is that while you can quit his band you don't ever completely sever your ties with the Hawk himself. B.J. came back to sing with him on occasion. Years later, Foster would realize that some of the tricks and tactics he was using in the recording studio he'd learned while playing with the Hawks in the old Le Coq D'Or, on Toronto's Yonge Street strip.

XIII

JESUS, JERRY LEE, NOT THE LOUIS QUATORZE

Flying to London, the Hawk Parties with the Killer and Is Tailed by the KGB

RONNIE RARELY MISSES OUT on anyone new or different — not in his town at least. He started listening to Gordon Lightfoot in the sixties when the singer-songwriter was still mostly making the rounds of Toronto clubs. "Hell, Gordon hadn't even recorded yet when I met him," says Ronnie. "He came into the Le Coq D'Or several times with Ian and Sylvia, when they had just signed with Albert Grossman. They were mostly just song writers then. Grossman had Peter, Paul and Mary and he was getting songs for them from Ian and Sylvia, Gordon and eventually Bob Dylan. Then I'd go over and listen to Gordon when he was down the street at Steele's Tavern. I'd taken people out of my bar when I'd have to break and we'd go down and hear Gordon. Mel Tillis was around then, and I'd take him down."

Eventually the pair started hanging out together, Toronto's odd couple in their way: the big, call-your-bluff Hawkins with the more introverted all-Canadian country boy from Orillia. Lightfoot wrote "Home from the Forest" at Ronnie's place. The Hawk recorded it; Ronnie was a fan, pure and simple. In fact, at one point he was so turned on by a new batch of songs Gordon had written that he phoned "Cowboy" Ray Thornton, the attorney-general of Arkansas, late one evening — he even got him out of bed — just so that Gordon could play him the new songs. "Listen to these," Ronnie bellowed down the line. The next thing Ray heard was a one-man concert by folk music's rising star.

Lightfoot, for his part, thought the Hawk was fascinating and wrote "The Silver Cloud Talkin' Blues" for Ronnie, a long and complete account of how the Hawk bought a brand new Rolls. Talk about being a legend in his own time.

"But he used to drive Gordon crazy at times," says Cathy Evelyn Smith, who was living with Lightfoot then. "Ronnie was forever trying to steal Gordon's women and Gordon knew it. I remember Gordon would go away on one of his canoe trips and Ronnie would call.

"'C'mon up,' he'd tell me. 'Goddamn, I can chase you around the house all night.'

"It got to the point where before Gordon would go on a trip he'd phone Ronnie asking him to leave me alone."

As Ronnie says: "I was always short on money and talent, but I was always long on nerve. Well, Cathy would come up and tell how tired she was of being den mother to Canada's leading poet. Gordon was being temperamental, I guess. He was going through changes like everyone else does. Now, at the time I didn't know what was wrong. Gordon wasn't doing his job or whatever and she was stepping out. And a lot of those young kids in my band — 'Cocaine' Carl Mathers was one of them — were extremely interested in her. But why not? When your dick gets hard, your brain goes soft.

"Anyway, around 1975 or 1976, we had to got out on the road, and Cathy followed us because she was crazy about Carl. She was carrying Gordon's credit card. Here the rest of the band was sleeping four in a room, and she and Carl had penthouse suites. Or something almost as good. They must've spent $20,000 on that trip and I was starting to worry that Gordon was going to think I was carting his old lady around the country.

"So I told her she couldn't do what she was doing, she had to go back. Well, she was always a gutsy lady. She left us and we started driving on our way to Calgary. And there she was, standing on the side of the road, hitchhiking. And you know, she got to Calgary before we did.

"I liked her, still do. She had paid some terrible dues in her time. She hung around The Band all the time, and got pregnant. She was terribly in love with Levon, but she ended up with Richard Manuel because he needed a lot of help and she likes mothering people. Later on, Richard called me after The Band had broken up and he said he'd gotten himself back together.

"'I knew you were great when you were with me,' I told him. 'But I've since seen you when you weren't so great, because of all those goddamn bad habits of yours.'

"Well, he said he hadn't touched a thing in months. Goddamn, his nose was running into his mouth. He really did need help. Richard needed Cathy, I guess. And she needed him. For a while there she ended up being his nurse — like she did with John Belushi."

After a while Ronnie was starting to hear about another up-and-coming songwriter — a lanky devil of a ladies' man with hooded eyes and a bear rug for a voice who was country music's only Rhodes scholar — Kris Kristofferson.

"Kris first arrived at the Riverboat in Toronto, when he was getting really heavy with 'Me and Bobby McGee,'" remembers Bernie Fiedler, who opened and closed the 'Boat and in between saw most of the sixties generation of songwriters, from Joni Mitchell to Arlo Guthrie, peer out into the narrow room from its little stage. "And Ronnie started coming around back then. I remember we'd all go back and hang out at Lightfoot's house. There was a real little clique developing at the time. Eventually, Kris started going out and staying with Hawkins, so he could get away and write in the little cabin Ronnie had."

"Ronnie was already a legend when I first met him," says Kristofferson. "I'd heard his name mainly in connection with the bands that he had — with The Band and with all the guys who'd been with him and who'd worked with Janis in her last band, the Full Tilt Boogie Band. It seemed like he was just Albert Grossman's farm club. Here was this rock 'n' roller from Arkansas who'd gone up to Canada and carved out a little empire up there. How many people have had Robbie Robertson in their band?

"Well, there are some people you hit it off with right away and Ronnie was one. He just loved life so much. Christ, he was driving a Rolls Royce and everything he did and said was funny. He'd have us come over to his club where he had these guys working for what he said was five cents a night. 'You can't get musicians to work anymore,' he'd say. 'I give them forty bucks a week, man.'

"So we'd stay at his place out in Mississauga," continues Kristofferson, "and listen to him tell all these tales about John and Yoko staying out there. I know there had to have been some down times for him. Some sad times. I know that there's times when he's probably foul — that he's a grizzly old wolverine, but whenever we were together he was a silver-tongued devil.

"I once told a guy that was playing bass for me at the time, Terry Paul, 'Man, you should just follow Ronnie around with a tape recorder because he's got the most colorful language of anybody I've ever heard.' He'd walk up to me with some little girl he'd introduce me to in his club and say, 'Look at her Kris, she's clean as an angel's drawers and sweet as a mother's love.' Just listen to that — 'clean as an angel's drawers' — I have no idea where he gets all that stuff.'"

"Now right off I could tell Kris had a good mind," Ronnie says. "He was blessed with a good cerebellum, he was. More than anything he was a real lady killer. Goddamn. Women would follow him everywhere. I knew I could get a lot of pussy following this fella around. I remember this one time this actress came up to visit him. This was before he met up with Rita Coolidge whom I already knew when she was singing backup with the Mad Dogs and Englishmen tour. I wrote a song about this ol' girl. It's called 'Patricia':

I had me a woman in Memphis
Had me one in New Orleans
I even made love to a twelve-year-old Cajun queen.
I've been higher than the mountain tops
I seen World War Three
I once slept with a Salem witch
In Sixteen Forty-Three
I thought I'd seen and done everything that there was to do
But I know I was just an infant child the morning I had you.

"Well, this Patricia was something, I tell you. She had a big job in the record business. And I'd met her and asked her to come up to our place in Mississauga. Well, Kris was there at the time so I fixed her up with him.

"So they went into my cabin together that evening. Well, eight hours went by, then twelve hours — then twenty-four hours. They hadn't come out. They hadn't eaten. Nothing. On the second morning I said, 'Goddamn, they may be dead. I'd better go out there. She may have killed Kris by now.' So I went out and there's Kris yawnin' and stretchin' and sayin', 'I gotta have a drink of Jack Daniels.' But she came out of there looking like she'd been gang raped by Communist China.

"'Pat, you okay?' I asked her.

"'Reckon I can come back next week?' she asked.

"I don't know what he did in there, but I knew it was pretty good. 'Kris,' I told him, 'Kris, you're a pretty good songwriter. And you're a pretty smart guy. But you're in the wrong business to make money. I'm going to show you how to make money, man. Those women are going to pay a lot of money for your special treatment, man.' Hell, I wanted to manage him.

"But besides the women," Ronnie continues, "all he was doing was writing. These were the days when he was scared to death to play. Back then they had to trick Kris into playing. He saw himself as a writer so he thought he couldn't sing, couldn't do this or that. To get him to record they had to tell him it was only a demo session. Then he'd come in straight and play and sing and do everything right. I know others like him. It's a complex thing only entertainers know about. They want to entertain so badly they get scared. I've gone through it all my life. I still get butterflies in my stomach and a little nauseous. You worry that you can't go on.

"Now at this time, Kris was known mostly as a writer, so he wasn't booked into many clubs. He had this little circuit of coffee houses he'd work in. Still he was worried about everything.

"'Kris,' I told him, 'it doesn't make a difference how bad you sing, or how bad you do this or that. If they had Mario Lanza in the Riverboat singing your songs they'd throw bottles at him. They want to hear you. It's your image, it's your thing. It doesn't make any difference. You're Kris Kristofferson.' I had to work on him for months."

But as much as Hawkins was watching Kristofferson, his guest was watching him. Left alone, Kristofferson could disappear into himself, dark and brooding. He'd been so desperate to be recognized as a songwriter that's he cleaned ashtrays in Nashville recording studios just to be involved. Now there he was, staying with his exact opposite. The legend. Larger than life, thought Kris, as easy with socialites as with shitkickers.

Kristofferson wrote about Hawkins, his ear in tune with the Hawk's language and his unique set of social graces: "A formidable businessman, he has the instinct of a born horse-trader, more into the joy of dealing than the outcome. He's generous to a fault, and he could retire on the bread he's scattered bailing various and different friends out of various and different kinds of trouble."

What Kristofferson had found in Mississauga was a world that was absolutely right for Ronnie, a place where he'd found some measure of peace after years of non-stop turmoil. After the failures — the festival, the Cotillion album — here was a season of calm weather. So Kris took it all in. He sat back, watched the Hawkins clan and wrote:

"Cruising around checking his traps in his chauffeur-driven Rolls Royce in Levis and cowboy hat, cigar clamped in his teeth like a smiling challenge, rolling down the window to sing a few bars of 'Forty Days' at the smiling young snuggy on the sidewalk. Until showtime. All spaces filled with stories. A dangerous fighter, a disarming fool, a loyal friend. One minute he looks as deadly as the devil, the next he's smiling as innocent as an Arkansas school boy."

By now the "school boy" had closed the book on one chapter of his life. He'd left the Le Coq D'Or for the last time, and was at the Nickelodeon. And there he was like a magnet for every star, every would-be star and everyone who just wanted to hang out.

"One night Kris was supposed to be up at the Riverboat," remembers Ronnie. "He was really hot at the time, and both shows were sold out. But he'd been drinking so he walked in and said, 'Folks, sorry, but I've been drinking too much. We're all going down to see the Hawk at the Nickelodeon. Give 'em all their money back, Bernie.' Now, Bernie had a Mona Lisa grin on his face when he heard that. Well, they all ended up at our club. Then Gordon

Lightfoot came in. I think he may have had a cocktail or two by then — he doesn't drink now, you know — and he ended up on drums. David Clayton Thomas came in later the same night."

To the late Bernadette Andrews, then a columnist writing in the Toronto *Telegram*, the scene was straight out of Las Vegas: "It could have been the good old days at the Sands Hotel," she noted, "when the 'clan' used to arrive at every Sinatra opening and there would be Dean and Sammy 'spontaneously' clowning it up, gratis."

"Racket time," Ronnie yelled from the stage, as the audience hooted. Since this was also bikini contest night, he beckoned all "the sweet young *hors d'oeuvres* to show off their money-makers." In this case, the *hors d'oeuvres* just happened to be from the nearby Lori Lane's Le Strip.

"Gordon joined one girl on the dance floor and even made an attempt to join her in nudity," reported Andrews. "His lace shirt was off to his navel, but Kristofferson just sat on the edge of the stage with his cowboy boots out, long, in front of him."

"Gordon Lightfoot and Kris Kristofferson go electric," shouted Ronnie, joking: "It took two hundred dollars worth of dope to do this."

Then Kris started to sing his quiet ballad, "Me and Bobby McGee."

Only a few months later, his life now centered around session-singer Rita Coolidge, Kristofferson found himself one more time borrowing Ronnie's mike at the Nickelodeon. Coolidge's Massey Hall concert with Marc Benno and the Dixie Flyers had been cancelled due to poor ticket sales. It seemed Kris's days of inviting girlfriends back to Ronnie's cabin were over when they sang "Help Me Make It Through the Night." To Bruce Kirkland, then with the Toronto *Star*, it seemed that "they sang it for each other, with the audience like some collective peeping tom, but sharing the magic."

"The club was really rockin' by then," continues Ronnie. "On another night, I remember we had on stage at one time Kenny Rogers and the First Edition, David Clayton Thomas, Gordon, Ian and Sylvia and Frank Zappa. Well, you know what happened? The manager of the club came up to me and asked me to have them stop playing so they could sell some drinks.

"'Damn it,' I told him, 'you couldn't buy this much talent at once for a million dollars.' I mean, nobody had seen anything like this in their life! I wanted to build this club up with the college crowd. We weren't far from Ryerson. 'Jesus,' I told him. 'You couldn't buy this much free publicity for a million dollars.'"

Around the time he was causing a ruckus on Yonge Street, Ronnie was also shaking up the London, Ontario, city council. After years of playing for other club owners in the area, in the mid-sixties he'd opened his own club, Campbell's, in London. But in the early seventies, when the city council announced it was expropriating the land for the new city hall, Campbell's had to move. And Ronnie knew exactly where it should go — smack dab into the middle of the city's old city hall which, he and his restaurant manager, Leo Sitter, found out, could be had for under $300,000.

Although it was only indirectly connected with a rock 'n' roller buying the old city hall, the sale of the old site was delayed by a fit of aldermanic furor. Finally, in July 1971, it was settled; Ronnie got the old building for $275,000. Later, friends and journalists would say that it was the beginning of his troubles. But at the time he felt it was a good deal. With a brand-new Campbell's he now owned his own base of operations away from Toronto.

Meanwhile, Kristofferson's first album, *Border Lord*, had become a hit for newly established Monument Records and its chief producer, Fred Foster. Foster had produced Roy Orbison's boomingly big sixties hits. "Fred's a good man with a good heart," Kristofferson thought, "and so's Ronnie." He wanted to put the two together. Ronnie, one of Orbison's contemporaries, was sure ready for the kind of international success Foster had provided Orbison. Foster listened to what Kristofferson had to say. Ronnie Hawkins? Foster knew about Ronnie's Roulette material. Sometimes he felt he was the only one old enough to remember that period; even so, with the success he'd had with Orbison, Ray Stevens and even Willie Nelson, there was nothing wrong with that.

"So I thought, well, I'll go out and check this out," says Foster. "Besides, I'd been hearing things about what was happening up there — nothing specific, just things, from all over." Yes sir, the legend at work.

Well, after all the hassles Foster had in getting from Nashville to Toronto in those days he found that the bouncer at the Nickelodeon wasn't going to let him in.

221

"Look," said Fred Foster, "I've come all the way from Nashville to see Ronnie Hawkins. What do you mean you're not going to let me in?" Now, Foster wasn't all that thrilled having to leave home in the first place. As urbane and worldly a man as you'll find in or out of Nashville, he remains a southerner through and through. "You know how dumb the Yankees are?" he'll ask you. "Hell, they won the Civil War — and kept the *North*. That's dumb." So his patience with this big dumb northern bouncer had just run out and he snapped, "I *am* coming in. Go call Ronnie."

"I'm not disturbing him," returned the bouncer.

"Well, he's going to get disturbed, I damn well tell you that."

Just before they got into a serious fist fight, Ronnie suddenly appeared to cool things down between the two. By now Foster was getting more and more impressed with the Hawk's mystique. He'd heard stories. Jesus Christ, thought Foster, if that dumb-ass bouncer only knew the stories *he'd* heard, there'd be no fooling around at the door. Being on Yonge Street for as long as he had had given the Hawk, free and unwarranted, some of the strip's notoriety. Foster had heard about the time Ronnie had particularly impressed one of Heavy Andrews's desperado friends because the desperado thought Ronnie had had a guy bumped off. Ronnie hadn't, of course. It just happened that another ruffian had come to the Hawk asking for a favor. The ruffian said that he wanted a certain guy "dumped" because he was messing with the wrong women — namely the ruffian's very own woman. This ruffian thought Ronnie had the kind of connections that he didn't.

"Say no more," said Ronnie who, today, will admit to being "half drunk" at the time. "There's no goddamn problem."

What he meant was that, given enough time and the right approach, the aforementioned guy could be talked out of this liaison. It was the civilized approach. That night, however, the guy was bumped off for some entirely unrelated reason.

It mattered not a bit that Ronnie was in no way involved. The ruffian was mightily impressed. Ronnie tried to tell him he had nothing to do with it — that he had no such connections. But the ruffian wouldn't believe it. Ronnie was his hero and he'd remain his hero come what may.

Fred had also heard about the night that a Volkswagen was torched. As it happened, the Volks belonged to brothers who had been incorrectly informed by their sister that this singer named Ronnie Hawkins had impregnated her at his very own birthday party. To show their displeasure, these brothers had cruised by the Le Coq D'Or one night and had taken several shots as Ronnie happened to be walking out. The torching of the Volks was carried out by several of Ronnie's distant friends who in due time informed the brothers that not only hadn't Ronnie done anything naughty with their sister but that he'd never even met her.

Ronnie had become used to this swirl of danger about him. In truth, he was fascinated by the thieves, hustlers and assorted riff-raff who drifted through his clubs and was just as capable of asking them to come up on stage for a bow as any visiting rock star. Hell, it wasn't long before Ronnie was trying to talk Foster into a sweet little deal of their own. Foster would announce he was going to write a book about everyone he'd recorded, produced or otherwise dealt with. All of Nashville would be "mentioned." He would announce he was going to tell all — all about the sex, all about the drugs or any juicy combination of the two. What Ronnie would do "would be to go around to everyone involved and take donations for keeping their name *out* of the damn thing."

The more he heard Ronnie, the more he talked to Ronnie, the more Foster was convinced that he had the wildest, wooliest potential superstar he'd ever met.

"Give me a year," he told Ronnie, "and do what I tell you — and I'll give you a million dollars."

Well, now, Ronnie didn't need much more convincing than that, although he balked when Foster asked him to move to Nashville. "Wanda wouldn't like living in Nashville," he said. What he meant was that he really didn't want to leave home.

Recording the first album for Foster in Nashville without Wanda — it was released in 1972 as *Ronnie Hawkins: Rock 'n' Roll Resurrection* — became something of an event. The producer had lined up a who's who of Nashville session payers: Fred Carter, Grady Martin and Dave Kirby on guitars; bassist Tim Drummond; drummers Ken Buttrey and Jerry Carrigan; Stan Szelest on piano; percussionist Farrell Morris; David Briggs and Charlie McCoy both on organ, with McCoy doubling on harmonica; Peter Drake on steel guitar; a sax section with Boots Randolph, Norman Ray and William Puett; trumpeter Don Sheffield; as well as a string section and a small choir. Wagner would have felt comfortable with these numbers.

Now, Foster's approach to all this was to relax and let talent take over. As he watched from the control room, talent took over all right. It ran amok. The playing went this way and that and the songs weren't coming together. The crowds of visitors were making matters even more chaotic. Kris and Rita dropped in. A reporter from *Rolling Stone* wanted in. Chaos! Another night went by and still nothing was happening. Finally Foster exploded, kicked everyone not involved with the sessions out of the studio and tried to make some sense out of everything. He even posted a guard at the door.

But even when the *Resurrection* album was finally finished, the chaos didn't end. No sir. Ronnie was happening. Monument Records and Fred Foster were happening. And when the chance came up for them to promote the album in London, England, where Ronnie had already stirred up so much press attention and where Foster had to go on business, why, nothing was going to stop them. Both felt they were riding a wave. Everything was going their way.

When they arrived after a terribly rocky flight up from Nashville to catch Kristofferson's Lincoln Center gig in New York, they were treated like visiting royalty by Clive Davis, the charismatic music mogul who then headed Columbia Records. They looked like something that had just blown in from the backwoods of Alaska, but Davis had practically dragged them into his limo, leaving other chief CBS executives standing on the curb. From New York, Hawkins and Foster flew on to London. Sitting near them on the plane Foster happened to notice Sir Lew Grade, the powerful British show business tycoon, then head of Associated Television Corporation Ltd. (ATC), "the one-man shadow image of the BBC," as he was dubbed by critics. Their talk led to Sir Lew's promise that if Foster ever needed anything in London, he could just give him a call at his *private* private phone number.

They arrived in London on a Sunday to find a penthouse suite at the pricey Four Seasons Hotel had been set aside for their disposal by Foster's company. Ronnie couldn't believe the thick white rugs with inches-deep shag. What you could do on that! Still wired after their flight, they decided to walk around the deserted town, buying a London *Sunday Times* along the way. As he glanced through it something caught Ronnie's eye. Jerry Lee Lewis was in town and he was playing that night.

"We have to see the Killer," said Ronnie.

"Why?" asked Foster. "After all, I've seen Jerry Lee forty-eight times already. Why one more?"

But the Hawk insisted, and back in their room he phoned for tickets.

"Tickets?" laughed the clerk at the Palladium. "The Queen herself couldn't get a ticket for tonight, sir. We've been sold out for months."

Ronnie sweet-talked, cajoled and bragged. He did everything else he could think of to get a pair of tickets. No luck. Foster, however, was now interested in the hunt and phoned back to ask who owned this theater.

"Sir Lew Grade."

"Right," nodded Fred Foster.

"I'm terribly sorry," said Sir Lew on his private private line. "But not even Her Majesty the Queen could get a ticket tonight." The vision of Her Majesty wigging out to "Great Balls of Fire" tickled Foster's imagination.

"But what I can do if you're willing," Sir Lew went on, "is to sit you on the stage for the first show."

Well, now, Ronnie immediately raced out for gifts for Jerry Lee, returning with a fistful of £5 cigars. The Killer did like a good cigar. Looking around the suite, the Hawk then noticed a glistening, unopened bottle of Jack Daniels Black Label bourbon whiskey.

Foster caught his stare. "Uh-uh," said the producer shaking his head. "No way. That bottle of Jack Daniels is going to my publisher over here. He'll kill me if he doesn't get it."

Ronnie just smiled. What the Killer just loves to have along with a good cigar is a sip or two of Jack Daniels.

There was pandemonium at the Palladium. Locating the stage manager, they told him, "Sir Lew called you about us."

"What's your name?" the stage manager yelled back frantically.

"Ronnie Hawkins and Fred Foster."

"Oh," he grumbled darkly, tearing back a rope barring their way to the dressing rooms and stage area. Ronnie looked back over his shoulder to notice that just outside the back door they'd come through was Wild Willie and what looked like the rest of the Ronnie Hawkins fan club lined up out on the sidewalk. But they too had been informed that not even the Queen could get in.

The Killer, sitting in his dressing room in his shorts, saw Foster first, nodding that he could be let into the dressing room. "He's my friend," he snapped. Then he saw Ronnie. "Man," said Jerry Lee, "he's come to see me, too."

Fred watched as Jerry Lee took the bottle of Jack Daniels Black Label. He caressed it like it was the most beautiful woman in the world, thought Foster. Next Jerry Lee saw those cigars and exclaimed, "Oh man, my friends." Firing up a stogie, he poured himself a water glass about half-full of Jack Daniels. "My friends have come to see me," said the Killer, leaning back.

"The BBC are here," announced Judd Phillips, who was managing him then. The show's producer looked on anxiously.

"So what?" barked the Killer. "I'm busy with my friends. Can't you see I'm busy?"

"But," sputtered the producer, "but they have a camera crew of nine and they're going to document your entire tour of the British Isles. This is a very big thing. They're waiting. They want to come into the dressing room prior to your first show."

Jerry Lee picked up a cigar and looking at the matches in his hand, said: "I think at about fifteen thousand pounds I might consider it."

Foster thought the producer "was going to be sick. I think he was. The woman who was from the BBC fled. Someone went after her. Jerry Lee got up — and this was the truth — but the minute he turned his back, he wheeled around again and said to Judd, 'You touch my whiskey, I'll break your fucking arm. What the hell do you think you're doing?' How he knew that his manager was reaching for the whiskey I'll never know. Judd asked, 'Can I have just one sip?' And Jerry Lee said, 'No, drink that damn British slop, that's my whiskey.'" As the Killer walked by the window, he glanced down at the street. "Hey, look at the black and gray Rolls," he said. "Whose Rolls Royce is that?"

"It's mine," said the promoter.

"And you sent a bus to get the Killer?" shouted Jerry Lee. "Well, I'm going to tell you something. The Killer ain't singing one fuckin' note until there's another Rolls just like it parked right out there. The Killer does not ride on buses." The promoter was by now entirely panicked. "No, I can't get one of those," he complained.

"No show then," said Jerry Lee.

The next thing he knew Ronnie Hawkins was down on his knees. "Let the BBC in, Jerry Lee," said the Hawk. "If you don't want the publicity, shit, I can sure stand it."

By then Foster was absolutely convinced the show wouldn't go on. "Jerry Lee hasn't been to sleep in at least four days," Foster was thinking. "He's still wired. And now the whiskey is double-clutching into overdrive and going into unknown time zones and zip codes and everything."

"He'll never make it," Foster told Hawkins. "There's no way. It's over."

Fred was shaking his head as they found their way out to their seats on stage — red velvet seats. "The Queen's chairs?" they both wondered. "We sat down," Foster still remembers, "and watched as that son of a bitch gave the greatest show I have ever seen in my life. Greater than anybody'd ever seen. That London Palladium went totally berserk. You'd have thought it was Madison Square Garden and Rocky Marciano had come back from the dead and knocked out all the champions at once. He dedicated every song to us. Every goddamn song he sang. Every song."

After the show, Ronnie said to Jerry Lee, "When you all get through, why don't you come over and have a drink? Fred's got this real Louis XIV suite."

"Where are you staying?" was all that Jerry Lee asked.

"When Ronnie and I got back to the hotel we got us a couple of drinks," remembers Foster. "We talked about what a show he'd done and how the hell he did that. We didn't know how he could last like that. We put on our pajamas and got ready for bed. There was a knock at the door. Well, we'd ordered something from room service so I figured it was room service.

"I opened the door and Jerry Lee and the band came in. The Killer sat down on the couch, which was about fifteen feet long, and leaned back and said, 'I got my Tennessee sipping whiskey my friends brought me.'

"'You did a great show, Jerry Lee,' we told him. 'Did the BBC ever get in?'

227

"'Fuck the BBC,' said Jerry Lee. 'The Killer will tell them when they can come in.'"

More drinks were ordered, and Ronnie noticed that the Killer's bass player was out cold on the couch. A complete zombie. Now it was Foster's turn to notice something. The guitar player was down on the floor on his hands and knees. "What's the sucker doing?" Foster wondered. He watched as the guitar player took a big box of kitchen matches and started sharpening several of them to stick in one of the zombie's boots. All the way around the boot he lined them up, a ring of at least forty matches.

"Wait a minute," Fred said, jumping up. "You can't do that. You're going to hurt the guy. In the first place you're going to set this damn hotel on fire."

"Aw, don't worry about it," replied the guitar player. "I'm just doing this for fun."

Well, figuring he was indeed just joking, Ronnie and Foster ignored him for a few minutes. All of a sudden they were startled to watch as the guitarist reached down — and lit the matches. *Whoosh*, the rug was on fire.

"It's blazing like a brimstone field," thought Foster. "The guy's legs are on fire."

The zombie came screaming up off the couch. He had second-degree burns on his foot. But Jerry Lee didn't even look around.

"Me and Ronnie got the cushions off the couch and started beating the fire," says Foster. "We're opening windows, trying to do everything. And Jerry Lee is still arguing with somebody else about something or other."

Finally at four in the morning, Foster turned to the Hawk: "Ronnie, I can't take it any longer, I've got to go to bed."

"Me too," said Ronnie.

What they found the next morning horrified even such hardy party people as Hawk and Foster. Not one piece of antique furniture was left standing. The couch was over on its back. The tables were all turned over. There were huge black burn spots everywhere.

"They got into a fight," Foster told Ronnie. "Jerry Lee will not rest until he gets into a fight."

He surveyed the destroyed television set. "Oh God, Ronnie," said Fred, "we're going to be put into prison. Roy Orbison didn't sell enough records to pay for this goddamn suite."

But Ronnie, more used to the sight of total carnage than Foster, had a plan. He called the hotel's head maid to the room. After she nearly fainted at the sight of the mess, he handed her some money. A lot of money. "Do what you can do and I'll give you more money later."

Within minutes a crew of maids was crawling all over the suite, sudsing this, soaping that. Meanwhile the head maid herself was down on her knees, clipping the burn marks out of that inches-deep white shag rug. Ronnie sniffed. The smell was still there. They'll never get that out, he thought.

Broken armoire legs were taped together. Lamps were fixed. The couches tilted back into place. The crew of maids had no sooner left when there was another knock on the door — the assistant manager himself. He'd heard that there might be a problem in the room. "Was everything satisfactory?"

"Hmmm," said Ronnie. "Something's been burnt. I can smell it."

The assistant manager looked dutifully appalled. "I will check into that for you, sir," he said. "It will not happen again."

The bill for the suite was four thousand pounds. "There would have been two more zeros on that number if we'd been caught with that room before it was fixed," Foster said to Ronnie as they headed to the airport for a flight to Copenhagen where Kristofferson was playing.

By this point Ronnie was tired of being a mere spectator at someone else's party. So after Foster took care of business in Copenhagen and Ronnie had finished some interviews about their new album, they headed out to dinner.

"I want to go where the action is," the Hawk told the representative from Foster's publishing company. "I want to see something."

But what? Foster wondered, knowing that Copenhagen offered wide-eyed tourists more carnal delights by far than either Nashville or Mississauga. Live sex shows?

However, their guide had another plan in mind and after dinner they were taken to what Foster thought was "the most exquisite, luxurious, rich, high-class, architecturally brilliant" part of town he'd seen. After visiting one luxurious brothel after another, they found themselves inside a third. Inside it they viewed a scene out of a movie: a long table groaning under the weight of a sumptuous buffet; the beautiful people chatting over cocktails. Soft music. "What the hell is this?" Foster whispered. It looked like a scene out of Fellini.

Ronnie, he soon saw, looked particularly prepped for the night. "Some of Jerry Lee's killer bees," explained the Hawk, showing Foster a tiny pill. By now Foster had realized that the kind of elegant debauch he might have in mind could be found exactly where they were. But suddenly Ronnie was edgy.

"Somebody is following us," said Ronnie.

"Oh, come on," said Fred.

"I'm telling you, son. Someone is following us. He's been in the same three different spots we've been in. He's got a trench coat and the whole number."

Soon they were in the move again, to an even more stunning mansion two blocks away with even more food, with people even more beautiful and the possibility of even greater sensual activities.

No sooner had both of them secured a drink than Ronnie wheeled around.

"That son of a bitch is *still* following us," said Ronnie. "It's the same cat and this is the fourth place. I'm telling you son, it's the KGB. I tell you what," he went on. "I'm going to leave. If that son of a bitch follows us, I'm going to kill him."

By the time they reached the fifth stop, Foster was ready for anything. Yet this place was even grander than the others. Just as he was about to go in he glanced over his shoulder and there indeed was the shady gent in the raincoat. As soon as they inside, Ronnie walked over to the buffet table to begin looking for a carving knife. Not finding one he picked up a regular dining knife.

"What are you going to do?" whispered Foster.

"I'm going to knife that cat," said Ronnie.

"Not with that you're not."

By now the raincoat was just about through the door when Ronnie started to move up to him. "You son of a . . ."

"Mr. Hawkins, Mr. Hawkins," exclaimed the startled figure.

"What's wrong? I'm your biggest fan. I just didn't have the nerve . . . could I have your autograph?"

"I'll sign the son of a bitch ten times," sighed Ronnie. "I thought you were the KGB."

XIV

STAY WITH ME AND I'LL HAVE YA FARTIN' THROUGH SILK

A New Use for Honey, or How Rompin' Ronnie Founded the Women's Movement

SOME WOMEN THINK THAT RONNIE'S SEXIST. And they have a point I've never heard him say, "Goddamn, lookit that sweet li'l ol *person* over there, boys." As far as I can tell, he likes women as women, first and foremost. Ronnie has great difficulty being objective about sex and to this degree is entirely, and happily, out of the step with the times. Then there are those who can't understand how he's been married to the same woman all these years, spends so much time talking about his family and all that and . . . well, you know, have such a roving eye. The assumption behind Barbara Frum's piece about "eight wives who have achieved status through the reputations and power of their husbands" in the August 1971 issue of *Maclean's* magazine was that there must being something odd — at least by the enlightened standards established by Simone de Beauvoir and Betty Friedan — with any woman, i.e. Wanda, who'd choose to live with Ronnie Hawkins. Wanda was furious. Frum noted how Wanda "keeps repeating

'Oh boy, I'm going to be famous, too.'" Wanda, we're told, is one of the "big winners in the marriage sweepstakes." Her husband comes home with lipstick on his shirt but Wanda — so her own words indicate — goes along with it. "As long as he keeps coming and telling me about the orgies and the parties they have I don't mind," she's quoted as saying. "The day he stops telling me about them, then I'll worry."

To this day, Wanda can't think of the piece without wanting to shred it into bits. And no wonder. In most ways Wanda is as much a survivor as her old man; as savvy and tough-minded as he is. Besides, what Frum could not have known was that the women who over the years were closest to Ronnie would also be closest to her. Like B.J. Cook. Like the young singer from Ohio who looked so pale and frail, but was anything but — Bev D'Angelo.

These days Bev is most often seen opposite Chevy Chase in a series of broad Hollywood farces in the National Lampoon's *Vacation* series about the world's least successful holidaying yuppie family. After leaving Ronnie's band in 1974, she starred in a number of musicals, notably as Marilyn Monroe in *Hey Marilyn* for CBC Radio. She then appeared in *Rockabye Hamlet*, a failed Broadway musical. In 1977 she began her movie career with a bit part in Woody Allen's *Annie Hall*. D'Angelo went on to play Patsy Cline opposite Sissy Spacek in *Coal Miner's Daughter* and was also the embittered wife opposite Peter O'Toole in *High Hopes*.

She grew up in Columbus, Ohio, was a pig farmer in British Columbia, a cartoonist in Los Angeles and a student in Florence, Italy, at the American School of Contemporary Arts. She has hustled all her life, she once told me happily. She was, she figured, always adventurous. "I think I was the first girl in my class to get laid.

"When I came to Toronto," says D'Angelo, "I was working as a singer, which didn't require a lot of work because my room was only twenty-five dollars a week. It was a great time to be in Toronto. I played the Zanzibar — it was called Circus Circus at the time — from seven at night till two in the morning, forty minutes on, twenty minutes off. I sang 'The Girl From Ipanema' repeatedly. Every forty minutes I'd say, 'Now, gentlemen, it's swing time' and topless girls would get on the trapezes and swing over everybody's head. I thought it was pretty great. I also knew I needed something more."

Before D'Angelo came along, Ronnie was struggling to get and keep a band together; it was after B.J. Cook and David Foster had left. The glory days of John Lennon's peace festival were followed by a return to basics for the Hawk. "But there were some of those young cats who wanted to stay around and learn some rock 'n' roll," says Ronnie. "So I put another new band together. I had Hugh Brockie, who played guitar. He was an excellent musician but he knew too much so I put him on bass to slow his ass down. I couldn't find a drummer, so because Dwayne Ford was playing too many notes on keyboards I put him on drums. I brought in a little old rockabilly picker from down South named Terry Tyler — Terry Pitts was his real name. Stan Szelest was on piano again. Well, when I got back from my travels with Fred Foster we started touring and damn, but if it didn't sound better than The Band.

"Well, about as good. You see, the reason why I changed everybody around was this. You put a cat on drums who hasn't played them for years and years, he has to keep things real simple. He has to keep that ol' back beat just as simple as anything, which is exactly what I'm prone to. Hugh had to slow down on bass because he had to keep the groove going. As for the guitarist, well Terry was from Arkansas — he played around Fayetteville — by way of Texas, so he didn't play anything but rockabilly and it all worked out perfectly. With bands, its like it is with sports teams: you've got to get the right combination. That's what counts."

"Those nights at the Nickelodeon!" says Dwayne Ford. "The band changed and changed again. Terry Danko — Rick's brother, who was straighter than Rick and had at least as much talent — became the new bass player. Jim Atkinson became the guitarist. And we became incredibly tight and for months we packed them into the Nickelodeon. They were lined up around the block to get in. There were fights inside. The place held maybe five hundred people, and it was always packed. It was an incredible introduction to the whole scene for me.

"And all the time I was getting more and more fascinated by Ronnie. I mean, he could be tough on people, but I was still fascinated. He could be tough on women especially. He was never cruel to them but he could be condescending and patronizing. Yet in a way he was old-fashioned and chivalrous. He went through a lot of rough times around then. But I remember he had his pride. One night he and Terry Tyler were having an argument. I don't know what it was about. I do remember Ronnie saying, 'I can put a rock 'n' roll band together. I can do that.' And he could.

"To produce good rock 'n' roll, you can't compromise. That was his lesson. When the song calls for eighth-notes, you can't play quarter-notes, even if it means you arm's falling off, even if it means two more weeks of practicing. And he insisted on it. If you came up to him and said, 'Well, I'm sorry, I can't rehearse tonight,' he'd say, 'Well, I'm sorry, you're out of the band.' So we got really good as a band, just like his earlier bands. We just listened to old rock 'n' roll records to cop their licks, and we got better. Sometimes he'd stay to learn a new song. He was hard-working.

"Having a beer, maybe a little pot, was tolerated — within reason — with the band. If it became a problem and you weren't carrying your weight, he'd nail you. None of us really liked to smoke dope because of the intensity of the music. If we smoked we simply couldn't function. Drugs were never a problem with him then.

"By this time there were a lot of hangers-on around Ronnie. A lot of so-called friends. Hangers-on were regarded by band members as less than human, like lost souls to be pitied. Well, you're young and you're in a hot band, it's an ego thing. On top of that we had Ronnie saying over and over, 'When we make the big time . . . when we get to the big time.' I don't know what he thought about that but he used that phrase over and over and he conveyed the idea to us. Back then I didn't know anything about the rock 'n' roll business. I didn't know any of the politics of getting a record deal. There is no big time; I know that now. But back then whenever *we* made reference to it, it was to keep our dreams alive. To keep us going. The big time. Ronnie knew all along that to dream was okay.

"Then one night he was driving with the beautiful Airstream trailer he had. He had a matching Ford van, and he totaled the thing on the highway. He hurt his leg and he couldn't play for a couple of weeks. So we ended up sitting around not doing anything. He wasn't paying us; I was getting up to around $175 when we were playing. We were unemployed and we were bored. So I said, 'Hey, let's put the band together. Let's work.'"

That was the beginning of Atkinson, Danko and Ford. This in turn evolved into another band, Bearfoot, and finally it evolved into a brief solo career for Ford complete with an album, *Needless Freaking*, produced in no small measure by . . . David Foster.

Once again, the Ronnie Hawkins college of rock 'n' roll knowledge had helped fill the musical marketplace. Not that Ronnie was at all pleased to lose another band. "He was really pissed off at me," says Ford. "He made some reference to the fact that he'd kept me working for a long time but when he'd had his accident, when he needed us the most, I bailed out on him. But I didn't feel that was the way it was at all. The whole thing was falling apart. There was no leadership, no direction. Nothing."

Gary Lucas had flirted with rock 'n' roll all his life. He loved the style of it all, the action And when he met the Hawk, he knew, just knew, he'd encountered all the style and action he'd need for the rest of his life. Starting as a rock promoter — he'd brought Alice Cooper into Sudbury — he began booking the Hawk into various venues around Georgian Bay like Wasaga Beach, and places like New Liskeard in northern Ontario. Ronnie made him an offer he couldn't refuse: "Quit the promoting business, son, and work for me." Now, Lucas played a little guitar, but that's not what Ronnie had in mind. He needed a right-hand man, someone to be there. When Ronnie was on the road Gary would stay back in Mississauga or at the huge spread Ronnie had out near Peterborough. Wanda and the kids needed protection; besides, there was lots to do in the Ronnie Hawkins empire.

"When I arrived I couldn't believe what I was seeing," says Lucas, now working at a Nissan dealership in Burlington. "He was living the life of a man making one-hundred times what he could afford, cars alone. He had four Rolls Royces. Four! Then there were his antique cars: his '50 Merc and '37 pickup, his '26 Model T Ford and a Mark III Lincoln Continental. At one time he also had a 1956 'gull-wing' Mercedes, which he later sold to Don Tyson. Hell, these days that car alone is worth a quarter of a million dollars."

But Lucas was bothered by the Hawk himself. He was heavier than ever — "up to 278 pounds at one point," Lucas remembers.

"He was drinking a lot and at night, after a gig, he'd done what Elvis was doing. He'd eat tons of stuff, hot dogs, onions, he'd just stuff it in. He was depressed. He was having trouble with his bands. I remember he stayed upstairs in his room at Peterborough for months at a time, and wouldn't come down. But then he started hearing about Al Brisco, a steel-guitar player, and he went to Toronto to hear him."

Ronnie wanted musical stability. He had too many other things to worry about: Campbell's in London wasn't doing as well as he'd hoped, he was still looking for that breakthrough hit record, and he didn't want to have to worry about his band. So the more he kept hearing about Al Brisco, the more he felt he'd found his man. Now, Brisco was a lot more of a country musician than Ronnie was used to. But that was all right, Ronnie reasoned. "I'll just adapt my band to go in that direction."

Al had left his home base in the Ottawa valley in 1965 to tour with a number of country bands. He could play some piano, bass and guitar, but it was a steel-guitar player performing country swing where he'd made his reputation. Ian Tyson was interested in him, so was Gordon Lightfoot. But *they* didn't call him. Not then, anyhow. Ronnie Hawkins did. "That was the biggest break of my career — a memory maker," says Brisco. "It meant I'd arrived. Right away we went to Ronnie's club in London to rehearse for a month or two. Then we went to the Nickelodeon in December. By then I was not only his steel player but was keeping his books, as well.

"The band had changed. A drummer named Dwayne English was playing with us. Later Ronnie got him a job with Mel Tillis; he's still playing with him. Mike Francis went with me to join Ronnie. His nickname was 'Peppy.' Ronnie liked to have characters around him, even though I certainly wasn't a character. He gave everyone nicknames. He called me 'Alimony' because I didn't get married until I was thirty-eight.

"Another thing about Ronnie," Brisco says, "is that he likes to keep good-looking guys in the band to attract the girls. That's why he wouldn't allow wives or girlfriends to come to the gigs. He might allow it one night a week, but that's all. Business was business. Anyway, Mike went on to become one of the busiest session guitar players in Toronto — and an award-winning producer. We played the Nickelodeon for a year or so and in 1973 we moved to the Embassy Tavern. At the start we made about $200 a week. Before my tenure in 1975 was over I was making about $400 a week."

With Brisco, the band found some measure of stability. And when The Band returned to town in 1974 in triumph with Bob Dylan, Ronnie could flaunt his new band in front of the old.

No sooner had Dylan and the boys finished their Maple Leaf Gardens concerts than they headed south in their limos the few blocks to the Nickelodeon. It was early January, and Dylan in his fur hat and fur coat, with dark sunglasses, looked as if he'd just returned from the Russian front. Bill Graham looked on as the Hawk ran through his vintage hits, "Who Do You Love," "Bo Diddley" and the rest.

"Now hold on, Bob," Ronnie said. "I know you're just itching to get up here and sing, but you can't. This is my show."

Dylan smiled slightly. The crowd murmured. Dylan didn't budge.

"Things haven't changed much," said the Hawk. "We're just ten or twelve years older now."

Graham, who owned the Fillmores East and West, was promoting the Dylan-Band tour which he confided that night, "had gone perfectly." He looked around, and allowed himself a rare smile. "But it's really sweet here now. We rarely get a chance to do something like this."

The crowd had heard the rumor that when Ronnie had finished his final set of the night there'd be one massive jam session with Bob Dylan and The Band. But when Ronnie was through, they headed back to their $120-a-night suites at the Inn on the Park. Ronnie hung out most of the night at their hotel, talking with Levon and the boys and listening to Dylan's new album. The flattery flowed: "If Shakespeare and Lincoln were still around," said Ronnie, after hearing one particular Dylan cut, " they'd have to pick up their pens again and try a little harder. They were good writers but Dylan's got 'em."

Ronnie's praise must have made the impression he intended. The next time Dylan came through Toronto he booked Ronnie a suite at the Harbour Castle on the waterfront and spent most of the night hovering around the Hawk.

"What the hell is he doing that for?" Hawk asked Levon privately.

"You used to be one of his earliest idols," said Levon. "He loves you."

The Nickelodeon had become exactly the kind of club the Hawk had wanted it to be. His spot. Anybody who came through town dropped in at the Nick. Al Brisco remembers: "Even Frank Zappa came up once. He actually wanted to hire me. But I wasn't interested. He's pretty straight and narrow but his band members burn themselves out every three months. The Hawks kept busy. We played a few gigs in the States, too. One time we went down to Ronnie's hometown area for a concert in a hotel — the whole hotel was rented by Don Tyson. Rick Danko and Levon were there, too, and sat in. There was a real good reception.

"We kept changing personnel, though. We went through sixty-seven musicians during the three years and four months I was with Ronnie. A lot of the young guys would get bored with the material. And of course Ronnie was a disciplinarian — the licks had to be done the same way every night. You had to play your part. An awful lot of retraining went on. It's too bad we never did any studio recording: if anyone should have live albums, it's him. When I left in '76, he was shutting down for a while. There were problems with some musicians and Ronnie just needed a rest."

Bev D'Angelo was hearing through the grapevine that Ronnie Hawkins was looking for a new singer. By now she knew his band. Most of the musicians she came across had played for him, and the Nickelodeon was the place she ended up at whenever she had any free time, although she thought going that far south on Yonge Street was going into "no-man's land."

"So I went down to him one night after hours," Bev remembers, "and I sang 'Compared to What' — I was doing a lot of jazz at the time, lounge stuff. He was impressed. He had a big Cadillac and he drove down to my house and I was totally impressed. That weekend I went up to Peterborough with him and I just fell in love with the guys. He had to answer for everything and was the embodiment of everything glamorous and exciting to me. He was a full-blown character. He was inimitable. When you're eighteen years old, you're looking for the real thing. He was the real thing."

Which is pretty much what he thought about her. In some ways, Ronnie Hawkins is a complete snob. It has nothing to do with lineage, pedigree, social position. It has everything to do with character. He's a connoisseur of character and right off he knew "this little lady" with the startled eyes was someone special.

"I guess she'd got the idea from my reputation," says Ronnie, "from what she'd heard about me, that she had to do something for me before she could have a job to start with. That wasn't the case. I knew she was the real thing. But anyway, that's what she thought. So right off the bat she said, 'I'll do *anything* I have to do to get this job.'

"And so I suggested a few things to her. And being funny, she said. 'We'll start with that. Then we'll *improve* on what you want.' Well, here was this little ol' eighteen-year-old girl saying this. Goddamn, I had to listen to her. Because you never know. I mean, that got my *attention*. After she said that I'd have hired her if she was a mute."

"I sent a lot of love in his direction, truly," says Bev. "I thought the world of him in a lot of ways. Emotionally I was a kid, running around on my own since I was sixteen, and here's this guy who's got the keys to the highway. And he wants to show you how. He had the ability to make you think you were in on something that other people didn't really know about.

"Still, he's a southern boy at heart. Ronnie always seemed to have the idea that women had it over men because they had certain powers that would render men helpless. He's a sexy guy and he made me aware that there wasn't anything wrong with that — that if anything, a woman should have as much fun with it as anything else. He went to great lengths to make sure I knew exactly what I was doing. At one point he sent me upstairs in Mississauga with a trumpet player who tried very intellectually to explain to me how to give a blow job. It was like Ronnie Hawkins college.

"We're also talking about a different time. It was women's lib and everything at the time. Ronnie was hip to all that kind of stuff. But he never neglected the fact that women were women and men were men. If anything, he kind of exulted in it. Ronnie was after good times *all* the time.

"And it was a very good time for Ronnie. A lot of people who'd worked with him were being recognized. A lot of people had come into their own in a big way, who had been in contact with Ronnie and had been on his long path. He was also very much of a musical authority figure, certainly in Toronto.

"On a professional level he gave everybody a sense of showbiz — that was a different idea at that time. Everywhere else it was a real 'natural' period. But he had rules. You couldn't bring your girlfriend or boyfriend to a gig. You had to talk to everybody between sets. Some people rebelled against this. But it never occurred to me to rebel because everything he said made sense. He was talking about professionalism. I didn't do my first movie until 1977; I wasn't into acting at all. So Ronnie's my background in show business in a lot of ways. Very many important ways.

"He found a voice teacher for me in Hamilton. I studied opera with him, which was a basis for my entrée into acting. No matter how wild the content was, the structure Ronnie maintained was extremely professional. You worked from nine to one; you re-hearsed from two to four and then there was your R and R time from four-thirty to seven in the morning. In all of its wild, wild ways it was very structured. The thing Ronnie imbued everybody with was the sacred place of entertainment. Ronnie understood that concept. I think that as wild as those times were, that was the first professional experience I had."

"Bev started singing with us full-time," remembers Al Brisco, "after February 1974, when we moved from the Nickelodeon — Ronnie had a falling out and that was the end of things there — to the Embassy. Bev got fifty dollars a week, because she was on a kind of training program. Right off we all thought her voice was fantastic and when she got onstage she sparkled. The band liked her. And she could really play up to the audience. She'd flirt with them yet she'd still be the innocent — innocently coy. Whenever anyone got out of hand, she could give them a verbal blast over the mike. She could come on like a freight train but we later found that in truth she was really very modest."

D'Angelo suggested that they hire her girlfriend from Columbus, Ohio, Nancy Kreider. Bev was singing Patsy Cline numbers as well as tunes sung by Bonnie Raitt and Linda Ronstadt. "Ricky Don't Lose That Number," by Steely Dan was a pop hit she sang a lot, too. And Briscoe liked the way she could belt out a blues tune. So would two voices be better than one? The first time he heard them, Ronnie was knocked out by the combination. They'd been singing together since they were kids, harmonizing old country songs and pop hits. It was perfect, like they were sisters singing. "Nancy had that low voice, kind of raspy. It blended right in with Bev's. They were a real good duo."

But Al Brisco wasn't sure how to handle the two characters: "After the gig was over the night Nancy had first landed in town we were heading out to my place in Mississauga for a party. I had some people with me in my car and Ronnie's chauffeur, Gary, was driving the Lincoln; Bev was in the front seat and Nancy in the back. As they passed us, both girls had their asses out the window, mooning us. Both of them. I learned later, don't dare Bev to do anything — because she'd do it."

Indeed. The "later" came later that night. For after the party was over both women ended up in Brisco's bed. Ronnie found out soon enough that Bev and Nancy were forever "clowning," as he puts it. Ronnie remembers that the two women and Gary Lucas were stripped to the buff "and acting real casual" when a writer arrived for an appointment in Mississauga one day.

And there was, for instance, what D'Angelo still remembers as "the honey treatment." To Ronnie, it was something every man's dreams were made of: "They grabbed Gary Lucas one old day and spread honey all over him. And then they started licking that honey right off him. I believe they had some sort of race."

With the Hawk, D'Angelo found a friend, fellow rabble rouser, mentor and boss — all the things she needed at the time: "There were so many firsts with Ronnie," she says. "He was the first person on so many different levels in my life it's hard for me to think of him as being into one particular thing or another. Because for me, everything was new. He was the first full-fledged character that I'd met. He was also one of the original rock 'n' roll guys. One of the credos of the old time rock 'n' roll is that you live it. The whole thing with Ronnie was you lived what you did. You didn't go home and have one life and then go to the club and you've got another life.

"One of the things I respect about Ronnie as a person is that Wanda is no small ingredient in his life. I was never Ronnie's girlfriend, ever. Wanda was always a friend. I was a singer in Ronnie's band. The affair we had wasn't a big thing. He wasn't some old codger trying to get it on with the back-up vocalists. Not at all. It was a different time. You can go into great detail about what happened at his house one night in Mississauga with fifteen monkeys and a trampoline but that really isn't the point with the guy. If people want to see him and be with him then they're getting to the real thing. Ronnie's the kind of person you really have to be around.

"He never had any intentions at all but to relax and drop the bullshit," D'Angelo adds quickly. "He'd do that by getting millionaires to take their clothes off or he could do that by putting a band together that played music so well that people wanted to dance until three o'clock in the morning. I was a pretty liberated person when I met him. He never judged me wrongly for that. The basis of my relationship with Ronnie was all about entertainment. There's nothing that I wouldn't do for him. There's nothing that I didn't do for him, is more to the point. When I look back at my experience with Ronnie I keep coming back to the fact it had to do with music and the way he taught me how to integrate that into my life. The extension of that experience is the way I've been able to integrate any kind of creative thing into my life.

"When I think about him the first thought I have is, why doesn't everybody know about him?" wonders D'Angelo. "Why isn't he that same kind of influence? He was always a scene-setter. He always set the stage. He put the bands together. He put the people together. He guided the conversation. He was like a magician, an alchemist. He liked to cook up things. Everybody I know who knows Ronnie says they don't think they really know him. Everybody. Ronnie is the kind of guy who can talk to you for five years. He can tell you absolutely everything and you can walk away and you don't really know anything. In some ways he's very traditional — he's been married for thirty years, right? At the same time he pushed against boundaries all the time. Rockabilly was about pushing a barrier. Rock 'n' roll was about extending the boundaries and therefore creating something new. To be with him was definitely a plunge into the deep end. He was always a mythical person and always will be. That's his grace."

Ronnie's temporary fall from grace came just before Bev left him. They called their band Elephant, named after the particularly potent strain of cannabis nicknamed "elephant sticks." Ronnie was strict about dope — just a little and only pot; still, a lot of it was around. The way Ronnie sees it, if it had been any other time than the free-wheeling seventies, he would have had a major public-relations problem when the headlines read: "Rock singer Ronnie Hawkins arrested on three drug charges."

To D'Angelo it was a set up. To Ronnie it was plumb strange. On April 5, 1974, the Toronto *Star* ran the bare bones of the story: "Six policemen searched the Hawkins home, several cars, including his Lincoln, and the grounds of his estate on Mississauga Road. [He] was charged with possession of cocaine, possession of marijuana for the purpose of trafficking and the possession of marijuana." Included in the drugs seized, the report continued, "was a quantity of 'elephant sticks' — 6-inch-long braided strands of tender tips of the cannabis (marijuana) plant, held together with thin strips of cotton." The following day the stories stated that "Gary Edward Lucas, 29" also was charged on a number of counts.

"The big shock was that all the police in Mississauga had to know I had a little grass," says Ronnie, "but that I never ever kept over an ounce, and that was *only* for myself. They should've known that because three or four of them had been at my house smoking my grass. I don't know what happened, though. I did not allow my band to have anything heavier than marijuana. I would tell them up front, 'Don't do it because it'll be an embarrassment for us. Don't do it or don't take the job.' I said that I'd allow a little grass, though. And the more you buy the cheaper it is. Otherwise the price was too high for our income."

In short: yes, there was a great big bag of pot, but no, it wasn't for selling, but using. Everybody was going to have some. When the case came to trial in February 1976, Ronnie admitted that he had "used marijuana regularly for the past three and a half years but denied that he had ever sold or given any to anyone else." John Finlay testified that while he'd seen the Hawk smoke pot, he'd never been offered any. John F. Bassett, Joe Bagnato, writer Earl McRae and Ron Stewart, once of the Ottawa Rough Riders football team, all gave character testimony.

Gary Lucas testified earlier that he had bought "about a pound of marijuana at a Toronto tavern and that Hawkins and about fifteen other people were involved in the deal." Ronnie explained to the court that he taken his share "and put it in a jar labeled marijuana." When asked by David Humphrey, his trial lawyer, if he'd ever given marijuana to anyone, Ronnie told the court: "If you started giving away marijuana you'd be pretty popular. I don't think ten acres would hold all the people and that's all the room I had on Mississauga Road."

To this day, he sees nothing wrong with "a little marijuana." Indeed, he's in favor of legalizing it. "I'd be in favor of banning tobacco and cigarettes," is his position. "And I'm a smoker who can't quit. But I don't think marijuana hurts anyone if you get to where you can control it. Instead of taking valium, instead of taking all that other shit we take, smoke a good joint and relax for a little. It lets your nerves settle down for a little bit and lets you start thinking right. It still works for me and for everybody I know. I still smoke a little grass. I don't like to take pills. I don't like to do *anything* else."

What bothered him the most was the way all the charges hit the papers, charges which included references to cocaine and weapons possession. "It made everybody think I was a cross between Al Capone and the Loch Ness monster," Ronnie complains. "Of course, even before it went to court the first time they dropped three or four charges. I was charged with guns. Well, those guns were all registered in their police department. When they got to check it out they found all my stuff was legal. It hit the papers anyway, that they'd found unregistered guns by the hundreds. It was as if they'd found an S.S. troop or something.

"Then there were four or five other of those big-worded charges that they try to throw on you, about 'too much of this' and 'over-the-limit that.' So right off I made sure we gave everyone's names because we had all decided that if anybody got busted getting the pound in or out we'd all take the bust together. I also told the police that it was not supposed to be on my property, that it was put there by mistake because I do not allow that amount on my property. I had told Gary Lucas that it was not supposed to be on my property and he told the court that he had done it.

"But the publicity! For three or four days it was on the CTV news and the CBC news. Films of my house! I thought, oh my God, if it had been five years or more earlier, it would have ruined me. The

Band got busted too early and it hurt their reputations. They had to cancel jobs, that's how bad it was in the late sixties and early seventies to get busted. But it wasn't so bad for me. When it says you're let out on your own recognizance you know you ain't killed nobody. A lot of people didn't know that. They just saw all the charges — guns and traces of this and traces of that. Dang. It looked like they were looking for Patricia Hearst, who was rumored to be in Canada at the time."

"Ronnie got set up for a drug bust and that's when Elephant split up," says Bev. "That particular band was never together again, although it went through more changes. There were times I'd go back and we'd do stuff together but it was the end of that band. It was in springtime. That summer I went to Prince Edward Island and the following winter I went to New York. About a year after that I started acting.

"I think deep down inside Ronnie's a very romantic man. This guy knows how to love people. I think that's the basis. You never get an unemotional thing from Ronnie. He makes you feel things. He's got an opinion and a point of view. He's got an amazingly strong character. He's a very emotional person. I think that's one of the very things that communicates with women. They know there's feelings there."

For Ronnie, the fallout from the drug bust didn't provide the measure of freedom it did for D'Angelo. The band continued for a while at the Embassy, but the club didn't like the bad publicity and eventually Elephant was put out to pasture.

Then there were those other worries. Campbell's wasn't working, and when Hawkins went over the ledger he realized he'd spent hundreds of thousands of dollars to keep the club going. Later the grand total was reported to have been one million. People were coming and going in his life too quickly. His kids were growing faster than he could keep track of them. Heavy Andrews, out of the joint one last time, died of cancer. But Ronnie, who hates funerals, wouldn't even go to Heavy's.

It was a down time for him. The release of the second of his Monument albums, *The Giant of Rock' n' Roll*, received little fanfare and any further help Fred Foster could give him stopped when the company folded. But when Earl McRae, an admitted long-time Hawkins fanatic, wrote for *The Canadian* magazine a moody portrait of Hawkins at age forty-one with the evocatively gloomy title, "Last Boogie in Sturgeon Falls," Wanda was furious.

"Ronnie Hawkins has been down and always he's come back, but this time the climb is steeper than he's ever known before," began the third paragraph. The picture of Hawkins — "fat, depressed and weary" — was pitiable. Wanda thought it made Ron look like a loser. And he wasn't. She knew he wasn't, and for a time Earl McRae was banned from the Hawkins household.

XV

"LIVING THE LIFE
I CAN'T AFFORD"

"IT'S BEEN REALLY WEIRD WITH ME and recording," says Ronnie. "I'd signed three three-record deals in a row starting with that one with Cotillion. Each time, something strange would happen."

Ronnie shakes his head. He's been dealing with the music industry for more than thirty years, and each new record deal has been a struggle:

I'd done my second album with Cotillion when everything stopped. Just like that. Atlantic, the parent company, was bought out and about the only artist they kept was Aretha Franklin. The whole business was being run by accountants, as the record business so often is these days.

The same thing later with United Artists. I went with that company because I knew the people in it. That's how I've always liked to do business, by knowing and trusting the people I'm doing business with. But the two guys, Artie Mogul and Jerry Rubinstein — I'd known them for years, how they worked and how they hustled — were offered a deal and they sold the company for several million dollars' profit.

Then my boss became a computer in Amsterdam. That was hard to deal with. Robbie Robertson was going to produce my album for United Artists, too. Robbie had arranged to meet whoever was running the company at that time. Three meetings were arranged and nothing happened. Finally Robbie said, "Dammit, but I'm busy." And he was. He'd already produced Neil Diamond by this time. He was hot a producer. Goddamn. Three meetings! That was the time everybody in California had a dipper in their nose. *Nobody* was making any meetings. I mean, the big wheels were out of control in the record business in those days.

But United Artists had already given me money for the first album. Altogether they gave me $125,000 to do the album. It was a hundred-grand deal but they gave me another $25,000 to fine-tune it. I saw a chance to get five albums out of it, if everybody worked at it. I thought everyone in the band had a shot with their own album. So I took the guys I had at the time down to Fayetteville. Biscuit Boy was back with me and I thought I could get an album out of him. I had this great guitar picker, Jack De Keyzer, and I thought there was an album in him, too, because he could play that great rockabilly stuff.

I rented a house from Don Tyson and we did like The Band did at Big Pink. We put foam up on the walls for insulation. It was a perfect set-up, just like The Band had had when they'd set up in houses where you could stay after you were finished rehearsing. I had a good engineer. I even had bought the equipment, figuring to keep it because there were other people who could use it to get their albums out. That was the time no one could get a record deal for the kind of music we played, so I thought this was the best way.

I bought a beautiful sixteen-track set-up. Sixteen tracks means sixteen separate bits of music — a drum part, or a guitar part or whatever — can be recorded at the same time. There were bigger set-ups — twenty-four tracks — but to me, having sixteen tracks was just right. The Beatles had recorded *Sgt. Pepper's Lonely Hearts Club Band* on sixteen tracks, which meant you could do a lot with it. You just had to practice a little harder before you went in there and know your parts a little better. I like a smaller set-up like this because when they get much bigger, when they get to be forty tracks, all that means is that it gets so complicated that it's the recording engineers who are running things then. Folks around Fayetteville still remember the session.

Goddamn, soon enough they were practically backing the Budweiser beer trucks up to our front door.

They brought in barrels of beer. They must've brought in three hundred gallons of every kind of whiskey in the world. What I'm trying to say is that there was a lot of liquor in that house at that time and to those boys — well, that was just like putting a blind, hungry dog into a butcher shop. As it turned out, I never got a goddamn thing done. I'd wanted to cut this album down in Arkansas because we'd be with people I knew. I brought in the engineers. I brought in everything and everybody we needed. What I hadn't counted on were all the guys around bringing all these *other* goodies to the house.

Things started getting delayed. So I moved the rehearsals back to two o'clock in the afternoon. But I'd come into the house and there'd be whiskey bottles and beer bottles piled to the ceiling. Everybody would be unconscious. Nobody had rehearsed. Nobody could do anything. I told Biscuit that he'd better straighten this out because there was a chance for him to really accomplish something with these sessions. "Who knows?" I told him. "Maybe it'll be a hit."

But the whole thing started getting screwed up really bad. So I'd had it. I'd wasted a month. So I canceled the whole thing and sent them all home, and I headed to Los Angeles. I got this kid, Keith Allison, to be the producer. Instead of my band, I got all kind of heavyweights to be on the album: James Burton on guitar, Waddie Waddell, Linda Ronstadt's guitar player, Garth Hudson, Terry Danko and the Eagles.

There he ran into B.J. Cook, who was in the process of getting a divorce from David Foster. She was worried. The Hawk, she found out, was living with a dope dealer and he was increasingly bothered by it. He wanted out, as he told her on the phone one day:

"'B.J.,' he said to me, 'It's just a matter of time before somebody gets killed or busted and I can't be here anymore.' So I moved him into my apartment in North Hollywood, in Cold Water Canyon. We were just friends, you know. Now, at this time I had the

Mercedes — David Foster had the Jeep. One day Ronnie and I were driving along and David pulled up alongside of us. And Ronnie said, 'Son, nice wheels. Next time I'd like a Jag!'"

"Now, I was finishing the album," Ronnie says, "when Kris Kristofferson came by one time. He had to go down to this shop to get his costumes made for this movie he was making, *Heaven's Gate*.

"I didn't know much about it but I said I'd go along with him. This was the time he'd smoked that gorilla shit so as we were parking out front of that costume place, Kris raked four cars and didn't even look at the damage he'd done. He was backing into a parking spot and he was scraping cars with his bumpers, causing gashes two inches deep on all those cars. He was telling me a story all the while and never even stopped to look outside at what was happening.

"I had to sit and wait for him to get his costume done. Because I was stoned and on a bit of a roll, I was cracking wisecracks and Arkansas bullshit. And Kris was just laughing his ass off. This young guy was sitting there taking it all in. Hell, how was I to know that this was Michael Cimino, the director of the movie?

"The very next day I got a phone call from just about *everybody* — at least ten people on this one day — asking me if I'd do a part in *Heaven's Gate*. Cimino had liked my Arkansas bullshit, I guess. I said, 'Goddamn, I don't know. It all depends on how heavy the part is. I don't want to mess you up.'

"Apparently, Ned Beatty was Michael Cimino's first choice for the part they wanted me to have — Major Walcott, which was a major role. They had two good guys, which were Kris Kristofferson and Chris Walken, and two bad guys, Sam Waterston and me. Beatty and Cimino had gotten into an argument over this and that and the other, because Cimino is one of those directors who wants you to do it the way he wants you to do it. He's got the whole picture in his head already. But those heavy actors insisted on doing *their* thing.

"'You know,'" I told them, 'I've got a little brain damage. I've been in bars, *acting*, all my life. But there I don't have to memorize two or three pages of script. I don't know about this.'

"Then Michael Cimino himself came on the line and said: 'Can you repeat three words at a time, after me?'

251

"I said, 'I can do Shakespeare *that* way, sir.'"

"Michael liked Ronnie," Kristofferson remembers. "I've always thought Ronnie would be good in a movie. He's a colorful person. Because of his presence, he makes a strong impression on you."

"So I was out of L.A. right away," says Ronnie. "I went back to Fayetteville to get some business done before the movie started, then up to Calisville, Montana, where the filming was going to take place. The snow was still on the ground when I left, seven and a half months later. In all that time, I took only one break. I came back to Canada for a week. Young Ronnie was in trouble and it was becoming too much for Wanda. I flew in, straightened everything up, then took Ronnie back with me so Wanda wouldn't have to worry about him."

B.J. Cook had her reasons for being grateful for Ronnie's participation in the movie. "Now, with my marriage over, I was in the middle of the heartache, the worst headache of my life. Then Ronnie called and said, 'What are you doing? I'm in Montana making a movie. I've gone from imaginary idol to matinee idol overnight.'

"'Hmmm,' I was thinking, 'it seems he's there for every important moment of my life.'

"I was skinny, long-haired and tanned. He told me to get on a plane and come up. He said, 'I've got nothing but heroes around me — Chris Walken, John Hurt, Sam Waterston, Jeff Bridges, Kris Kristofferson. B.J., they'll go crazy over you. If you've ever trusted me, now is the time.'

"He told me Michael Cimino was going for complete authenticity: hairy armpits, bushy eyebrows. They were supposed to be Slavic immigrants. Ronnie said, 'Come looking real good 'cause the women here are looking like real dogs. So wear your sexist clothes and bring your high heels.'

"Because David had our daughter Amy for the summer, I went up to Montana, initially only for two weeks. I arrived at the airport with my red hair, suntan and skinny body. I got off the plane and twenty guys went to pick up my bag. It was one of those times. 'Thank you, Ronnie,' I thought.

"The principal actors were all staying at the Outlaw Inn, a beautiful rustic old hotel. The rest — that's us — stayed across the freeway at the Thrifty Scot Motel. It had cement walls and two double beds in each room. It was a bedroom, period. It had a phone but that was about it. Wanda called the first day I was there and I answered. My immediate reaction, woman to woman, would have been, Why were Ronnie and I in the same room? That's what I would have thought if it had happened to me. But she also knew we were best friends. She was so cool. I thought, You're so hip.

"But as time went by there was a real problem. Ronnie was in agony. I made him promise he'd go to the doctor. Two days later he did and it was diagnosed as a ruptured hiatus hernia. All that horse riding had done it. He was simply abusing himself to where his body couldn't take it anymore. But being around Kristofferson began to pay off in another way for Ronnie. He started eating what Kris was eating, lots of salads, and lost so much weight that he needed extra padding to do his scenes."

"Yeah," says Ronnie, "but what I almost didn't survive, though, was this battle scene we did. The way it was to work was this: I was supposed to come out — as it says in the script — 'guns a-blazing.' I was supposed to kill Jeff Bridges and wound Kris. Then Kris was to let fly with — again, as the script says — several rounds, and kill me.

"Now, Cimino had all kinds of charges set up in the ground, for explosions and special effects. And there were three hundred head of horses in a circle. It looked like Vietnam all over again. Those horses were going crazy, man. They were scared for their lives. And I was scared, too. Me? Try to get on one of those wild-assed horses and ride out of there? Dammit, when I tried to mount my horse, it started going round in a circle. John Wayne couldn't have gotten on that goddamn horse. Finally I got on and it went in the right direction and the charges went off when they should have, after I'd gotten through the gate.

"But for the second take, I guess Cimino whispered something to the cameraman and something to the rest of them because, baby, when I got on the horse and just started to go through that gate the charges went off right under that horse. Blew it three feet in the air. I went one way, the saddle went the other; the horse had to be destroyed.

"And damn, but I landed in the only spot in that circle where I couldn't have broken something because there were wagon wheels and wagon tongues everywhere."

"It's amazing that more people weren't injured in that battle scene," interrupts Kristofferson. "There were a lot of animals and a lot of explosives and a lot of wagons going around and people lying on the ground. Ronnie's horse happened to get into one of the holes they dug for the explosives. When the explosion went off he went flying through the air about twenty feet and landed like a ton of bricks. Everybody was scared to death."

Ronnie remembers, "It rammed my cigar right down my throat. What the hell happened? I was wondering. Everybody ran over and Cimino was undoing my top buttons and saying, 'Bring him a drink of water.'"

Kris Kristofferson remembers what happened next: "Hawkins, lying flat on his back, says, 'Water? Bring me some heroin! I need something heavier than water.'"

For Ronnie, *Heaven's Gate*, with all his pains and its confusion — for this was the movie accused of bringing down a movie company, United Artists — was an escape: from the grind of the road, from all the financial pressures brought on by his London club investment, from having to deal with *another* record company which wasn't sure how to deal with him. He wouldn't have been the first rocker to try the movies but it seemed to those around the sets that he had a shot at being one of the few, like Kristofferson or David Bowie, who could make it work.

For Wanda, though, *Heaven's Gate* was a crisis. It meant she was left alone to deal with young Ronnie. And she didn't know what — or sometimes, who — she was dealing with. Her son was moody, angry, sometimes almost violent. He was pushing her away from him and pushing away from his dad, too, even though there was little question that at one time he'd been his dad's favorite. Ronnie could remember what promise this moon-faced little boy with the deep, dark eyes had shown early on as a guitar player.

Oh sure, he'd played what his dad had wanted him to — it was always that way living with Ronnie Hawkins, that's for sure — but he was listening to Jimi Hendrix and "he had Jimi Hendrix down as good as Jimi Hendrix can be put down," says Ronnie. "He was just gifted. He had it. He said something from day one. At twelve years old I knew he was above average.

"Now, with all my kids I did the one thing I think you should *never* do. I wanted them to steer away from what *I* did. It's a rough business to get into. I wanted them to get a college education, you know. That's why I put them in a private French school first because I wanted them to learn French. This is Canada, right? And for a while it worked. They could all read and write French as good as de Gaulle. Then I put them in Lakefield College so they could meet the future leaders of the world. But they got into music. Then they started playing and putting little bands together. Then there was nothing I could do but help them all I could.

"When Ronnie was just a kid, I got him the records I thought he should listen to. He was into the Rolling Stones and all that stuff, though. But he's also had all of Chuck Berry's stuff, and Fats Domino. The roots! I told him, 'You learn your roots first, then you advance it. At sixteen years old he could play better than Robbie Robertson could. I got him all the help I could. What we've since found out is that he was suffering from a chemical imbalance, something that happens to one out of ten kids."

Along with brother Robin, two years his junior, Ron Jr. had been going to Lakefield College when Prince Andrew was there. But Ron Jr. started to rebel, and his parents felt that maybe it would be better if he went to a nearby high school.

"There were a lot of drugs in Lakefield at that time and Ron became involved," says Wanda. "Much later we found out that the drugs — and we know he really didn't take very many — had brought on schizophrenia. Later the doctors told us that the schizophrenia might have appeared anyway, but the synopsis of it all was that the drugs had brought it on."

Ron Jr. had had problems before this, certainly. "Spreading themselves too thin" financially, Ronnie and Wanda had finally sold their Mississauga house. Instead of moving to their 180-acre spread on Stoney Lake, near Peterborough, they spent the year at 196 High Park Avenue in Toronto, the house which had been in Wanda's family for thirty-five years, the one Ronnie had gone to when he was courting her. They loved Stoney Lake and went there every weekend and all summer if they could. But they had to be in Toronto to get help for young Ron.

But help for what? What was wrong? They had no answers at this point. What Ronnie and Wanda realized was that one of the worst problems was not knowing what was wrong with their son.

They had taken him to a hospital in Texas but all they were told was that as an adolescent he could be expected to get over his condition in time. So all that Ronnie could think of in the meantime was to take young Ron with him to Montana. And that, for a while, looked like a good idea. There was even talk of young Ron getting a part in *Heaven's Gate*. But that didn't pan out and when Ronnie had to move to a temporary location, Ron was put in the care of one of Ronnie's band members who in turn left the boy with friends of his in Albuquerque, New Mexico.

The next thing Wanda knew, she heard from some friends in Arkansas that young Ron had somehow found his way to the Albuquerque airport, had scored drugs there and was wandering around lost when the police picked him up and admitted him to a local psychiatric ward. Eventually Ron Jr. was sent back to Toronto, but not before even their friends knew that something more than adolescence was bothering the boy.

Although he tried not to show it, Ronnie was growing increasingly worried. He knew that it was beginning to wear Wanda down: "I was taking Ron to psychiatrists and clinics but no one could help at all. No one knew what to do. God, it was heartbreaking. Wanda, she could barely handle it. For a while I thought she needed help almost as much as Ron. It was hard on us, real hard."

Wanda noticed that at some of the places she approached, as soon as they knew whose son it was their attitude changed, as if what was happening to young Ron was what you might expect from a rock 'n' roll family. Wanda tried not to let it get to her, but it did. "They thought we were all taking drugs," she says. But that wasn't the case. Sure, the kids had seen some pot smoked around their house. "When John and Yoko were there they were smoking all the time," she knew, "but that's all. A little smoking. Nothing more. No coke. No pills. No one was shooting up." Good heavens, if they only knew how demanding a father Ronnie was. How much he believed in work and family. How really old-fashioned he was. Ronnie had even told Michael Cimino he'd quit the picture if he couldn't get back to care for his son. What did those psychiatrists think the Hawkinses were all about anyway?

Maybe things would have been better, Wanda started to think, if young Ron hadn't been named after his father. "I don't think anyone should name a son after a father, especially if the father is a bigger-than-life father." That was one source of pressure on the boy. "And maybe with Ronnie being away so much Ron felt he had to take on the responsibility for the place. Maybe. I don't know."

Wanda found help from an unexpected source — Ron's younger brother, Robin: "He was my strength. Ron never did anything to me, but whenever it looked like he could have, Robin would jump in there and keep him from it. He'd help control Ron. We went to the drug abuse center in Toronto and they told us that he was a 'difficult' child. We went to another in Quebec where they sat everyone in a circle and make the person sit in the middle while everyone tells him what's wrong with him. We were told it would either make Ron or break him. It broke him. Eventually we found a place which would help him, a clinic in Collingwood, Ontario. But before that he regressed. He became a nine-year-old child. It was a terrible burden for all of us."

It was Ronnie's manager Steve Thomson who drove the Hawkinses to Montreal. It was Steve Thomson who seemed to be involved more and more in their lives, back then. For whether Ronnie was aware of it — or Thomson himself for that matter — Steve was gradually becoming the one thing the Hawk had never had: a genuine manager.

Ronnie was used to straight people, but Thomson gave straight a good name. He rarely drank, didn't hang out, was genuinely happily married — Margaret, his wife, was John Finlay's bookkeeper — and he loved to handle all those little details that used to drive Ronnie bananas. He was quiet, wore a suit and tie and loved the suburbs. This could be a manager? For Ronnie Hawkins?

Ronnie had known him for years. Thomson, a student at St. Michael's College, had been in a band called the Verge. When the Verge made a little name for itself, it signed with Heavy Andrews's Agency, Baby Blue Productions, and it was upstairs above the Le Coq D'Or where Steve first met the Hawk. Typically, the Hawk started offering him advice even before the two had really come to know each other. And the Hawk's advice was to stick to music.

The problem for the Verge was *its* manager — Heavy. When the band tried to get a date at the Colonial, the Colonial's manager Mike Lyons told him he'd never get booked into his club as long as Heavy was involved with the band.

Because of Heavy, Thomson eventually started spending more and more time at the Hawkinses' Mississauga home. He came to know Wanda well, and the kids. But Ronnie was never around. At first Steve couldn't figure out why Ronnie spent his time at home away from people. Later, he came to understand. Home was the Hawk's only escape and even here he needed his own private refuge.

Steve was learning the music business on his own. After the Verge changed its name to Fat Chance he'd developed an interest in booking acts and was developing a small circuit of his own in Ontario. So he started thinking about booking Ronnie. And he couldn't believe how little Ronnie was charging per night — *the* Ronnie Hawkins.

He was appalled, and the closer he looked at the way Ronnie's career was going the more shocked he became. Christ, thought Thomson, no wonder Ronnie's Cotillion records didn't sell. No wonder "Down in the Alley" was only a moderate hit. No wonder the Monument albums were stiffing. Look at the bad planning. When Hawkins had just come back from his world tour, *after* John Lennon had stayed with him, *after* a major story in *Rolling Stone*, *after* getting more press in Canada than anyone this side of Pierre Elliott Trudeau, where did he play? Not in Maple Leaf Gardens or on his own CBC special, but in some godforsaken town way up north. What a waste.

What finally got the Hawk listening, Thomson figures, was the day he helped him firm up a booking. The offer had come from a Palmerston, Ontario, club Thompson knew. He knew how much other acts were getting there. He knew how much more the Hawk should be worth. So he sat in Ronnie's office, cradling the phone in his hand, as the owner wondered down the other end of the line exactly what the Hawk would want for a date.

Cupping his hand over the receiver, Thomson asked Ronnie how much he'd take.

"Hmmm," thought Ronnie, "Nine hundred bucks maybe?"

Taking his hand from the phone, Thomson said, "Three thousand five hundred."

"No problem," came the voice down the line.

This impressed the Hawk, for sure. "In a way they're probably made for each other," says a friend who's known both for years.

"If Hawkins was managed by anyone who lived the way he lived, God knows what would have happened — neither would be alive. But Steve couldn't care less about the bright lights and big city stuff. He goes home. A beer will put him under the table. He keeps everything in perspective."

Another area where Ronnie and Steve agreed was the direction of Ronnie's career. Both knew that after *Heaven's Gate* he had to slow down. And Wanda, although she tried to keep it to herself, trying to be the dutiful wife and all, knew it, too. Oh Ronnie kept bitching — sometimes in print, sometimes in private — about all the work he had to do. But Thomson knew that he could never entirely quit the road. Never would. It was in his blood. Somehow, they all had to figure out how to get Ronnie's career to the level where he made more money for less time on the road.

The key to it was publicity. Not that Ronnie himself was any slouch at getting publicity. He knew how the press worked. Better, Ronnie knew what the press wanted to believe. He had landed key solo spots on The Band's Last Waltz concert and Bob Dylan's Rolling Thunder Revue show when it stopped in Toronto, yet in both cases he was careful to show his deference to all the great stars around him. He knew what was expected of him, good ol' boy that he was. That was his given role, so that's how he played it.

The problem with all of this exposure was that it always came on someone else's terms. Hawkins began to cast around to start making his own big breaks. The first chance to appear on the horizon was prompted by the Canadian government's offer of substantial tax breaks for those who invested in Canadian film-making. In taking advantage of the tax write-off, John F. Bassett, the late sports entrepreneur and son of CFTO TV owner John Bassett, found he could indulge his passion for the Hawk's music by underwriting a documentary about him. *The Hawk*, produced by Henry Less and directed by Martin Kahan, started bravely. Kahan saw it as an opportunity to pay tribute to Ronnie's faithfulness to rock 'n' roll.

So all of the Hawk's old buddies were lined up; the faithful fire was going to be rekindled. The more than $300,000 that Bassett invested in the project was supplemented by the Arkansas Arts Council and the state's motion picture development office. The crew arrived in Fayetteville to shoot local color such as the Bethel

A.M.E. church and the local twenty-one-voice choir from the Opportunities Industrialization Center. Everything looked great — then, inexplicably, things started falling apart. The money fell short of what was needed. Expected big-name guests couldn't make it. Frantic calls were placed and Tanya Tucker was rushed into a set to fill in. When the crew arrived back in Toronto, B.J. Cook, now living in Toronto after her divorce, whirled around town keeping interest alive in the project.

Eventually, *The Hawk* did appear on television. But it wasn't sold to an American television network. It wasn't the definitive work Ronnie was looking for. And in the end, he likely benefited more from the publicity drummed up about the making of it than from the thing itself. Ronnie was disappointed, deeply disappointed, mainly because of all the old friends who'd promised to help but in the end didn't. The fiasco of *Heaven's Gate*, doomed by enormous delays and cost overruns, was easier to take in stride, he told Marni Jackson, writing a major profile on him for the May 14, 1981, *Rolling Stone*.

Jackson understood what his run for the big time was costing him. "I can't help it," she remembers him saying. "I keep dreaming something will happen. I've been on the rise for so long now, I'm getting tired of bubbling *under*. Every year they say I'm making a comeback. Back from where? That's what I say."

To Cheryl Hawkes, profiling him for the Toronto *Star*'s *Starweek* magazine, he complained: "The stress and fatigue, that's the only trouble I've had. I'm really tired right now. I'd like to stop for three or four months. But we're just getting some momentum." The question was, was anyone listening? In the pictures with the article Hawkins was shown singing, smiling, flanked by women — Tanya Tucker and Jennifer Warnes. The Hawk tired? He's just joshing us, right?

"Oh Lawdy," he told Jackson, moodily. "Life is funny, ain't it?"

No it wasn't. As the seventies went and the eighties came, the Hawk gave his greatest performance. He hid his hurting. Time and time again I'd see him, and while he looked tired he never seemed beaten. Father Christmas, I started to think of him as his hair went increasingly gray. But life wasn't funny. Life was hard, very hard, and he started to give in to it. On the one hand he and Thomson were finally landing the very kind of high profile gigs —

television, movies, prime summer concerts at the Ontario Place Forum — that he'd always wanted. On the other hand, something dark and awful had settled in his soul.

To Wanda it had grown worse when he was appearing at the Club House, up on Toronto's Merton Street. He'd started drinking every night and she was afraid he was going to kill himself. "It was working in a bar and hating it," she says. "It was six days a week and he'd been doing it for so long. It was as if he felt he'd failed in some way."

Wanda met with Thomson. "Steve," she said, "we've got to confront Ronnie and let him know how we feel. I don't care if we have to live in a little room, I want him out of the bars." As much as she liked all the houses, the help and celebrities, she didn't want Ronnie to drink himself to death just to keep things going. As far as Wanda was concerned, "if he was drinking and going to kill himself, then he'd have to leave me and kill himself somewhere else. Because I couldn't stand watching him kill himself. I knew what he was doing was trying to make it better for us. But 'better' was okay a long time ago. He didn't have to go on trying to still make it better."

What made it worse for her was she knew how much he'd prefer not to have to be hustling all the time.

"His background is home," she says. "Family. That was how he was brought up. He went out on the road because he had to make money. You do what you have to do. That's why he turned down Albert Grossman. That's what he's still like. It was only that it got harder as the years went by. You see, in our earlier years he taught me so much. He taught me how to roll with the punches. Nothing ever flustered me. I just rolled with it, went with it and didn't think much about what I was doing. It was, okay we're here, now we're there, we have to take care of this, now we take care of that. There was pressure in trying to take care of all our places. I've always had to take care of the bills, the books and the house.

"I never had any expectations of what it was supposed to be like living with him, or what marriage was supposed to be like. To me — it's because I come from a Ukrainian background, I guess — the husband goes to work and makes money the best he can; whether he has to go to war, whether he has to go away, whatever he has to do, he has to do. And I have to do my share to help out to keep everything rolling. I wanted him home. But I never would say, 'I wish you'd stay home.'"

"Wanda was amazing through all this," remembers B.J. "I've tried to figure out how she's managed to be so stable all these years, and I still don't know." Another friend observes, "Wanda's entire life has been Ronnie. Always has been and if she gets her way, it always will be. You see, she worried about him on a basic level. She put out of her mind all that business about him and other women. To her it simply didn't matter. What did matter was that she felt he was killing himself."

"I knew he'd come home to me," says Wanda. "Although I didn't always feel that way. In the early years I was confused about it, but I learned that it was part of the business he was in. After a while we'd learned to trust each other. Part of his business was to flirt. When he was with Bev or B.J. they were playing to him and he was playing to them. It was a show. What wasn't part of the show? So that wasn't a worry. What really worried me was how he was driving himself so hard."

John Bassett's fascination with Hawkins didn't end with his involvement with the movie, *The Hawk*, although word leaked out that he was disenchanted with Ronnie when more superstar guests could not be corralled for appearances. Nevertheless, Bassett listened with interest as Thomson laid out plans for a TV series featuring the Hawk. It would start with an hour-long special called "Honky Tonk"; if that made it in the ratings the series would follow. Well, the special made it and a series did follow, but the pressures mounted and mounted.

Hawkins found taping the "Honky Tonk" series even more exhausting than going on the road for one-nighters. Why not slow down? he wondered during a break in the taping. He'd gone back to his old-buddy network for the show's lineup: Conway Twitty appeared on the opening show, Roy Orbison shot another one. He also kept the legend alive one more time for any reporter who'd buy it. "I've got musicians in my band who haven't been as lucky as me. Some of them are forty, you know. I could retire if I wanted, but they can't afford to. They've paid their dues. So I'll keep working to honor that."

He was jiving, of course. He wasn't through paying *his* dues. In some ways he was just beginning. Yet another project with "Johnny F," as everyone called Bassett, Jr., was to have been Ronnie's biggest real-estate deal. It proved to be the most expensive. Ronnie was planning to sell his unprofitable restaurant in London, Ontario. "I could've made over a million dollars, too, that's net profit over a million — when Bassett and all those came along with their idea for a new restaurant."

Bassett and John Finlay thought they saw the wave of the future: rib houses. Ronnie's old restaurant would be the first of a chain of rib houses across the country. So with Finlay, Bassett, Hawkins and Steve Thomson as equal partners, $600,000 was sunk into the first Johnny Finebones, named after John Finlay whose passion had always been to be in the restaurant business.

Bassett, "who was always star struck," remembers Finlay, "loved being near the center of the action, and Ronnie was the action."

"We were all going to be millionaires," remembers Thomson. "The first week we did $30,000 in business. The second week was as good. It looked absolutely great." But it did not last. When business started to slacken off, the partners had another idea: an upstairs club for Ronnie, called the Hawk's Club. Ronnie would guarantee to work there so many times a year. They'd get the overflow crowd from downstairs. They'd be on their way.

They were. In six months, they were on their way out of business. "The food was terrible," says Thomson. "People were getting served cold hamburgers." To Finlay the problem was that none of the principals could be on hand to oversee its day-to-day operation. "You can't run a restaurant that's 120 miles away, and none of us could get down to watch it."

The collapse of Johnny Finebones ended the partnership and for several years divided friend against friend. Thomson and Hawkins felt the other two were "cutting their losses," something they themselves couldn't afford to do. Although Ronnie, as landlord, ended up with less of a straight cash loss, he was still stretched past his financial limit. "Until that restaurant came along I could always count on about $40,000 a year from my building. Before that, in Campbell's before it was expropriated, I was making over $100,000 a year," he says. "It was only after I lost everything that I had to go back and grind for everything to save the farm. So I went back in and ground the six- and seven-nights-a-week jobs and that's when I started drinking a bottle of cognac a day. All those li'l old clubs I had to stay in all the time, all those li'l old gut-bucket honky tonks. It didn't matter how good you were, there wasn't anyone in there most nights who could appreciate it. So I'd just drink a half bottle of cognac and go on. I blew up sixty pounds in weight. But I couldn't take it any other way. You see, now there was a difference in my life. I was forced to play, anywhere, for any penny I could make, to keep things afloat."

Complicating Ronnie's financial matters were the soaring interest rates that affected a line of credit he'd secured for his bus. To Ronnie, the 1955 Scenic Cruiser was a work of art. It was as pretty as any one of his vintage cars. And he saw nothing, absolutely nothing wrong in dropping $200,000 to bring it up to current standards. He loved to bring his old cars back to mint driving condition, why not do the same for a great tour bus? Besides, he'd been on the road long enough to know how wretched it is to break down somewhere. He'd had *that* happen to him enough times, that's for sure. To Steve, the bus was a bottomless financial pit, although Ronnie was happy to spend money on one of his vehicles.

But the collapse of Johnny Finebones put the squeeze on everybody. "It was a hellish time," remembers Thomson. And for Ronnie, "things went from bad to worse. I just call it Karma. Bad Karma. The restaurant went under and I ended up losing the whole building."

The collapse of Johnny Finebones was kept a private matter, and the press for the most part didn't get wind of it. What was made public was the Hawkinses' auction at Stoney Lake of a lot of their excess — some of the vintage cars Ronnie had amassed, extra crystal, a barn full of memorabilia. In part the auction was intended to raise some cash for the place in Florida they were planning to buy for Wanda's mother. In part, as Ronnie says, "it was to pay debtors off." The press was left to speculate. Something was obviously going on with Ronnie Hawkins. Something no one fully understood. Things were ending. Things were beginning.

Like music, for one thing. For years Ronnie had been threatening to go to England — permanently. Like many North American musicians before him, particularly jazzmen, Ronnie found Europeans, and especially the British, unstinting in their passion for his music, and for him. That wasn't the way it was at home. So in 1980, in order to test the water across the Atlantic, he flew his current edition of the Hawks eastward for their European debut in Holland; shortly after, they played Belgium. Going back for a second time around he added the "legendary guitarist" Lonnie Mack to the band, before recording a live album in London.

Anticipating the Hawk's arrival at a rock 'n' roll revival festival in Perranporth, Cornwall, Ian Wallis wrote enthusiastically in *Music World* magazine that "top of the bill . . . and undoubtedly the main attraction will be the long-awaited British debut of Ronnie Hawkins and the Hawks." Well, damn! Ronnie was sure impressed. Back home he was fighting this hard, hard battle — although in April 1982, he finally won a Juno award as the Canadian male country singer of the year — while over here, in England, he was a genuine goddamn hero.

The Juno awards, given annually to the best-selling and — sometimes — the best musicians in the country, had almost been a jinx for him. Although probably one of the best-known rockers in Canada, he'd been overlooked for years. Then, in 1981, he provided the Junos with the single most embarrassing moment in their history.

It was a set-up. He was supposed to get out of the Rolls he arrived in along with country singer Carroll Baker, and both were to get mikes and start singing live to a dazzled nation. Well, the Rolls arrived, the door opened, Ronnie moved to get out — and the pants of his tux caught on a door handle and ripped open right down his leg. "My ass was hanging out there in the breeze," he remembers. To make matters worse — and funnier — he had to go straight up on stage. By now he was too disoriented to be able to see the cue cards.

"Well, I can't see," he admitted live on air "I can't hear and I can't read those cue cards."

The following year, Juno in hand, he admitted, "I thought I'd never get an award, except maybe for best body. After twenty-five years I'm a teenage idol — the working girl's favorite and the housewife's companion." Then, for a brief moment he stopped joking — at least for those who knew him. His special thanks, he said, went to "all the drunks who came to see me."

Thomson, trying to capitalize on the Hawk's legendary status, decided to go for the last remaining old-style élite nightclub in the country, the Royal York Hotel's Imperial Room. Ronnie, to say the least, was not pleased: "I love the hotel but I knew it was the wrong clientele, the wrong staff, the wrong attitude — because it was fifty dollars a head to get in. Well, the folks in my market, they'll out-drink anybody but they won't pay fifty dollars to get in somewhere then pay six dollars for a beer. Well, of course the first time I went in there it was a novelty and we set the record for the Royal York. All those heavy rollers filled her every night. Later on — and this is after Steve had hustled his ass getting press and everything — well, we played for four hundred nuns one night. It was tougher. It came out in the papers that way. It was, 'Ronnie's only good habits.'"

As much as playing at the Royal York bothered him — "Damn, people tipping a hundred dollars," he mumbled at one point — it was still, for him, a key date. "To get ready for it the next year, I'd been on the road playing honky tonks, but I'd needed this playing time, just like a dress rehearsal, because I knew what I had to do to go over in the Royal York. Man, I was pushing it too hard. So I said, 'I've got to have four or five dates somewhere, just playing in any honky tonk — so we went to Sudbury. Dang. You've got to be in the right frame of mind to survive in Sudbury. So we played Friday, Saturday — well, whatever it was up there — and I started feeling bad. Then I got to the Royal York and it was time to open. Opening night, Monday usually, is the time when all the press comes out. So I had to get up at about nine o'clock in the morning after about three hours' sleep to talk to the press. Well, my blood pressure started coming up, higher and higher. Already I felt like the ol' Royal York was a jinx for me. Finally the ol' blood pressure sped up. I felt my heart fluttering a little bit. It was then I said, 'I ain't pushing it no further for any amount of money.'"

"Because he'd had the problem with his heart, I ended up singing half a dozen songs that night," remembers Larry Gowan, the singer-keyboard player who as "Gowan" later had a successful recording career on his own. "Our 'Bo Diddley' lasted about an hour. It was pretty hard to keep that beat going for an hour. Nobody knew me then; my first album was a commercial failure. Ronnie didn't play the rest of the week and he didn't come back to the band for two weeks.

"I'd only known him about a month then but I was starting to see what he meant to people. When we were up in Sudbury he tripped on a step going up to the stage and fell face down. It was about a quarter after one in the morning, and there he was, trying to bring himself to his feet, grabbing at tables and everything to bring himself up. Instead of helping him get up, a couple of people come through the crowd and shoved a piece of paper in his face and shouted, 'Ronnie, can we have your autograph?' As he was trying to get up, he kind of grabbed the pen with one hand. He didn't sign an autograph. It was more like a scratch across the page. They said, 'Thanks a lot, we've been listening to you for twenty years,' or something like that. With anyone else but Ronnie there'd be gasps and a lot of concern and people saying, 'Okay, get him up, is he okay?' and all that. But nope, they thought this was a good opportunity for an autograph. And Ronnie — he can't say no, now.

"Backstage at the Imperial Room were people from Hollywood and politics. I watched what was happening. There were a lot of these famous faces, not musicians, but people in other walks of life who knew him back when I watched and I saw people who had probably compromised themselves hundreds of times to attain the stature they'd attained.

"Yet they've somehow retained this link with Ronnie because this guy's been true to what he started out doing when he was eighteen. He's done it at different levels of success all through his life and he's still doing it. Through him I think those people feel they're getting back down to what they really were like years ago. It's more than simple nostalgia."

Larry Gowan remembers that "he played a show for Peter Pocklington at one of his meat companies. The joke around the show was that he was going to start another meat called Ronnie Hawkins — a bologna line. I thought, That's perfect, absolutely perfect. He's going to be like Colonel Sanders. Years from now you're going to see him on the front of a bologna package.

"I met Pocklington at that show," Gowan recalls, "and I asked him, 'What's your connection with Hawkins?' It turns out Pocklington was a roadie for him years ago. Here's someone else who's been extremely successful and in Ronnie he's able to take himself back to when things were simpler, before he had to make all the ugly decisions he's had to make. Nobody gets that rich just by being himself. People have to make compromises, certain decisions that perhaps they never foresaw way back then. But somehow with Ronnie, they feel they're with a guy who never made those calls. A guy who just remained true. I mean, Ronnie can shoot the shit when he feels like it. But he's always himself as a person. I don't think there's anybody more honest as far as understanding who he is and what he does in life. I know this is one guy who *never* ever thought, 'If things don't go well, I'm going to take a shot working at Eatons.' or, 'I'm going to see what accountancy holds.' A thought like that would never get in his brain. That's something to be admired.

"Ronnie has a fatalistic attitude. He's one of the most self-deprecating guys I've met. He's very humble but he's also the ultimate rock 'n' roll ringmaster. If it were the circus, he'd be the guy who'd set up everyone coming on stage. Without him there wouldn't be a show. Without him, it'd be chaos. But I've sensed he's a little uncomfortable in the spotlight. Every time he's had a chance to grab it, when he's had a real legitimate shot at things, he's shied away from it in some way.

"The night he had the heart problem at the Royal York I went to his room to say good night," Gowan says quietly. "He was sitting on the bed in a track suit. He didn't look at all well. He felt doing the Imperial Room was like doing a gig in somebody else's living room as opposed to doing it in the real type of roadhouse that he's at home in."

But it was work! He felt he couldn't stop. "Go, go, go," Ronnie says. "I wasn't hearing anybody telling me to slow down. Besides, I felt it was important that I kept doing the things I was doing. I'd keep telling Steve Thomson, 'I think I'm going a little too hard.' 'Cause your body tells you when you're going too hard. I wasn't sleeping but two or three hours a night. Now, everybody kind of thinks they're indestructible. I guess I thought that, too. But when my body starts giving me warning signals, baby, I slow down. It'd already been giving me signals for a couple of weeks, but I just tried to push it past that Royal York job. So I just stopped it. Patti Janetta, Bo Diddley and my band finished off the week."

But as Gowan remembers, as soon as he was better, the band was back working again. "That was around the time I needed a bit of confidence and he gave it to me," Gowan recalls. "I remember the story about what he said to Elvis: "Son, with a name like Elvis, you ain't goin' no place! Well, I asked him — we were in Montreal at the time — about that story because my record had just come out. I was wondering how it was going to do.

"'Ronnie, what do you think of my name?' I asked.

"'Gowan,' he says. 'Hmmm. Gowan. I like it.'

"I was hoping he'd say, 'With a name like Gowan, not a hope, son.' I was hoping he'd say, 'That's worse than Elvis.'"

Like their non-playing contemporaries, many musicians felt that tug of pleasure basic rock 'n' roll can provide. So, more and more, Ronnie found he was getting calls from the likes of Jerry Penfound, the saxophonist who'd left him when The Band did, and Stan Szelest who, when not playing for Levon, would play for the Hawk. They want to come back to him; they want to get back to real rock 'n' roll. Szelest — "Lon Chaney on helium" Ronnie calls him — is probably the greatest pure rock 'n' roll piano player alive. But as good — even great — as some of these players could be, they weren't the cohesive band, the one that was always together, the one that he could shape. He only found the heart of the band when he looked for it . . . at home.

Growing up, Robin Hawkins had no idea who his dad was when he was away from the house. He was just his dad. All the famous people who came and went were just friends of his dad or his mom. That's all. He'd watched his brother Ron get better and better on the guitar and thought if *he* was going to play anything, it might be the drums. As the family moved from Mississauga to High Park, then to Stoney Lake, he never really got around to doing much with the expensive drum kit his dad had bought for him from Levon, so it was eventually sold. Besides, he knew his folks would be just as happy if he never ended up in music. His brother — before his problem — had the talent. Little sister Leah had talent, too. Robin thought he'd do something else. A wild ride one night changed all that.

He'd been out roaring around the back roads in an AMC Eagle, and had driven it off the road going seventy miles per hour. He was just seventeen; he nearly died. In the slow months that followed as he recuperated at home, he started picking at one of the guitars he found around the house. Ron, Jr., taught him some simple chords, so he did what he could with them. And he kept working on it and working on it. Ronnie could see how much easier things had come to Ron, Jr., and to Leah than to Robin. But as he watched Robin work at the guitar, he began to be reminded of another kid guitarist he'd known who'd worked his ass off to get where he wanted — Robbie Robertson.

For a while Ronnie worried that maybe Robin had started too late. "Most of them nowadays start at nine or ten years old," he worried. His son was just too late. But damn, could that kid work, just like Robbie.

Robin knew he was getting somewhere, at least in his dad's eyes, when he started hearing all about the importance of "roots," and playing the right songs the right way. He had to learn how to make the music say something. It was the Hawkins method, the Hawkins school, and for better or worse, he was now part of it.

Sure, it frustrated him at times. Like Leah he wanted to do his own music. The two eventually even put a band together, to play around the Peterborough area. Leah was particularly rebellious. Wanda would see how she could frustrate her dad with her insistence on doing her thing her way. And Wanda could understand both sides.

"She was the princess," says Wanda. "Princess Leah. She was the apple of Ronnie's eye. She could do no wrong. But then she became a teenager and you know, as teenagers will, she resented living out here in the country. She didn't want to do what he wanted her to do. She didn't want to do *his* songs. She wanted to do *her* songs. Well, I could see she's very, very much a Hawkins and very, very much like him. Robin was like that too. They had that determination that they could do it without him."

One day Robin confronted Ronnie: "Nobody could tell you, dad," he said, as Wanda watched, "so however much it hurts you, I have to make my own mistakes myself."

Still, Robin was gradually learning something more than how to be part of a band. He learned about being in a band that could trace its roots back to a bunch of Arkansas boys who got a call from a honky tonker called Harold Jenkins telling them that if they wanted to play rock 'n' roll, they'd better come to Canada to do it.

Robin was coming to understand what it meant to be a Hawkins.

XVI

I Ain't Been Half So Intelligent Since I Stopped Drinkin'

Proving You Can Go Home Again, Our Hero
Heads Back to Arkansas for a Mess of
Herman's Mighty Good Ribs

ALL THE FIGHTIN', CUSSIN', FEUDIN', jammin', rockin', and yarnin'; the long days and longer nights of playin' and still more playin' were finally worth it. Ronnie had the band he wanted — "Tighter than a frog's ass stretched over a boxcar" — and he had his life where he wanted it when he decided to go back to Arkansas to revisit all of the good ol' boys who *didn't* pile into the old car the day he drove north all those years long ago.

Now, Ronnie loves to talk about the past. "Son," he'll say, "I've been playing since the Dead Sea was only a little bit sick," or, "I've been doing this so long I remember having Jesus on rhythm guitar."

And he loves old cars, old towns and old movies — shoot, he'll spend days after tours doing nothing but looking at movie after movie.

Yet he is not hooked on nostalgia, a prisoner of his past. Rather than linger over the past, he re-invents it. It is alive in his head. But only to the degree it means something to him today.

At least this is what I saw on that trip back to Fayetteville, as we rolled in our Don Tyson-provided car over the snug, low hills around the city. *I* thought he was showing me the past. On the contrary, he was showing me what was very much alive for him, today. On the way, I noticed something about him. He was at peace with himself now. Things were in place for him: the annual New Year's Eve blast at Toronto's City Hall which he hosts; his weekly club dates at the Deer Park Inn near Toronto; Robin leading his band; and his Variety Club benefit shows for charity.

Soon, I understood why I was here and why it was time for him to think about what the good ol' boys were up to today. For all that he had accomplished, it had started here.

Ronnie has come back to Fayetteville again after all these years, looking for that log cabin he and Wanda are going to settle in when they're ready to, and looking out for the boys in the very first band he ever had.

They aren't "boys" anymore, he knows, but in a way, they will always be. They'll always be the boys in *his* band.

As much as Ronnie and I have any real direction this day, we're heading to Herman Tuck's Rib House out on the Arkansas Interstate. But first we roll through downtown Fayetteville and along the way, he remembers, out loud and proud, the old band: "There was Herman 'Killer' Tuck on drums," he says, looking out the window, "and Harold Pinkerton, who's sort of the king of the air-conditioning business around Fayetteville, on guitar; Bobby Keene, who became an electrical engineer and is now working in Texas, was lead guitar; and Claude Chambers, who studied music at the University and played classical-style music was on upright bass. This was the first band I ever made any noise with at all: I couldn't been more than nineteen or twenty years old at the time."

There must be something in this log cabin thing. Something in the Arkansas genes: down the road Levon has moved back to his cabin. But Ronnie's search for a cabin first takes us back through a lot of memories; around the neatly laid out streets of Fayetteville, around the university, then down past where the Rockwood Club was — the building still catering to baby boomers, only now as a day care center — then down into the Hollow, or "Holler," as it's called, where JoJo Thompson, the pint-sized blues-playing keyboard wizard, has his dining room filled with speakers — waiting, forever waiting, for another club to call him.

Bob Thompson, Jr., as he was born, went to Dallas to try his luck. That was in '66. He was back in Fayetteville four years later. Got homesick. So on occasion he pops up seemingly out nowhere to startle the local students with some real blues. Hence one critic on the student-run *Grapevine* reported not many years ago: "After years of semi-obscurity, JoJo can suddenly sing with nearly any band in town. He is, as Blue Boy Orliss says, the star of the show."

The Holler is not much more than a collection of squat little houses where the black residents live, with old trees leaning alongside several wandery little roads. Nothing is well kept: everything looks lovely and comfortable. Don't leave, it says. You don't want to leave. For the young studs of Ronnie's generation, the Holler was an escape — somewhere you could get a cold beer on a Sunday, or, in Ronnie's case, where you could hear the blues.

"The end of my grade schooling and all of my high schooling was in Fayetteville," he tells me as we look at all the old buildings. Modern Fayetteville is now out on the highways. "During my high-school years I put a little band together, and we played around locally. That's when we really started listening to black music. There were a lot of radio stations around, but there is only one I remember getting — from Gallatin, Tennessee — and on a clear night you could get the station really clear. So we'd listen, and think about making trips to where we heard there were really good blues pickers. We always dreamed of Memphis, so we went to Memphis in the early fifties just to buy the records. We were all listening to the blues."

I discover this: Get Ronnie Hawkins moved enough, or happy, sappy or tipsy enough, and he'll start extolling the blues. The blues started it all, he'll tell you. Black music! Damn it all, black music is at the very foundation of everything anyone has ever done in rock 'n' roll — anyone! The Rolling Stones! Even Rompin' Ronnie Hawkins, his own sweet self. The blues! So damn it all, son, stop the car. We are going to see JoJo.

The Holler has its own rhythm, its own sense of history and fair play.

"Like there is the story of Sherburne Morgan, Jr." says Don Tyson, who can claim two distinctions — he's one of Ronnie's first fans and he is, far and away, the richest. "First, there was Sherburne Morgan, Sr. He had the only beer joint in the Holler where we all used to go and have a beer before we were of age. Sherburne Morgan, Sr., was just a super guy. But then there was Sherburne Morgan, Jr., who got into a spot of trouble once.

"One Sunday in the summertime, Sherburne Morgan, Jr., was out running around somewhere when a black friend of his came over to his house and extracted a watermelon from his refrigerator. He just entered his house and extracted this watermelon and when Sherburne Morgan, Jr., got home, about five-thirty in the evening, he noticed that his watermelon was gone. So Sherburne Morgan, Jr., went out and asked around the neighborhood about who exactly had extracted this watermelon from his refrigerator.

"Two or three of the neighbors testified that a particular fella had done it. So Sherburne Morgan, Jr., took his trusty pistol and went over to try to discuss it with this gentleman and after three shots the gentleman just dropped to the floor and died. You just don't steal a watermelon from a fellow black American. All the participants here were black Americans and they concluded it just wasn't right on a Sunday afternoon to extract a cold watermelon from a man's fridge.

"It went to trial and the Washington County jury retired for thirty minutes. They said it just wasn't right and that Sherburne Morgan, Jr., was innocent."

Down in the Holler as the hours go by, JoJo and Ronnie make small talk. At first it doesn't make sense to me. JoJo wasn't Ronnie's mentor. Ronnie never brought JoJo up to Canada to play. Then it *does* make sense. To each the other is special — a legend in his own time, as Ronnie is given to saying. "I thought 'bout movin' on," says JoJo. "But I thought 'bout it again and didn't." You know he's never going to leave it again. Later, he walks us back to the road, and after some talk about everyone getting together to have one mammoth meal just like in the good old days, "with them beans and peas, and ribs and all that," we say goodbye and Ronnie grows quiet for a moment. He doesn't look back as we drive up the little hill, back into downtown Fayetteville.

Along the way I begin to realize something about the Hawk: I've never met anyone who knows so many people, and knows them not in the superficial sense of just remembering them but in having had experiences with them. I've never met anyone who has lived his life so thoroughly as he has. So with these experiences come the stories, the tales tall and true.

Back on course to Herman Tuck's Rib House, we head down the interstate away from the old Fayetteville, past a series of new plazas with their Radio Shacks, coin washes, tanning emporia and classy, beefy-looking rib joints which from the gargantuan proportions they whip up should have neon signs flashing in blistering Day-glo pink: BIG FAT CHOLESTEROL. But don't look for Herman's among these establishments. No sir. Look on the other side of the highway, near a couple of bent-over trees, where you'll see this . . . well, this shack, with slivers of ancient white paint peeling from its old boards, a sign you can't read and a whiff of smoke bringing promises of to-kill-for ribs — finger-sticky suckers tasting so good they make you want to slap your granny.

"We did have a big sign and a tornado blew it down," Herman will tell you. "We was all sitting here when it happened. Later some older person asked me why I didn't have a sign and I told him I had one once and God blew it down so I figured God didn't want me to have it."

Around Herman Tuck's Rib House when the boys start talking about the old days and their wild old ways over their ribs and pork chops and Herman's world-class, dynamite chili, inevitably at least one Ronnie Hawkins story comes up. Herman, maybe the wildest of them all a long time since, stopping popping pills and drinking one day years ago to find he had a fine wife, Irene, a fine daughter and this little restaurant he could be happy with. He stayed put. So did Don Tyson. Each in his way is settled, so to each an uncommon experience — like a visit from Ronnie — is always welcome.

So when the Hawk and Don Tyson are at Herman's at the same time the stories start, and these stories will inevitably lead someone to remember what the Hawk did to Tom T. Hall. It's their way of razzing Tyson a little, seeing that he's richer than God, has no end of pretty women all around him and maybe could use a bit of razzing now and then. So Herman will set his elbows on his counter and the women will pretend to be busier then they are, seeing this story is a touch risqué and some newcomer will hear how Tyson had brought Tom T. to town for some business.

It all started when Tyson Foods Inc. thought they needed a spokesman. A face. A presence. Tyson Foods Inc. may not be the instantly recognized name that MGM is, or Ford or Pepsi, but as *Forbes* magazine and the *Wall Street Journal* have noticed, Tyson's is one of the fastest growing companies in the Fortune 500. That's a lot of money. That's a lot of chicken (around Fayetteville it's usually referred to more pointedly as "a damn lot of chicken"). Don Tyson himself, who made a billion-dollar business out of his family's measly old million-dollar business, can usually be found around town dressed like any of the old boys in his plant, in his khaki work clothes with his name, "Don Tyson," stitched over his heart. That's when he's here. When he's not, which is two weeks every month, he usually can be found on his yacht deep-sea fishing off the west coast of Africa or off Chile or some other such romantic place where very rich guys with the very big ocean-going yachts go, with the phones not far away. With Tyson, the phones are all linked back to chicken central at Springdale, near Fayetteville.

So maybe he doesn't actually chase chickens anymore, but Don Tyson hasn't entirely forgotten the country roots of the chicken business. He helped bankroll Willie Nelson's Farm Aid shows. He was a big Jimmy Carter supporter and threw a party at the Watergate Hotel complex for Carter's 1977 inauguration that is still famous in circles where real wild wing-dings are appreciated. That was the party where Ronnie saw Cher drag a comatose Gregg Allman outside.

Tyson Foods' need to project its down-home image with a down-home kind of guy you'd trust selling you some good heat-and-serve Chicken Kiev, led it to Tom T. Hall.

Tom T. Hall, we can recall, is that nice Nashville songwriter who wrote "Harper Valley PTA" and "The Year That Clayton Delaney Died." Tom T. Hall is a regular straight arrow who Don Tyson figured would be perfect to advertise Tyson Foods. After Tom T. had finished a meeting on one particular day, Rompin'

Ronnie, Fayetteville's own, showed up for a real nice long talk. *Well, Tom, how ya doin'? Fine, Ronald, and you? Real good. That's nice.* It was real pleasant, this conversation, until Ronnie says he's got to get going and Tom T. says something like, "Well, it was real nice," and, "Next time," . . . then — Good goddamn! There's the Hawk, out on Tyson's manicured lawn, neighbors all around, waving bye-bye to Tom T. with his . . . pecker.

By the time we arrive I've convinced myself that Ronnie and the guys at Herman's just have to be tired of the Tom T. story and all the old yarns. But such is not the case. Ronnie has come home for the first time in years and this is all the excuse everyone needs to remember the good old days. And that's just fine. Ronnie sits back as the old stories roll around the room, absorbing it all like some big old workhorse warming to the first sunshine in spring. He's old enough for nostalgia. So he's thinking about it all again: about The Band, named to the Juno Hall of Fame more than thirty years after he first called them all together; about Levon getting back in his band again on occasion — they were first together in 1957; about the bands he had before he'd ever heard of such a place as Toronto.

"You're sure lookin' good," Ronnie says to the women behind the counter, Herman's waitresses and his wife Irene. Herman himself thunks the plates down in front of us and pretends to look gruff, as if what we think of the food won't matter to him, not one bit.

At this moment, Herman's not buying any of Ronnie's yarns. "You wait," Herman whispers to us, "he'll tell the one about me takin' every pill there was and us playing seven songs for five hours. Well, that's not the way it was at all. It was only three songs we knew."

"Herman," announces Ronnie, "makes the best ribs in the world. But I tell you he was crazy. Because of him that first band I ever had broke three records in Arkansas which will stand forever. You see, in Herman's wild days, he once took every pill that Colliers Drugstore ever had. He also broke every drum head in Guy Singer's Music Store. Hell, with him drumming we could play a five-hour dance and only use seven tunes. I don't think anyone will be able to do that again. We did a lot of repeating. There were a lot of long solos."

"Shit, we only knew three tunes, Ronnie," says Herman, adding quietly, "I told you he'd say seven."

"It's because I didn't know the words to all the others," Ronnie says.

"That's why the boys played for free," Herman goes on, as if the two have been through this routine before. "Like I said, he will tell you he knew seven but he didn't. He knew three. We'd play the same one fast, slow, intermediate, several times. No one knew any different. With him gyrating and masturbating with his little microphone — why nobody was paying attention to what he was singing. We were playing a teen hop at the Rogers Teen Center and that really was one time when we were asked to leave point blank — to get the hell outta there. The chaperones did not care at all for the way he was acting on stage. He was doin' his Elvis Presley imitation. Besides, I was drinking straight whiskey out of a bottle that didn't have a sack on it or anything else."

"They thought you weren't a good role model," Ronnie adds.

"Yeah," says Herman Tuck reflecting, "I wasn't setting a good example for any of them."

Ronnie grins. "Herman and I used to be particularly good-looking and intelligent when we were drinking, weren't we Herman?"

"Now, Ronnie was always against drinkin' too much," says Herman. "He'd say, 'You can stay out late as you want, but we're gonna run stairs when you're through.' Then he'd make the band get up early and run the stairs over at the stadium. So they'd get some rest. They'd want to. It could just kill you if you didn't get in at a half-decent hour, running up and down those stairs. Now Pink — Harold Pinkerton — could drink a little. As for Claude Chambers — sheeeit! There was no way for him runnin'. He looked like he was eighty years old when he started with our band."

Herman wipes his hands on his white apron and looks at wife Irene: "When we were young I never could tell when Ronnie was serious about anything. He never looked like it or acted like it. I tell you, one thing he was serious about was when he was running up and down those stairs over at the university. He was a health nut. He had one hell of a physique on him, he used to swim a lot and was into diving. After he moved to Canada he used to box a little and work out in the ring with some boxers. He was about 175 pounds, 180 pounds when I met him. I've never seen Ronnie drunk — well, maybe two times at the most. I managed to do enough drinking for both of us. I've changed since then, though. I've been sober seven years this time," sighs Herman Tuck. "I haven't been rich, intelligent or good looking since I quit drinking.

"That wasn't the way it was with Ronnie, though. He would get a gig and make five or six dollars is all, but he was serious about it. Although maybe that was all he was serious about then. He never got more than thirty miles away from town with this band but he got very worked up about it. My memory's not really that good all the time. I had a few things that were detrimental to remembering — things that contributed to mental retardation, like electric-shock treatments and a couple quarts of booze a day. That kinda, you might say, cuts in on the memory banks. But I do remember the first time I saw him really get with it. It was just after he picked up Levon and some other guys. He'd been in the army with a band I hadn't seen. But I'd get to see him each time he'd be through after that."

Ronnie nods, "I used to have what I called the 'Ronnie Hawkins Olympics.' We had to stay in shape. I used do this with The Band, particularly. They used to let us into the University of Arkansas football field whenever we were down this way. We used to train there, getting ourselves in shape. Oh, Robbie used to make all kinds of excuses how he'd have to fix his guitar. He didn't like running too much. For the rest of us it was running and jogging to keep in shape. We'd go every day, a couple of hours a day. We'd jog the 440. Hell, I couldn't walk the 440 now."

"Kid," says Herman Tuck, "you couldn't *drive* the 440 now."

More plates are produced: sizzling pork chops, ribs. Then Herman leans on the counter again, to clarify: "I was in a band before I was with Ronnie. It was just local stuff I was doing at the time. I never played out of town. It was just Pink — Harold Pinkerton — and me and someone else. Then I heard Ronnie needed a drummer. Just messing around one time, I asked him if I could come play with him. He said, sure. So after that it was Ronnie, Pinkerton and me and Claude Chambers. I never got paid for any of that. But if I got a free beer I was all right. I'm five years older than Ron. I was married and so I couldn't get into it too deep. Shit, I was making thirty-five dollars a week working for my dad.

I didn't need another job. Why, I had all the money in the world. I fantasized about goin' out on the road all the time. But I was one of the first married, so I knew I couldn't.

"We used to feel sorry for Irene," says Ronnie. "We'd wake her up and make her cook for us. She fed us every time we'd come through. We were always a little short. By this time mom had left Arkansas to go to New Mexico to teach. She went my sophomore year in high school, so I stayed at 519 West Maple. Oh, man, we used to have parties there that Caligula would be ashamed of. We practiced music there day and night. It got where we couldn't practice too late at night. The neighbors across the road called the police on us a few times so we set a curfew to stop about ten at night 'cause we'd been going pretty late for a long time."

The party's over — for the moment — and we find ourselves heading back through the University of Arkansas. Coming from a family of intransigent female teacher students — his mother, his aunt and his sister all finding school to their liking — Ronnie, rebelling somewhat, viewed education as less than his life's work. High school was more a matter of getting his band together.

"He was social," one classmate will tell me later. "He did all right at his grades, just well enough I'd say to get where he wanted to go. But that didn't seem to matter to him. He was always involved with something and that something always had to do with a lot of people. I saw him on and off by the time he was in university, and he was even more involved with things then."

Even back in the early fifties, the University of Arkansas viewed itself as a liberal college. Blacks were part of school life earlier here than most places, they'll say. President Eisenhower's decision to send in paratroopers in 1957 to prevent violent resistance to desegregation in Little Rock gave the entire state a reputation it didn't deserve, they'll add. In truth, the University of Arkansas was as good a place as anywhere to get an education and have a good time getting it. For Ronnie, and Pink, Claude, Bobby and Herman it was time to get a band together.

"We were playin' rockabilly and rhythm 'n' blues songs, by then," Ronnie remembers as we head back down the interstate to R.J.'s, the definitive good ol' boys headquarters in this part of the state — a dark, low-ceilinged place in one corner of a tiny plaza.

"And we were getting noticed. Well, one day Roy Orbison was coming through to do a concert in town. He had the Teen Kings and he wanted us to be his opening act. Well, damn, there weren't but two songs in our entire repertoire that weren't his. He'd just had "Ooby Dooby' and 'Go Go Go' out and we did both of them. I was in really good shape in those days. I was doing all those double backflips and was really selling those songs."

"'Goddamn it boy,' Roy said to me. 'You just did all of my songs and that goddamn monkey act of yours, what am I going to do?'

"So he got up there and started, then he stopped and said, 'Shit, I can't do anything.' And he got me back up there again. I did his act, too. But it wasn't just Roy's stuff. We were doing anything that came out on Sun Records or Chess. Around here everyone else just liked country music. That wasn't for us. We were into what was new."

But there was absolutely nothing new about drinking at R.J.'s. As soon as we're there I realize why Don Tyson and all the local millionaires gravitate this way, for despite the high gloss of its tables, R.J.'s is really an old roadhouse in spite of its best efforts to be new. You could disappear into a place like R.J.'s and with any luck, not be found for days. A lot of folks have done just that, I hear.

Word was out though, that the Hawk was back, and no sooner is he settled in a corner than this tall guy, with a kind of sweet 'n' sad, hound dog face, comes over — Harold Pinkerton.

"You know," says Pink, "I played with him even before he had a band. The first stuff we did was Roy Orbison stuff and some Elvis stuff. I wasn't any good, mind you, but that didn't matter. We had lots of women. Ronnie always had lots of women around him."

More drinks are set clattering down on the table. Heads are bent closer as the memories come. "When Ronnie would hire a musician," recalls another long-time friend, Dash Goff, "he couldn't pay anybody because he never had any money that night. So he'd say, 'I'll tell you what. I can't pay you very much but I'll guarantee you'll get more pussy than Frank Sinatra.' After hearing this a few times, I asked him, 'What do you tell the girls?'

"'Well,' he'd say, 'Stick with me, honey, and I'll have you fartin' through silk by the end of the week.'"

Adds Ronnie: "When we played around here, we'd be making

maybe ten dollars a night. We'd be watching that entrance door hoping that Don Tyson would come in. He'd make us all suffer till about ten minutes to quitting time before he'd come up and put a hundred dollar bill in everyone's pocket and ask for one more song."

Being with Don Tyson never impressed Ronnie more than the night both of them were out on the prowl and Don found himself in need of a bit of cash. Since the Tyson family, in the tradition of Fayetteville gentry, owned a bank or two in the area, getting cash proved to be less of a problem than it might be for other folks. "Don just went in the bank," remembers Ronnie, "turned off the alarm system, scooped up a handful of cash, left a note, then turned the alarm system back on. I didn't know bankers could do that."

"I was a music freak," says Tyson. He's a compact man, with a round face, and a direct, unblinking way of looking at you. "Ronnie would get all the good pussy so I'd get the castoffs. In those days if you played guitar and looked as good as he did, they'd just come up on stage for you. But after one or two of them, he'd get tired."

Again, I sensed they'd been through this routine before, maybe for the movie company which had come through town in the mid-eighties with plans to film the Blackhawks segment of Ronnie's life; or with the documentary team that in 1978 had gone south from Toronto, with more than $300,000 of John Bassett, Jr.'s, money and even more of his grandiose plans to do a documentary on Ronnie's life.

"Of course," Tyson continues, "this was long before he went to Canada. Some say he had to make a run for it," he adds in a wink. "Several girls' daddies asked him to leave."

"You mean Rex Perkins," says Ronnie, not at all abashed. "He was the number-one lawyer around here at one time. I was going with his little girl. The family finally suggested that they'd rather their daughter went out with someone else."

"She was good lookin'," Tyson remembers, "She would stay two or three days with Ronnie and her dad wouldn't like it. She was fifteen. Hell, Ronnie was old enough."

Hawkins recalls: "Her father told me, 'Son, either you quit goin' around with my little girl or you marry her — if you're that stupid. After all, neither one of you can get a job. Those are the options.

Either you take one of them or you can go to the Tucker Farm.'
That's the penitentiary around here. Well, it didn't take me too
long to figure out what I wanted to do."

By now the table's crowded. More drinks are splashed down on
the slippery top, although Pink turns one down saying that he's
driving. Driving's important to Harold Pinkerton, as any man
would feel who owns a pair of mint condition Jaguar XKEs. Before
this night was through, I found myself flying through nowhere
Arkansas in the prettiest little Jag I'd ever seen. I half hoped that
some stud cop in a lesser car would try to give chase. I'd like to
have seen what that little baby would have done. Hell, I'd like to
see what *I* would have done.

"I was in high school with Ron," says Pink. "I played with him
for three or four years but I never went to Canada with him. I never
went big time. I stayed in school. Now I'm an air-conditioner
repairman. I went into the business in '58. I've known Don as long
as I've known Ron. We all met about the same time. Don, he's a
good time guy. They both are."

Without doubt we're deep in the heart of what feminists would
describe as good old-fashioned male chauvinism. Yet it's not
entirely like that, despite all the rudeness, as the one woman at
the table, a friend of Don's, aims to explain. "Around here — and
I grew up with these two — it's definitely male-oriented," she says
across from me. "Maybe that's changing now but that's the way it
was. You have to understand things in that context. But" — she
sips her drink — "because the men are this way, it gives the
women a kind of freedom. They know definitely who they are." I
want to talk to her more about this, not the least because she is
attractive and obviously not as submissive as she might have me
believe.

Ronnie is forever rushing, usually mouth first, into trouble with
feminists and it always seems to start with his unstinting *fondness*
for women. "Damn," he'll say, "what's wrong with women anyhow? They've always been in charge. When you've got half the
money and all the pussy you're *definitely* in charge."

Yet I can find that he and the others — maybe me, too, although
being nearly a generation younger has altered my attitudes somewhat — are drawn into a kind of sexual subservience when it
comes to these women who they (we) would seem to treat so

casually. At times when they talk, I notice, sex and rock 'n' roll become almost the same thing.

There's a movement to have the party move on to yet another stop down the road but not before the last bit of carousing gone by is remembered. "You see," says Ronnie, "Don's wife at the time used to go away to a clinic to get a physical and she wasn't supposed to come back for three days. So Don loaned us the house to have a little party. This was in '56. Well, we were having a real good time, with maybe fifteen naked women, and no one else with any clothes on either, when in she walked, days early."

Tyson recalls, "It was like someone put a hose on the party. Some of the real heroes went out the front doors. The ones with good judgment went out the back."

"I went up the tree," Hawkins continues, "but that isn't the main story. Don had gone everywhere and bought antiques and furniture and expensive stuff from all over the world for this house. Well, she took every stick of those antiques and furniture and threw it in the pool."

"It seems she had a very narrow judgment on the whole thing," says Tyson. "For some reason, she wouldn't believe they were holding me captive. She didn't believe me either when I told her I was merely being socially gracious."

Later, across town, the evening's low and sweet and quiet as Claude Chambers walks us around from his front porch to his little shed in back. Claude pulls on his cigar as he shows us the old radios on his work bench. Claude "fixes things," Ronnie has told me. That's mostly all he does, too: "fixes things." His momma doesn't like him to drink, so he has to sneak some beer quietly into the house. For Claude Chambers that's about as wild as things get. He probably wouldn't have ended up in Ronnie's first band — not being the type to carouse and carry on with women — if Ronnie hadn't needed a bass player so badly. "So I talked him into it."

"Well," says Claude, "it wasn't that hard. Before Ronnie, I played for grass fires, dog fights. Everything. I played all-night square dances where there's moonshine. I played all over the country."

"He never played rock 'n' roll, though," Ronnie comments.

"He'd been listening to orchestras and stuff. But we got to practicing with him and we got to playing and he got to like it. The rest of us could hardly read and write music, but he could. He's got that old bass that's got to be worth a fortune."

Claude says, " I got it from Scott Price who played with Bob Wills's band for years and years and years. It's got a solid back and a solid front. I had some good times with it. But I didn't have as good a time as these guys."

Carefully he closes the shed door and we walk out on the sidewalk, heading back to his front door. "Claude played with all those bands but when he was with me he'd get where he'd have to tape his fingers," says Ronnie. "His fingers would blister. He amplified his bass later on. Claude was the first one to amp. You couldn't amplify a piano or an upright bass back then. But Claude knew how. He put in some kind of a bug pickup on his back of his bass."

"You know that '35 Ford you had?" asks Claude as if there's no apparent change of subject. "The real slick one. That thing is still out here someplace. Somebody put a Cadillac engine in it. It had a slant back."

"We played together till I left," Ronnie goes on. "Claude wouldn't leave. He wasn't the only one. Nobody would leave home."

"Well," Claude explains, his large, liquid eyes opening wide, "the temperature up in Canada was about thirty below. Besides, I had the chance to start playin' with some orchestras. I joined Harold Stewart's Enterprises out of Dennison, Texas. They had a rodeo band that followed the rodeos. So I played with that. It had horns on it. And whenever the rodeo season was over we went to play for the circus. We played with these prancin' horses."

"Besides, he had three or four little girls on the side," Ronnie interjects, causing Claude to fluster.

"Well, after I made some of those rodeo and circus trips, I came back to find a couple of them's already married. In a way I do wish I went to Canada. You gotta have a little remorse. You always make mistakes. I never been to Canada.

"Later on I toured with Anita Bryant. She was a nice lady. She wasn't hard to get along with. She told us, 'There's not gonna be any drinkin' or smokin'. When we have rehearsals here in the mornin' I don't want anybody to have a hangover or I'll fire you.'"

"But *we* got a little drunk didn't we?" remembers Ronnie. "Hell, there was one night Claude's a-playing on that bass. He's looking around. Killer's just whipping on those drums. Wired he was — Herman would take a pill or two. And Herman's grinding his teeth, hitting those drums when this old girl jumps up on the table and takes all her clothes off. Claude nearly fell over that bass, man."

Claude: "She's takin' off one piece at a time. She's out there dancin' and her partner missed her hand and she slid out in front of the bandstand and you carried her out."

"There were three or four girls who didn't have a stitch on in the club after," says Ronnie, "Claude said they didn't do that shit when he was playin' in all those orchestras."

"I never seen nothin' like it."

"That's what all my musicians said down here since I've come back. They said they ain't seen nothin' before like it and they ain't seen nothin' since."

It takes us a good five minutes to get around to the front of the tiny bungalow. Ronnie's enjoying the quiet, I see. It's a side of him that's rarely revealed in public, the side he prefers not to show. But something tells me Claude may be the person he misses the most.

Inside, we meet Mrs. Chambers. The room's musty with age and old wood with decades of yellowing newspapers and magazines piled in every available space. Claude's momma is brittle and stiff as if she herself were folded from paper.

"She used to feed us," says Ronnie joshing her a bit. "As long as Claude didn't make her mad."

"I don't do that anymore," says Claude's momma. "I'm over seventy years old now."

"Ninety," Claude quietly corrects her.

"I mean ninety," says momma. She looks up at me brightly. "I never want to hear them play."

"She never would go," says Ronnie. "I always wanted her to but she was religious like. She wouldn't go to honky tonks where they had booze."

"You should have heard him when he come home from the Jefferson School over here," says momma, looking at Claude. I see

Claude's beginning to fidget. "He said, 'Momma, I got to have some hot pants and a hot shirt. I'm gonna play in a band.' That was years ago.

"For seventy years I've been here. I'm from southwest Oklahoma. My husband was from Texas. The reason I'm here is he was goin' to university here in electrical engineering. This is the first bungalow in Fayetteville. We came down a big hill over there to take a look at it. I said I'm not goin' back up that hill. So he went and paid for it. But I'm not going to stay here forever. I always wanted to go back to southwest Oklahoma. Close to Fort Salem. That's where I'm goin'."

Outside, Claude looks sheepish. As if he's heard his momma's plans for the first time. As if he knew that she wouldn't be going anywhere.

Nor would he.

"Bye, Claude, bye." Ronnie says this softly. I see that damp cigar glow in the night as we leave.

A day or so later I find myself in the back of one of Don Tyson's corporate jets whooshing down out of rain clouds into Little Rock to meet one of the few of Ronnie's musical peers he didn't end up playing with, borrowing songs from, giving songs to — his cousin Dale Hawkins.

For both of them, Dale's dad Delmar was a hero. Dale, lean, contained, dressed in a suit, explains: "He started playing professionally when he was nine. There really wasn't any string instrument dad couldn't play." The primary shapers of both Dale and Ronnie's music were growing up around St. Paul and Huntsville, Arkansas, and Delmar Hawkins. Yet for Dale, his song "Suzie Q" — one of the biggest hits to come out of the South that was not from Sun Records — proved to be as limiting to his career as "Forty Days" proved to be extraneous to Ronnie's career.

"I'd meet Ronnie off and on, you know," says Dale. "The thing for our family on Saturday nights was going down to the little court house there in St. Paul with everybody just getting together and playing. But I only got to spend a little time with Ronnie when we were growing up. My dad was on the road most all the time so we lived in Louisiana where all my mother's people were. So I met Ronnie when I went back up there a couple times and went to school in St. Paul. As a matter of fact, each of us didn't know that the other was in the music business professionally until 'Suzie Q' was a hit. It was released in the latter part of '57, August or a little later. I was on a little label out of Chicago called Chess. I was the first white act on that label. Even so at that time, because of the music we played, they thought I was as black as the ace of spades. Ronnie told me that when he heard the record he didn't know it was me.

"I guess you could call these two musical careers a coincidence. I don't. I think it's inherited even though he was up in Fayetteville and I was down in Shreveport. We were both on the same track although neither one of us knew what the other one was doing. Like he did, I always liked Elvis, Jerry Lee — the early stuff. Because of Elvis and a couple of the black acts I said, 'I'm gonna do it, too.' I thought Elvis's early stuff was great. It opened doors. Every label was looking for a white artist that sounded black. I thought I could be it, like Ronnie.

"Chess Records heard about me and came down to Shreveport," Dale Hawkins remembers clearly. "For a while we just talked. I didn't sign any contract. Then we went to a radio station. During that period of time you could go into the radio station and record at night when they changed transmitters. So that's where we cut 'Suzie Q ,' at KWKH. It worked out well.

"After the record came out, Chess kept me on the road all the time promoting it. I was on the road until early 1960. I was in Philadelphia and did a TV show and then went back on the road for a couple of years. After a while you get burned out. It wasn't like today. We only had maybe a station wagon, maybe a U-haul trailer for the road. That's all. Ronnie, because he was in Canada and played in the same club for long periods of time, didn't get burnt out while we were doing one-nighters. The first time I saw him on stage was in Canada and he looked good. And I'll *never* forget the time I saw him in New York.

"Just a couple of country boys walking down Broadway in New York, that was me and Ronnie. Ronnie would walk with one foot on the sidewalk and one foot off and he would say it's just like walkin' on the mountains. Ronnie never got me in trouble. We just had everybody lookin' at us thinkin' we were crazy — which we were at that time. It was when Buddy Holly was coming up and I'd just finished the Apollo Theater and Ronnie came in to do a session with Roulette. That's when we got together. I think 'Forty Days' was just out.

"Just good ol' country boys in the big city havin' as much fun as they could."

XVII

WHO DO YOU LOVE?

In which Levon and the Hawks Come Home, and The Big Time Is Just Around the Corner

ON JULY 4, 1989, SEVERAL MILLION rock freaks, country buffs and those who were just curious caught a Pay TV special concert, "This Country's Rockin'." Filmed at Detroit's Silverdome, the country-rock blast struck *People* magazine to report that it was one of the great rowdy parties of the year.

It was a wild-eyed, brave attempt to revive the original spirit of rock 'n' roll, with rockers like Ted Nugent, the host, Gregg Allman, David Crosby and Steven Stills all sharing the stage with their mentors and teachers, the likes of Carl Perkins, Etta James and . . . Rompin' Ronnie Hawkins.

Levon Helm, Rick Danko and Garth Hudson from The Band all got up on stage, too. So did Ronnie. But in truth, not all the main action was on stage because as the performers wandered around backstage, giving themselves over to the mood of the day, the good time, "let's party" vibes, they started wondering where the action was. The *real* action. Well, some of them found it — in Ronnie's trailer. For there, sitting around the Hawk, quite comfy, as if it was the front porch back home in Fayetteville, were Carl Perkins and Levon and Garth and Rick and . . . well, anyone and everyone who drifted in. And everyone did drift in. I mean, it was the place to be. A reporter from *She* magazine in Britain had come to catch up with the enormous wave of nostalgia sweeping England for The Band.

But after a few days with Ronnie, it changed her outlook. Soon enough, the Hawk was the focus of her story as she watched from the sidelines in Detroit. And so more and more started to drift into Ronnie's trailer, because, as the tall tales grew taller and taller, as Ronnie and Carl and Levon hunkered down, heads together, laughing at all the old jokes, all the "youngsters" on the outside of this charmed circle were learning something.

That this was what their music was all about: this was where rock started. Their stories, their roots. It had nothing to do with big studios, big contracts or big deals. Rock was — folks.

But some had known this all along. Some had understood how the Hawk had been *teaching* this all along. To Sylvia Tyson, without Ronnie, Canadian musicians "would probably not be where we are." And she is not just talking about the record charts. Ronnie hit Canada like lightning zaps an old building. After he arrived, things were never quite the same — in music and outside of music.

Like, he had this attitude. "Shoot, son," he'd say, "do it. Try it. Get it. It's yours, if you want it — if you want it *bad* enough."

Before him, Canadians didn't want it because they didn't believe they could get it. We believed, of course, that rock 'n' roll had be annexed by the Americans and they were never going to let it go. It took some time but he proved us wrong. Shoot, he just took a little ol' Canadian band into the heart of rock 'n' roll and simply outplayed those old Yankees.

Burton Cummings watched it all happen and when it came time for him and a bunch of other Winnipeg kids to take on the Hollywood rock 'n' roll machine, he was just as cocky doing it as Ronnie, who, by example, had taught him to be.

But along the way, the teacher was learning, too. He was learning to see himself as others saw him. He was learning to understand what he had come to mean to so many people. For instance, there are few directors or movie producers who have spent any time at all with Ronnie without thinking what a great story he would be. Or, what a presence he is. I talked to Norman Jewison about the Hawk as we walked down Fifth Avenue in New

York and the director of *Moonstruck* started to smile just at the very thought of the legend in his own mind.

In an entirely unexpected way, this good ol' boy from Arkansas has become something of a Canadian icon through TV and the movies. And interestingly enough, it all started with *Heaven's Gate*. For Ronnie, the Cimino movie wasn't just one hell of a rocky horse ride and a lot of wasted time. On the set, as everyone sat around waiting for Cimino's next decision, they found themselves listening to the Hawk being the Hawk. By the time *Heaven's Gate* wrapped up shooting, word was around that Jeff Bridges was thinking about doing the Hawk's life story. Ronnie Hawkins was meant for the movies — somehow, in some way, it seemed.

But then, others had seen how well he came off in *Renaldo and Clara*, Bob Dylan's personal epic of music and mystification in 1976 in which, in the mask-behind-mask spirit of the movie, the Hawk played Bob Dylan. In 1986, after he scored a small appearance in *Lover Boy*, one of the *Meatballs* sequels, Ronnie was approached by John Brunton, an independent Toronto-based TV producer, who thought he'd be perfect for a role in Brunton's proposed series, "Rockit Records." The time was right, Brunton knew, for television to recognize rock 'n' roll. The larger-than-life Ronnie Hawkins would be perfect for the role of the larger-than-life owner of a record company.

By now, Ronnie was becoming used to playing . . . well, himself. He appeared in a variety of television concerts, notably "A Concert in the Park" for the Canadian Broadcasting Corporation in 1984, and in the movie *Copper Mountain*, with Rita Coolidge. More TV work followed: in 1985 he filmed a concert hour in Arkansas for Ontario's Global network. Then in 1986 he spent several weeks dictating the story of his days with the Blackhawks to George Mendeluk, a Canadian producer based in Los Angeles. To sell the project, Mendeluk dug up a quote by Dylan about Ronnie: "I love the man, he's my hero, the guru of rock 'n' roll," and the talk for a while was of spending "a million-something" to get Sean Penn to play the young Hawk.

Ronnie had high hopes for the project, but after waiting around for developments he took on another movie role, *Run for the Money*, a.k.a. Cannonball Run III, where he worked opposite Donna Dixon, Dan Aykroyd's wife. John Candy helped land him the job. When Candy and Aykroyd were both working with the Second City company in Toronto in the seventies, they'd get to hear the Hawk. "What I remember most," Aykroyd told me, "was how wild those nights were. What a band!"

Of course, Ronnie figures he's been acting in one way or another on stage all his life, and this attitude worked for his appearance in *Seeing Things*, the 1987 CBC whodunnit and on a segment of *Mount Royal* in 1988. But as he waits for the Blackhawks movie to come through he's taking on other projects and working on that band he wants to put together — this big band, the kind Levon had with the RCO All Stars, the kind he's always wanted. He's spent nights thinking about his band, dreaming about it. And the more he's thought about it the clearer the vision becomes. A modern-day minstrel show. A big band. Comedians. Jokes. Music. The blues, rock 'n' roll. Rat-ta-ta-ta!

"Yeah," he says, "that's it. Baby, oh baby, I can see it now. It's right there. *Right* there. The big time!"

APPENDIX I

The Recordings of Ronnie Hawkins:
A Complete Listing of
All Issued Records (1958-89)

A

1960	A Poor Wayfaring Stranger	Roulette
1972	Ain't That a Shame	Monument
1974	Ain't That Just Like a Woman	Monument
1979	Ain't That Just Like a Woman	Charly (UK)
1979	Ain't That Lovin' You Baby	United Artists
1964	Arkansas	Roulette

B

1959	Baby Jean	Roulette
1987	Baby Jean	Epic
1981	Back on the Road Again	Quality
1970	Bitter Green	Cotillion
1968	Black Sheep Boy	Yorkville
1971	Black Sheep Boy	Cotillion
1965	Bluebirds over the Mountain	Hawk
1979	Blue Moon of Kentucky	United Artists
1963	Bo Diddley	Roulette
1974	Bo Diddley	Monument
1983	Bo Diddley (Live)	Trilogy
1972	Bony Moronie	Monument
1964	Boss Man	Roulette
1974	Brand New Tennessee Waltz	Monument
1960	Brave Man	Roulette
1981	Brown Eyed Handsome Man	Quality

C

1959	Clara	Roulette
1960	Cold Cold Heart	Roulette
1962	Come Love	Roulette
1979	Come on Let's Go	Charly (UK)

1972	Cora Mae	Monument
1985	Crazy Music	Epic

D

1987	Days Gone By	Epic
1965	Diddley Daddy	Hawk
1972	Diddley Daddy	Monument
1959	Dizzy Miss Lizzy	Roulette
1983	Dizzy Miss Lizzy (Live)	Trilogy
1987	Don't Start Me Rockin'	Epic
1971	Don't Tell Me Your Troubles	Cotillion
1970	Down in the Alley	Cotillion
1981	Down the Line	Quality
1983	Down the Line (Live)	Trilogy
1974	Dream Lover	Monument
1959	Dreams Do Come True	Roulettte
1971	Drinkin' Wine Spo-dee-o-dee	Cotillion

E

1968	Early Morning Rain	Ozark (UK)
1981	Eighteen Wheels	Quality
1979	Elvira	United Artists
1985	Everybody Knows	Epic

F

1960	Fare Thee Well	Roulette
1959	Forty Days	Roulette
1970	Forty Days	Cotillion
1983	Forty Days (Live)	Trilogy
1979	Four Strong Winds	Charly (UK)

G

1968	Girl from the North Country	Yorkville
1987	Girl with the Dark Brown Hair	Epic
1965	Goin' to the River	Hawk

1979	Goin' to the River	Charly (UK)
1985	Good Timing Song	Epic
1964	Got my Mojo Working	Hawk

H

1981	Havana Moon	Quality
1959	Hay Ride	Roulette
1959	Hey Boba Lou	Roulette
1958	Hey Bo Diddley	Quality
1960	Hey Good Lookin'	Roulette
1963	High Blood Pressure	Roulette
1974	High Blood Pressure	Monument
1984	Hit Record	Trilogy
1968	Home from the Forest	Yorkville
1970	Home from the Forest	Cotillion
1974	Home from the Forest	Monument
1959	Honey Don't	Roulette
1980	Honey Don't	Ozark (UK)
1964	Honey Love	Roulette
1974	Honey Love	Monument
1959	Horace	Roulette

I

1960	I Can't Help It (if I'm Still in Love with You)	Roulette
1962	I Feel Good	Roulette
1960	I Gave my Love a Cherry	Roulettte
1970	I May Never Get to Heaven	Cotillion
1972	I'm in Love Again	Monument
1960	I'm so Lonesome I Could Cry	Roulette
1968	I Still Miss Someone	Yorkville
1979	I Still Miss Someone	Charly (UK)
1968	It's Alright	Yorkville

J

1960	Jambalaya (on the Bayou)	Roulette

| 1960 | John Henry | Roulette |
| 1983 | Johnny B Goode (Live) | Trilogy |

K

1959	Kansas City	End/Quality
1974	Kinky	Monument
1985	Kinky	Epic

L

1968	Lady Came From Baltimore	Yorkville
1971	Lady Came From Baltimore	Cotillion
1972	Lawdy Miss Clawdy	Monument
1971	Leaves that are Green	Cotillion
1979	Let it Rock	United States
1964	Let the Good Times Roll	Hawk
1970	Little Bird	Cotillion
1965	Little Red Rooster	Hawk
1971	Little Red Rooster	Cotillion
1987	Livin' a Life I Can't Afford	Epic
1959	Lonely Hours	Roulette
1974	Lonely Hours	Monument
1971	Lonely Weekends	Cotillion
1971	Lonely Weekends (Alt. cut)	Cotillion
1974	Lonesome Town	Monument
1960	Lonesome Whistle	Roulette
1968	Long Black Veil	Yorkville
1985	Look Out Time	Epic
1985	Look Out Time (Special re-mix)	Epic
1981	Louisiana Backroad	Quality
1960	Love from Afar	Roulette
1958	Love Me Like You Can	Quality
1959	Love Me Like You Can	Roulette
1987	Lucy	Epic

M

| 1985 | Making it Again | Epic |

1987	Mama Come Home	Epic
1968	Mary Jane	Yorkville
1959	Mary Lou	Roulette
1983	Mary Lou (Live)	Trilogy
1987	Mary Lou	Epic
1967	Matchbox	Roulette
1970	Matchbox	Cotillion
1983	Matchbox (Live)	Trilogy
1972	Maybelline	Monument
1972	Memphis Tennessee	Monument
1960	Mister and Mississippi	Roulette
1964	Mojo Man	Roulette
1979	My Babe	United Artists
1959	My Gal is Red Hot	Roulette

N

1959	Need Your Lovin' (Oh so Bad)	Roulette
1960	Nobody's Lonesome for Me	Roulette

O

1959	Odessa	Roulette
1971	Odessa	Cotillion
1983	Odessa (Live)	Trilogy
1984	Ode to a Truck Drivin' Man	Trilogy
1959	Oh Sugar	Roulette
1970	One More Night	Cotillion
1959	One of these Days	Roulette
1960	One Out of a Hundred	Roulette
1970	One Too Many Mornings	Cotillion
1981	Only the Lucky	Quality
1971	Ooby Dooby	Cotillion
1979	Ooby Dooby	Charly (UK)

P

1971	Patricia (Slow version)	Cotillion
1971	Patricia (Faster version)	Cotillion

1985	Patricia	Epic
1974	Pledging my Love	Monument
1979	Pledging my Love	United States
1980	Poor Me	Ozark (UK)

R

1960	Ramblin' Man	Roulette
1968	Reason to Believe	Yorkville
1968	Reason to Believe (Alt. cut)	Yorkville
1968	Rich Man's Spiritual	Yorkville
1959	Ruby Baby (Album cut)	Roulette
1960	Ruby Baby (Single cut)	Roulette
1983	Ruby Baby (Live)	Trilogy

S

1980	School Days	Ozark (UK)
1964	Searchin'	Roulette
1964	Sexy Ways	Roulette
1979	Shelter of your Eyes	United Artists
1959	Sick and Tired	Roulette
1971	Sick and Tired	Cotillion
1979	Sick and Tired	United Artists
1959	Someone Like You	Roulette
1979	Something's Been Making Me Blue	United Artists
1960	Sometimes I Feel Like a Motherless Child	Roulette
1959	Southern Love	Roulette
1979	South in New Orleans	United Artists
1981	(Stuck in) Lodi	Quality
1960	Summertime	Roulette
1967	Suzie Q	Roulette
1979	Suzie Q	Charly (UK)
1985	Sweet Wine	Epic

T

1983	That's All Right Mama (Live)	Trilogy

1960	The Ballad of Caryl Chessman	Roulette
1960	The Death of Floyd Collins	Roulette
1960	There'll Be No Teardrops Tonight	Roulette
1963	There's a Screw Loose	Roulette
1972	The Same Old Song	Monument
1981	300 Pounds of Heavenly Joy	Quality
1981	Travelling Band	Quality
1971	Treasure of Love	Cotillion

V

1960	Virginia Bride	Roulette

W

1960	Weary Blues From Waitin'	Roulette
1959	What'cha Gonna Do (When the Creek Runs Dry)	Roulette
1972	When my Dreamboat Comes Home	Monument
1963	Who Do You Love	Roulette
1970	Who Do You Love	Cotillion
1978	Who Do You Love (From "The Last Waltz")	Warner Bros
1983	Who Do You Love (Live)	Trilogy
1987	Who'll Stop the Rain	Epic
1959	Wild Little Willie	Roulette
1983	Wild Little Willie (Live)	Trilogy
1968	Will the Circle be Unbroken	Yorkville
1970	Will the Circle be Unbroken	Cotillion

Y

1959	You Cheated You Lied	Roulette
1964	You Know I Love You	Roulette
1960	Your Cheatin' Heart	Roulette
1960	You Win Again	Roulette

NOTE Years shown represent date of issue and not date of recording.

APPENDIX II
Q. & A.: A Little Help from My Friends

Ronnie, there were a lot of people interviewed and talked about in this book. In a few words tell me what some of them mean to you.

ROY ORBISON — One of the good ones.

ROY BUCHANAN —Great but just a little too weird to understand.

DAVID CLAYTON THOMAS — Tough and one of my favorite voices.

JAY SMITH — In the 60s he had the talent to be an international superstar.

KRIS KRISTOFFERSON — I love him . . . I hate him . . . I love him for all the good things he stands for, I love him for his talent and his brilliance and I love him because he is a friend. I hate him because he won't share any of that good Hollywood pussy with me and he could, if he wanted to.

LEVON HELM — The best! He was born rockin'.

ROBBIE ROBERTSON — Worked as hard as anyone can to be somebody.

GARTH HUDSON — Garth has always been ahead of his time and sometimes he would play so far out that I wouldn't really know what he was doing musically, but it fit.

RICKY DANKO — Great ear, great musician, great writer.

RICHARD MANUEL — One of the great voices, and a rocker's rocker. I really miss old "Beak."

BOB DYLAN — The "high lama" of the 60s. His writing has helped make a change. Bob would give William Shakespeare a run for his money.

BEVERLY D'ANGELO — A very talented lady and she can sing and act good, too.

MICK JAGGER — I never saw anyone that ugly make so much money in the entertainment business.

KEITH RICHARDS — He's a rocker. I'd like to play with him.

JOHN LENNON — John Lennon was a real fine cat.

YOKO ONO — You shouldn't criticize what you don't understand.

PAUL McCARTNEY — I don't know Paul but I've heard from musicians like Duck Dunn that he's real good.

RINGO STARR — Everybody I know loves Ringo.

GEORGE HARRISON — I would love to put a rockabilly band together with him.

FRED CARTER — That Louisiana farm boy can pick with the best of them even until this day, if you know how to handle him . . . and I do.

IAN TYSON — A tough cowboy and a great country song writer.

SYLVIA TYSON — I've always been in love with Sylvia.

HERMAN TUCK — The rocker's rocker.

ELVIS PRESLEY — Elvis Presley had the looks, had the throat and had the timing. Most of the world today calls him "king of rock 'n' roll" but that's not true, because you see in the kingdom of rock 'n' roll Elvis would have certainly been one of the royal knights, because there is only one king in the kingdom of rock 'n' roll and that is rock 'n' roll.

JIMMY RAY PAULMAN — The greatest rockabilly rhythm man I've ever seen.

JERRY LEE LEWIS — A rocker's rocker without a doubt.

CONWAY TWITTY — A great business man — owes me a guitar.

STAN SZELEST — The best rock 'n' roll piano player on the planet.

B.J. COOK — I love her but she talks too damn much.

DAVID FOSTER — He's one of the great ones.

BO DIDDLEY — Abraham Lincoln said all men were created equal but "honest Abe" never saw Bo Diddley in the shower or he wouldn't have said that.

GORDON LIGHTFOOT — Next to the "cat lady" I'm his biggest fan.

CATHY SMITH — She was beautiful and talented but she gave too much.

AL BRISCO — To have Al in my band was one of the greatest musical pleasures I ever had. It was an honor for me to have worked with him.

ANNE MURRAY — In my opinion she can sing a song as good as a song can be sung.

LARRY GOWAN — A great talent. I'd love to have him in my band playing rock 'n' roll.

DALLAS HARMS — Great humanitarian, great song writer and one of the best friends anybody could ever have. And he definitely ain't no sissy!

DON TYSON — Loves music and loves pussy. My kind of guy and he's helped a lot of people.

DON ROMAN — Could have been a great record producer.

FRED FOSTER — The smartest country boy I have ever seen.

TOM DOWD — An engineering genius — everybody knows that.

GERRY WEXLER — Treated me like a king and knows the record business probably as good as anybody in the world.

MORRIS LEVY — Morris is one of my heroes. He spent a lot of money on me and he probably saved my life. I'd do anything for him.

WILLIE JEFFERY — Willie is a rocker of the highest order! And one of my very best friends. But he's got a little bit of Ebenezer Scrooge in him when it comes to spending money . . . and he's got plenty.

SCREAMIN' BRIAN SIMMONS — When an entertainer's career is over, if he's had one fan like Screamin' Brian, all the work and effort in building that career would be worth it ten times over.

KEITH JAMES — One of the smartest radio men in the business and has probably helped me and a lot of other Canadian artists as much as anyone, but I like his old lady better.

MICHAEL CIMINO — Well, he won an Academy Award and you can't get any stronger than that.

STEVE THOMSON — If I had a choice I would not trade Steve Thomson for five of the biggest management companies in the world. I have never seen anyone in my lifetime work as hard and keep the faith as much as he does . . . It's hard to control a legend, you know.

Ronnie, you love women and obviously your wife Wanda is the number-one lady in your life, but if you could have any other woman in the world other than Wanda, who would that be?
I want five, and here they are: Joyce Davidson, Elizabeth Taylor, Catherine Deneuve, Brigitte Bardot and Jane Fonda. And that goddamn French movie director, Roger Vadim, was lucky enough to marry three of them, and that's as lucky as winning the lottery three times in a row.

Canada has been your home now for some thirty years. You've seen a lot of changes in the music business and because of you music has come a long way. What do you think about the music business in Canada today?
When I first came to Canada it was really tough. But then along came cats like Walt Grealis and Stan Kleese and now people like Flora McDonald, Lily Munro, Al Mair, Marcel Masse and programs like FACTOR. But I still think the music business is like slavery and human rights. It is getting better but it ain't good enough and all we need is just a little help from our friends and we'd bring into Canada ten times more money than CBC could lose, and Baby Blue, that's a lot of money.

Ronnie, do you think you will ever retire from the music business and retreat to that cabin back home in Arkansas?
You ain't a shittin'! If I don't hit the big time in the next twenty-five or thirty years, I'm gonna to pack'er in and, "Cabin, hear I come."

INDEX

Index